THE MARCH EAST 1945

THE FINAL DAYS OF OFLAG IX A/H AND A/Z

PETER GREEN

The History Press

Cover illustrations: Front: Captain John McIndoe (Otago Settlers' Museum, New Zealand); *Back:* Oflag IX A/Z walk down the main street of Dachrieden, 3 April. (Green Collection)

First published 2012 by Spellmount, an imprint of The History Press
This paperback edition first published 2025

The History Press
97 St George's Place, Cheltenham,
Gloucestershire, GL50 3QB
www.thehistorypress.co.uk

British Library Cataloguing in Publication Data.
A catalogue record for this book is available from the British Library.

ISBN 978 1 80399 939 5

Typesetting and origination by The History Press
Printed and bound in Great Britain by TJ Books, Padstow, Cornwall

MIX
Paper | Supporting responsible forestry
FSC® C013056
FSC www.fsc.org

Trees for Life

EU Authorised Representative: Easy Access System Europe
Mustamäe tee 50, 10621 Tallinn, Estonia
gpst.request@easproject.com

CONTENTS

FOREWORD

Every child has a question of their father – whether that father lived his life to the full or not. My father died when I was 20 months old so I was never able to ask the question. Had he been alive as I grew up I would probably have to ask the question now.

My father would have behaved as a father with me and as someone very different in Oflag IX A/Z. The essence of the person remains however and my very scant memories of him were as a larger-than-life person. All accounts from members of my family who knew him said roughly the same thing.

Through this book I have gained insights as to how his life as a POW may have been. I can imagine him having such a mixture of feelings, from extreme excitement that this Boy's Own event could be happening to him, to despair that his life might end after many years of captivity, when all he wanted to do was burst with life on the whole world. I don't think he would have explained it this way, I don't think he would have been able to explain his feelings. He just did what he did – take photographs – and his excitement is captured in the picture of the jeep moving through Wimmelburg, on 13 April 1945. In contrast, there is the wary relief in the faces of the two concentration camp prisoners; surely he and most of the other POWs would have shared that feeling.

I am sure that all who read this account of the journey in 1945 will gain insights into their fathers who survived something unimaginable. It helps to answer the question – who was my father?

David McLeod Hill, son of Leighton McLeod 'Lee' Hill
Pohangina, New Zealand
ANZAC Day 2012

ACKNOWLEDGEMENTS

The research for *The March East* has depended on the cooperation of many individuals and organisations. However the greatest assistance and encouragement has come from Björn Ulf Noll. Björn has unselfishly worked to provide a great deal of information regarding Oflag IX A/Z at Rotenburg and the work of Gunnar Celander. He could always be relied upon to overcome an apparent dead end in the research or open up a new avenue of inquiry; and his personal experiences from living alongside the camp have been beyond price.

The major individual contributors in the UK have been from four participants on the marches: Ernest Edlmann, who made his time available for interviews and provided access to his wartime diary and reports; Michael Langham, who sadly passed away before he could see the results of his contribution; and Robert Montgomery and William Watson, whose memories included insights into the detail of camp life at Oflag IX A/H Upper Camp.

Any reference to the march of Oflag IX A/Z has to include the contribution made by Muriel Roberts, the widow of Harry Roberts. Muriel refused to be thwarted in her efforts to publish her husband's account of the evacuation, which was one of the starting points for this book. She has very kindly provided access in addition to Harry's wartime log. Sadly, she passed away as this book went to press.

Jean Beckwith and Gillian Barnard have also been unstinting in their time and in providing access to Ted Beckwith and Rupert Holland material; as has Hugh Wilbraham with regard to his father's unpublished manuscript.

Björn Ulf Noll's contribution was in many ways mirrored by Harald Schlanstedt, another witness to events in 1945, who has also unearthed witnesses to the march in its later stages. The other local historians who have made major contribution are Eduard Fritze, Professor Hans Heinz Seyfarth, Thilo Ziegler, Peter Lindner and Fred Dittmann. Horst Ehricht, a family friend, for whom Oberstleutnant Brix was always 'Uncle Rudolf' has provided wonderful insights into the life of the Commandant of Oflag IX A/Z.

The contributions of other members of prisoners' families are very gratefully acknowledged, in particular: Eva Hill, David Hill, Megs Fawkes, Sholto Douglas, Kathleen Biddle, Anthony Foster, James Forbes, Michael Fuller, Thelma McCurchy, John McIndoe, Sheena MacDonald, Simon Mountfort, Sally Phun, Brenda Norris, Alan, Tim and Julie Redway, Sarah Rhodes, Mrs Henrietta Taylor and Grace Westcott. Marion Gerritsen-Teunissen for access to Kenneth Grayston White's YMCA log and his collection of Lee Hill photographs.

John Irwin, Bob Cardinall and Robert Patton, former members of the United States Army, have helped to explain the 'Other Side of the Hill' in a story that is predominantly set in a German context. Ann Sumners has kindly provided access to Charles Sumners' photographs of US 6th Armored in April 1945.

Ingemar Björklund generously contributed translations of Gunner Celander's reports to the Swedish Red Cross, whilst Tony Herbert willingly undertook an interview with a camp survivor in Shropshire at very short notice.

The staff of the Otago Settlers Museum, Dunedin, New Zealand, have been extremely generous with their time and in providing access to the John McIndoe material. Other archives, particularly UK's National Archive, the Imperial War Museum, ITS *Internationaler Suchdienst, Riksarkivet* and the *Bundesarchiv* have met all my requests for material with great patience and contributed ideas for further research. Valuable assistance has also been received from the Australian War Memorial, Australian Film Archive, Kings Own Border Regiment Museum and in particular Stuart Eastwood, Maidstone Museum, The New Zealand Film Archive, New Zealand Defence Force Records, Royal Army Chaplain's Museum, Royal Engineers Museum, The Alexander Turnbull Library, Ushaw College Library, War Art New Zealand and the Zoological Library, Oxford.

Fellow-researchers have contributed via electronic media, but in particular the *Feldgrau* bulletin board should be singled out for its ability to unearth the more esoteric data about the German Army in 1945.

Finally, I must acknowledge the support of my wife for her contribution and her forbearance in the face of a husband's obsession with somewhere in Germany in the spring of 1945.

INTRODUCTION

> We set off on a march that lasted fifteen days and took us on a zig-zag route across 230 kilometres. It was a march none of us will ever forget.
>
> Lee Hill, 'Forced March To-Freedom', *Illustrated* magazine, 12 May 1945

Leighton McLeod 'Lee' Hill was a remarkable man. A pioneer of the New Zealand Film industry, he recorded the march east by the Germans of Oflag IX A/Z in 1945 with his camera and diary. His entrepreneurial instincts took over when he sold his photographs and text to the British magazine *Illustrated* on his return to the UK. The story that appeared under his by-line has some elements of truth but large parts of it are fabrications. We will never know the role that the editorial staff of the magazine played.

What can be said with great certainty is that the article would have played well with its British readers at the time: the German guards were Nazi brutes with whips; it was the evil Germans who shot up Red Cross vehicles; and the prisoners were hostages on their way to the Southern Redoubt. All these stories are contradicted by Lee Hill's own diary and those of the other participants. The journeys of Oflag IX A/Z and its sister camp Oflag IX A/H do not form part of the canon of Nazi brutality. They were certainly not death marches.

John McIndoe, also a New Zealander, kept a sketchbook during the march and produced images that complement Lee Hill's photographs. In addition there are over 40 accounts of differing lengths by those who took in the journeys or witnessed them.

Contrary to the expectations of the prisoners, the German commanders were able to keep their prisoners out of the hands of American divisions travelling at many times the speed of the plodding columns. At the same time, the Germans kept the men safe from the rogue elements in the collapsing regime. Nevertheless, for both camps the evacuations became an ordeal that they shared with their guards and the civilians they met at each overnight stop.

This account helps to put the record straight and gives an insight into one small part of Germany's collapse into chaos in the last weeks of the war.

TIMELINE

22/23 March	Rhine crossings by Allies
27 March	First official warnings that the camps might be evacuated
29 March	Oflag IX A/H walks to Waldkappel, arrives after midnight
	Oflag IX A/Z walks to Rockensuß, arrives after midnight
30 March	Oflag IX A/H walks to Wanfried, arrives in the early hours
	Oflag IX A/Z walks to Oetmannshausen area
31 March	Oflag IX A/H rest day at Wanfried
	Oflag IX A/Z walks to Wanfried, the Kalkhof
1 April	6th Armored cross the Fulda
	Oflag IX A/H at Wanfried
	Oflag IX A/Z walks to Diedorf
2 April	US 11th Armored reach the Reserve-Lazarett at Obermaßfeld
	Oflag IX A/H walks to Lengenfeld unterm Stein
	Oflag IX A/Z walks to Lengefeld
3 April	6th Armored cross the Werra
	Oflag IX A/H at Lengenfeld unterm Stein

	Oflag IX A/Z walks to Windeberg
4 April	Americans reach Mühlhausen and Ohrdruf
	6th Armored liberates Oflag IX/AH
	Oflag IX A/H at Lengenfeld unterm Stein
	Oflag IX A/Z walks to Friedrichsrode
5 April	US Army repatriate the remainder of the patients from Reserve-Lazarett Obermaßfeld
	Oflag IX A/H at Eschwege
	Oflag IX A/Z walks to Nohra
6 April	Oflag IX A/H at Eschwege
	Oflag IX A/Z rest day at Nohra
7 April	German counterattack at Struth
	Oflag IX A/H at Eschwege
	Oflag IX A/Z walks to Uthleben
8 April	Oflag IX A/H flies to Paris
	Oflag IX A/Z walks to Buchholz
9 April	Oflag IX A/H flies to UK
	Oflag IX A/Z walks to Uftrungen
10 April	Oflag IX A/Z walks to Dittichenrode
11 April	3rd Armored reach Nordhausen
	Oflag IX A/Z by lorry to Wimmelburg, arrive after midnight
12 April	3rd Armored in action with AA guns between Sangerhausen and Wimmelburg
	US 9th Army reach the Elbe
	Franklin Roosevelt dies
	Oflag IX A/Z at Wimmelburg
13 April	3rd Armored reach Wimmelburg
	Oflag IX A/Z at Wimmelburg
14 April	Oflag IX A/Z at Wimmelburg
15 April	Oflag IX A/Z at Wimmelburg
16 April	Oflag IX A/Z flies to Liege from Esperstedt
17 April	Oflag IX A/Z at Brussels
18 April	Oflag IX A/Z flies to UK

1

PRISONERS, CAPTORS AND WITNESSES

> At last, we rolled into that fateful year 1944 and the invasion of Normandy and then the realisation that the British and Americans were really on the road to the conquest of Germany. Slow as it might seem, we realised at long last that they were coming.
>
> Major 'Peter' Brush, Rifle Brigade, captured Calais, May 1940.

In March 1945 the Western Allies had reached the Rhine. Across Germany prisoners of war could finally believe that freedom could not be far off. At Spangenberg and Rotenburg near Kassel, in two camps – *Oflags* – for British and Commonwealth officers, the inmates had been anticipating release ever since the momentous news had reached them of D-Day in the summer of 1944. Life in the camps was recorded by the prisoners, 45 records discovered in all, some long, some detailed, others very patchy. Those records, including drawings and photographs of the last two weeks of captivity in one of the camps, are amongst the most comprehensive of any camp. They include German, American and Red Cross accounts and show not just the concerns of the men, but also those of the civilians and soldiers in the countryside around them.

The men in the two camps were amongst the most fortunate of the many victims of the Third Reich. Despite the chaos in which they found themselves, German commanders were able, against all probability, to maintain control of their captives and keep them safe from extreme Nazi elements and Allied aircraft. To the prisoners, their experiences from March to mid-April 1945 were evidence of desperate, on occasions random, German attempts to prevent them from being liberated. In fact their captors were acting logically, whilst around them the German Army was fighting on hopelessly and German society was collapsing.

Oflag IX A/H at Spangenberg was an *Offizierlager*, a camp for officers. It was in *Wehrkreis* IX – military district IX. 'Oflag' was the German abbreviation of its full title. It was the senior camp or *Hauptlager*, hence the 'H' and Oflag IX A/Z at Rotenburg an der Fulda was its sub camp, or *Zweiglager*, hence the 'Z'. Rotenburg was eight miles south of Spangenberg. Somewhat confusingly, Oflag IX A/H was itself divided into Upper Camp, in the *Schloß* and Lower Camp in the former manor of Elbersdorf, a village on the edge of Spangenberg. Between them the three sites held around 900 British and Empire prisoners. Both camps also held Polish prisoners captured whilst serving alongside the British Army. In the camps the men called themselves 'Kriegies' from *Kriegsgefangener*, the German for prisoner of war. Once liberated their formal title changed to RAMPs.

At both camps the Kriegies included men captured at all stages of the war. The oldest group were men captured in Norway in the spring of 1940. They were about to start a fifth year in captivity. Lieutenant W.K. 'Butch' Laing, at Oflag IX A/Z, had been captured in Norway whilst serving in the Sherwood Foresters. In a regimental photograph taken just before the war, Laing appears keen, an enthusiastic teenager. In civilian life he was a teacher at an unnamed public school. He seems to have fitted

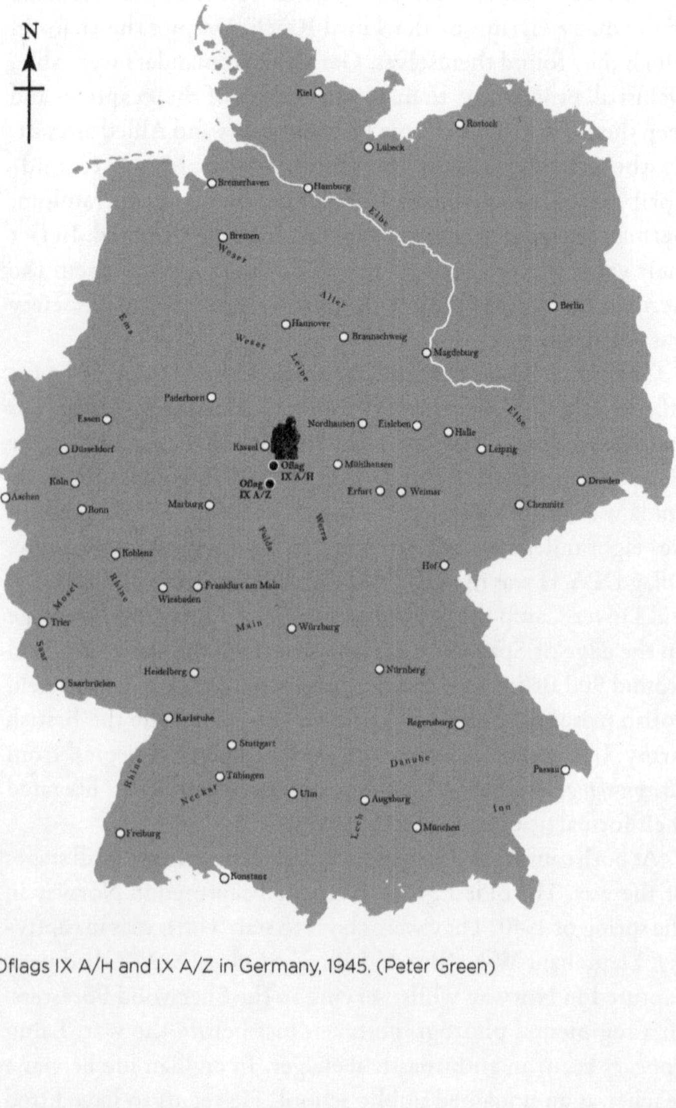

Oflags IX A/H and IX A/Z in Germany, 1945. (Peter Green)

The Upper Camp exterior of Oflag IX A/H, showing the entrance bridge that crossed the castle's deep moat. This picture was drawn in 1940 by Captain John Mansel, Queen's Royal Regiment, before he was transferred from Oflag IX A. Mansel spent time in camps at Thorn and Warburg; by April 1945 he was at Eichstätt in Bavaria. Mansel had trained as an architect at Liverpool University before the war, and his skills were put to use forging travel documents for escapes. (Gillian Barnard Collection)

easily into school and prison camp. Both were disciplined environments with lots of cold water and poor food. Certainly some officers compared their life in prison camp favourably with their time at public school. Laing also appears a little naïve. At one stage in the camp's evacuation he misidentified Russian POWs being mistreated by their German guards as French Moroccan and Indo-Chinese prisoners under their own French officers.

Laing's shooting war had lasted less than a month. He joined the Territorial Army in January 1939 and was called up in September 1939. In April 1940 he left Britain for Norway and was captured by the end of the month. On his way to prison camp in Germany, he and others were paraded before Hitler, who told them of his sorrow that Germany and Britain should

Spangenberg castle is now a hotel. (Ingmar Runge, Creative Commons Attribution 3.0 Unported licence)

find themselves at war. Laing might have been forgiven for having similar thoughts, as failure in Norway was followed by defeat in France and it appeared that Laing might not see England again for a very long time. Laing taught basic German at Rotenburg. One of students, Captain Theodore Redway, Durham Light Infantry, recalled that their text books were the children's stories Hansel and Gretel.

Laing's account of his capture and time in captivity is almost completely devoid of emotion. The occasional exclamation mark and reference to astonishment is the closest he gets to describing his feelings. Most of the men's accounts are factual and often dry, though emotion does burst through when liberation arrives and many admit to being close to tears or of finding a quiet spot to reflect on their recent past. The men's military training encouraged brevity. Occasionally they would admit to feeling tired or miserable, but when they do so it was only temporary. Stiff upper lips rapidly reasserted themselves. For example, Captain

The Upper Camp interior of Oflag IX A/H, inside the Schloß looking back towards the gateway and bridge over the moat, also drawn by John Mansel. The room where Robert Montgomery and the rest of the Wash Kitchen team boiled water for washing and hot drinks, and watched over the camp comings and goings looked down in this yard. (Gillian Barnard Collection)

Ernest Lorne Campbell Edlmann, Royal East Kent Regiment (The Buffs), wrote on Easter Sunday 1945, 'Woke up filthy and miserable. No Easter feeling at all. But wash and some porridge sends up morale.' Edlmann was a career soldier. He had been captured in France in May 1940. After the war he returned to his regiment, eventually commanding the 1st Battalion in Aden in the late 1950s. Ernest had made several attempts to escape whilst a prisoner of war. His final and successful one would come in April 1945. When interviewed in 2009 aged 95 he still retained his military directness and confidence. Aged 31 in 1945, he was one of the younger men captured in 1940.

The Lower Camp of Oflag IX A/H, Elbersdorf. (Imperial War Museum)

A watercolour of the Lower Camp of Oflag IX A/H, painted by Major Borrett, Royal Engineers. Lower Camp was a former farm in the village of Elbersdorf, which then become a hostel. Elbersdorf lay in the shadow of the castle and its hill, northwest of Spangenberg. Inmates of Lower Camp were imprisoned in close proximity with German civilians. In civilian life Borrett was an architect; he was captured when on leave in the Caribbean. His ship was torpedoed and he was rescued and captured by the U-boat crew and returned to Europe. (Green Collection)

Oflag IX A/Z from the east bank of the Fulda. It was originally a teacher training school, becoming a prisoner of war camp in the autumn of 1939. John McIndoe's watercolour was painted just above the main road running from Rotenburg towards Kassel. In front of the school building it is just possible to make out the wooden hut built to hold Red Cross parcels. (Otago Settlers' Museum, New Zealand)

The view from Oflag IX A/Z, painted in May 1943. In the foreground the Red Cross parcel hut is beginning to take shape, whilst in the distance above the trees is the spire of Rotenburg's Lutheran parish church, dedicated to St James. (New Zealand War Art Collection)

The building remains the home to Jakob Grimm Schule, a secondary school, on the outskirts of Rotenburg. (Peter Green)

Ted Beckwith produced a magazine, The *Quill*, at most of the camps he was held in. The magazine was original text and images bound between wooden boards and passed around its readers. Finding a reliable source of paper was a constant problem. (Green Collection)

One corner of Rotenburg's small parade ground in the autumn of 1943. Although by this time Rotenburg camp had only held British and Commonwealth POWs for a year, most of its inmates had been imprisoned for three years. (Otago Settlers' Museum, New Zealand)

Captain E.G.C. 'Ted' Beckwith, also captured in Norway whilst serving with the Sherwood Foresters and held in Oflag IX A/H at Spangenberg, was older than Edlmann. He was 40 years old in 1945 and had 18 years service in the Territorial Army before being captured in Norway. He was an employee of Imperial Tobacco in Nottingham and after the war he went on to become a director of the company, before retiring to Oxfordshire. Beckwith had a life-long interest in literature and prison life allowed him to pursue it more fully. He created and edited the *Quill*, a literary magazine. It was entirely hand produced, each edition a single copy that was passed from 'subscriber' to 'subscriber'. Thirty-one editions were produced in the various camps that Beckwith passed through. The 31st *Quill* was 'published' three weeks before he was liberated. Beckwith compiled an omnibus edition that was published by *Country Life* in 1947.

One of his poems, written on 4 September 1942 whilst he was briefly held at Rotenburg, discusses the contradiction between the prisoner's experience and that of the previous inhabitants of the camp buildings. The sorrow it expresses is melancholic, rather than desperate. Melancholia better matched the stoicism, the calmness under pressure, that were expected of an officer.

AUSGANG ZUM GARTEN
[Inscription over a door in the hall at Oflag IX A/Z, which was formerly a girls' school.]

What high ideals inspired its builder's minds
This nursery for Teutonic womankind
On Fulda's bank, hard by the little town
On which the sheltering tree-clad hills look down
We cannot know. Imagination plays
With scenes and sounds of bygone, happier days
When Mädchen laughter echoed through its floors
From roof to hall, and carried out-of-doors
Into the garden, green then, where the breeze
Stirred, as it does today, the chestnut trees.
Today! The smiling valley lies as green
Among its hills, and Fulda flows between
Its banks, as ageless as the summer skies
Which form their canopy.
But other eyes
Look on the new-reaped fields beyond the wire
(High, tangled barbs) – and in those eyes desire,
And wistfulness, shadows of private troubles,
Longing for other hills and farms and stubbles…
And other feet now tread the gravelled ground,
That once was garden, tramping round and round.

Beckwith combined his writing with breeding canaries. In a world where there was no privacy, there was also none of the intimacy that comes from family or pets, so Beckwith found some of that emotional satisfaction from his canaries. 'Canary' was also the nickname the prisoners gave to their secret radios.

Rotenburg held a man whose interest in bird life was more academic. It led to him publishing a monograph on the goldfinch after the war. Lieutenant Peter Conder, Royal Signals, had been captured with 51st Highland Division. After the war he he became Warden at Skomer Island field study centre, before becoming the Director of the Royal Society for the Protection of Birds. Whilst at Rotenburg he recorded seeing an albino buzzard for a couple of years, as well as irregular sightings of sea ducks and sandpipers on the Fulda. Conder was not the only prisoner with an interest in wildlife. His notebooks include a record contributed by Ernest Edlmann of a hare that, after being disturbed by a party of walkers on parole, had 'jumped into the river that was quite full and flowing, swam to the other side splashing a bit, on reaching the far bank resting for some time'.

The fall of France led to the capture of more senior staff than at any other time in Europe. In 1945 Spangenberg held 46 colonels, including Lieutenant-Colonel E.H. Whitfield of the Oxford and Buckinghamshire Light Infantry, whose German POW number was 1. He had been captured in France after the prisoners from Norway so the German prisoner administration was less logically organised than one might imagine. Rotenburg held more young men and by 1945 it had only seven colonels amongst its inmates.

The Senior British Officer (SBO) at Spangenberg was Colonel Rupert Holland, Royal Artillery. Holland had been the town commander at Calais in May 1940. He was captured with the rest of the Calais garrison on 26 May 1940. More fortunate than some of the others captured at Calais, he was moved by car, lorry and train to his first camp, Oflag VII C, in a castle at Laufen in Bavaria. Most walked to the Rhine.

As the SBO of both Upper and Lower Camps at Spangenberg, Holland was involved in negotiations with the Germans and in the absence of German camp records his diary provides the little that is known of German planning for the time when Allied troops might arrive. Holland's diary was written after the war. It is clear, concise, almost a civil service note of his time in camp.

Perhaps he was not such a stuffed shirt; Holland's nickname was 'Pixie', given to him whilst in his first camp at Laufen, where he made a hat from a greatcoat pocket that stuck up like a pixie hat. Although the men's accounts often lack emotional content, they certainly did have worries. The major one was how would the war end for them? Massacres or hostage taking had long been topics of conversation in the camps. In 1944 the Senior British Officer at Rotenburg had warned the War Office that there was concern in the camp that the Germans might massacre them at the end of the war. This might not have been done by their own guards, but more likely by retreating troops taking revenge for Allied successes or by diktat from Berlin. Following the bombing of Dresden, Goebbels suggested that Allied POWs should be shot as a reprisal, but with the Allies holding large numbers of German POWs and the risk that it might provoke the use of gas or biological weapons, the idea was dropped. At Rotenburg, after more senior officers refused to produce a plan to avert a massacre, Captain Richard Page, Royal Artillery, created a scheme for the prisoners to take over the camp, imprison the guards and move into the nearby woods to wait for liberation. His plan required prisoners armed with chair legs to overcome the guards with their rifles, so perhaps the more senior men showed more wisdom. Lieutenant-Colonel Frost, 2 Para, had urged a similar plan on senior officers at Spangenberg. To his disgust, his plan, which included doping the guards before an assault on the guard house under the cover of smoke bombs by prisoners armed with hockey sticks, was rejected.

The most immediate concern, however, especially in early 1945, was the lack of food. Article 11 of the Geneva Convention required that the 'food ration of prisoners of war shall be equivalent in quantity and quality to that of the depot troops'. By 1945 the Germans were finding it hard to feed their own troops and the destruction of the German railways by Allied bombing meant that Red Cross parcels were becoming rarer. During the war the Red Cross tried to provide each prisoner with the

The daily food ration, drawn by John McIndoe in August 1944, before it was further reduced. It demonstrates the essential role of Red Cross parcels in supplementing the prisoners' diets. (New Zealand War Art Collection)

Red Cross parcels supplemented and at times replaced absent German rations. A wooden hut had been built at the front of the Jakob-Grimm-Schule to hold the parcels and allow them to be searched for contraband – including escape equipment – before being released to the men. (Otago Settlers' Museum, New Zealand)

equivalent of one parcel a week and at Rotenburg the supply was at around this until the winter of 1944. It then dropped to half a parcel a week in 1945 and the supply had all but dried up by March 1945. The last batch of parcels for the two camps was sent in mid-March. It did not arrive. Instead it was diverted to the main prisoner of war hospital in the Wehrkreis, Reserve-Lazarett Obermaßfeld, 30 miles away, which was in greater need.

Harry Roberts, 24 in 1945, was one of the youngest men whose diary has survived. His account was published as 'Capture at Arnhem' in 1999. Like Ernest Edlmann, Lieutenant Harry Roberts, REME, wrote his account of capture at Arnhem and life as a prisoner. Unlike Edlmann, who wrote up his notes in 1945, Harry Roberts waited until 1990. The combination of the immediate and raw response of the diary with a later response that drew on his wider memories makes his record extremely valuable.

Harry Roberts recorded the amount of food provided by the Germans, or more likely that which was expected to be provided, from 5 March to 8 April. He estimated the average intake per day from German supplies was 1497 calories. The current level recommended by British nutritionists is 2550. Ominously his records are preceded by a table describing the effect of starvation on a cat, with percentages of tissue loss. The entry concludes with the comment that animals typically die when their body weight has been reduced by 60 per cent. During March 1945 Roberts recorded the expected German rations for the month:

Margarine	170g (6oz)
Sugar	140g (5oz)
Meat and wurst	200g (7oz)
Potatoes	2400g (5lbs)
Coffee	14g (1/2oz)
Bread	1780g (4lbs)

The bread was made from dark rye flour and had such an effect on the men that many former prisoners refused to eat any kind of brown bread after the war. A modern British sliced loaf weighs 800g. So the men were expecting the equivalent of two loaves of bread during the month.

Special meals described as 'bashes' are a regular feature of prisoners' diaries. 'Bashes' were often prepared by the men themselves from food they had managed to squirrel away. Captain E.H. Lynn-Allen, Gloucestershire Regiment, defined 'Bash' in a 'Glossary of Words and Phrases' for the *Quill*:

> Bash (To). 1. Indulge in gastronomic excess (if possible, at someone else's expense).
> 2. To consume at a sitting

Gastronomic excess would not have matched modern definitions of either gastronomic or excess and, with the exception of

The former Manager of the Droitwich Spa Hotel, Lieutenant Robert Lush RASC had been captured whilst serving with the Expeditionary Institute in France in 1940. According to John Logan in *Inside the Wire*, Lush was appointed catering manager at Rotenburg after a scandal with the existing catering. His portrait was painted by David Feilding. (Imperial War Museum)

meals to celebrate the Rhine crossings in March, were few and far between after Christmas 1944.

Some meals were provided by a central kitchen and others by the men themselves in their dormitory messes. Both relied heavily on Red Cross food parcels. From the summer of 1943 Rotenburg's kitchen was run by Lieutenant Robert Lush, Royal Army Service Corps, who, pre-War, had managed the Droitwich Spa Hotel. It is not clear who provided a central food service at Spangenberg. However Captain Robert Montgomery MC, Royal Engineers and Commandos, was part of a team heating water for washing and afternoon drinks at Upper Camp. The team used camp rubbish as fuel for the boiler. The Wash Kitchen was close to the main gate and was a useful vantage point to observe the guards. Also near the main gate was a group of small rooms that housed colonels and senior majors in groups of around four to a room. The other men were housed in communal rooms. Montgomery remembered that Room 19, which predominately housed young subalterns, was the source of most of the jokes and stupidity in the camp. William Watson, Black Watch and Commando, recalled that this room was also known as the 'Arab Quarter'. Montgomery and Watson were survivors of Operation *Chariot*, the raid on the dry dock capable of holding the *Tirpitz* at St Nazaire. The leader of the raid, Lieutenant-Colonel Augustus Newman VC, was also held in Spangenberg. Their presence is a reminder that although many in the camps came from France in 1940 or Greece and North Africa in 1941, there were men captured throughout the war, including some taken when the Allies were in the ascendant in North Africa and Italy – and of course during the disaster at Arnhem.

Lieutenant-Colonel John Frost was one of the men captured at Arnhem who were sent to one of the two camps: 55 to Spangenberg and 36 to Rotenburg. These last additions were younger and fitter, even if many were wounded. Lieutenant-Colonel Frost was the most senior, but unlike the older Colonels captured in Norway or France, he was only 33. His wartime biography has little to say on his time at Spangenberg or at Obermaßfeld hospital where he was transferred when his wounds proved reluctant to heal. He was certainly disappointed by the lethargy of many of the men he met at Spangenberg. In March 1945 his suggestion that the prisoners seize control of the prison hospital as the Americans approached was overruled.

Lieutenant Hugh Harry Langan Cartwright, 2 South Staffs from 1st Airborne Division, published his experiences of Arnhem and in prison camp afterwards in a piece for the Airborne Museum at Oosterbeek. It has only a few paragraphs on prison life.

Lieutenant Alan Thomas Green, 1 Border, kept a prison diary in great detail until January 1945, when it stops with no explanation. He later compiled notes on his experiences after this date. Of all the Arnhem captives Harry Roberts' account is the most detailed.

The Swiss Government made what was to be the last inspection of the camps in early March 1945. They found the prisoners in good spirits. The prisoners' concerns over their use as hostages or of a possible massacre were perhaps not best raised with the Swiss in the presence of the Germans, who included officers from Berlin. Several prisoners comment on the reassurance they got from being marched out of the camp with their usual guards. Had they been replaced by SS troops the prisoners' mood would have changed. The splendidly named Lieutenant Terence Cornelius Farmer Prittie, Rifle Brigade, remembered at Oflag IX A/H that one of the few things they were told in advance of the evacuation was that they would be under the escort of their own camp guards.

Only slightly less alarming was the idea that they might be held hostage, perhaps in a redoubt in the mountains of Bavaria. The idea of a Nazi last stand based on underground factories, stockpiled supplies and SS divisions became prevalent amongst the Allies in 1945. An intelligence briefing for the British

21st Army Group, prepared in March 1945, suggested that the Redoubt was centred on Salzburg and Berchtesgaden, 'a region from which the most persistent reports emanate concerning the arrival of ammunition, food and other supplies'.

Nazi redoubts were illusory; but they had a strong hold on the minds of Germans and Allies alike. It was therefore only natural that this would be a concern to all POWs. John Logan, Argyll and Sutherland Highlanders, published his wartime experiences as 'Inside the Wire' in 1948. 'We often try to visualise the end as it concerns us ... Some visualise the Germans carrying on a guerrilla war in Bavaria and the Tyrol and our being moved down there.' Logan's diary covers almost the whole period of his imprisonment from 1940 until the day before the camps were moved. On his arrival at Rotenburg, in July 1943, he thought it a 'pretty dull spot' with low morale caused by too many of the men being older prisoners. By November he describes it as a 'most comfortable building'. Logan was 38 in 1945, so he was not one of the youngest prisoners himself.

Optimists in both camps believed that they would be abandoned by their guards and peacefully liberated by Allied troops as the front line rolled over them. The belief was based on the argument that the Germans would not want to burden themselves with moving prisoners when they had more than enough problems in moving their own troops. Though logical, this overlooked the high value that the Germans attached to their prisoners. During one of Hitler's military conferences in January 1945, the fate of Allied airmen, prisoners at Stalag-Luft III, who were now close to the Eastern front, had been discussed. Göring suggested that they should be left for the Russians. Hitler's response was, 'They must leave, even if they march on foot. The *Volkssturm* will be mobilised for that. Anyone who runs away will be shot.'

Stalag IX A at Ziegenhain, a grossly overcrowded camp for NCOs and other ranks, was liberated by American troops with its inmates in situ. Stalags were intended to be administrative centres for the working parties – *Arbeitskommando* – in German agriculture or industry. In the confused conditions of spring 1945 Ziegenhain simply filled up with men as the Germans were unable to allocate enough of the incomers, many Americans from the Ardennes, to external kommandos. In the end the German attitude to their prisoners at the two Oflags was simple. The men as officers were a valuable resource, even if many were old and out of touch with modern warfare.

Like Harry Roberts, Captain John Humphrey Sewell, Royal Engineers in Oflag IX A/H, had been employed by the London and North Eastern Railway, also in York, before he was called up and then captured in Greece in 1941. John Sewell's diary is perhaps most interesting for its almost obsessive attention to meals and food. This entry is typical:

> **Wednesday 14th March**
> Breakfast 8.45: 2 slices bread (incl. 1 crust) with Ger. marg and Ger. jam
> cup of tea with RX dried milk.
> Lunch 12.30: the usual – 1 plate vegetable soup, ½ slice bread with Ger. marg cup RX cocoa with cond milk RX and 2 sacherins.
> Supper biscuits and 2 ovaltine tablets.

Sewell retained his railway associations as a prisoner of war. Included in his papers is a photograph of fellow prisoners that has, along with their signatures, the names of their peacetime railway employers.

Sewell shared a room at Spangenberg with Captain Ralph Venables Wilbraham MC, Pioneer Corps. Ralph Wilbraham was born in 1893, making him at 52 one of the oldest men in either camp. He had won the Military Cross whilst serving as Brigade Signals Officer with the Cheshire Yeomanry in Palestine in the First World War. Called up in 1939, he went to France as a Captain in the Auxiliary Military Pioneers and was captured near Rouen in June 1940. After time in various camps he eventually arrived at Oflag IX A/H. After the war he became the Director of the Cheshire Red Cross.

Another older officer, who had also seen service in the First War, was Lieutenant Edward Baxter, Royal Army Ordnance Corps. He was 48 in 1945 and in Oflag IX A/Z. Baxter was captured in Greece in 1941. In his liberation questionnaire he gave his pre-war occupation as 'writer'. Baxter's account of his life as a prisoner, which he wrote later, provides more background than others but is still light on emotional content. Baxter was one of the prisoners who did not believe that the Germans would move them but did record rumours that they would be marched away. He attended a lecture given by one of the survivors of the appalling winter marches through the snow from the East, 'It had been a terrible thing, and several men had died. We did not relish the prospect at all.'

Two men from Spangenberg captured in France in 1940 wrote an account of their time in captivity and their attempts to escape that became a best seller in the early 1950s. *South to Freedom* was written by Terence Prittie and Captain William Earle 'Bill' Edwards, Royal West Kent Regiment. Lieutenant Prittie went on to be a more well-known writer than Edward Baxter. He had been captured at Calais along with Colonel Holland in 1940. He made the first of his six escape attempts whilst still in France being marched eastwards. In January 1943, as a repeat escapee, he was to have been transferred to Oflag V C at Colditz, but at the last moment it was found that Colditz had no space and he was sent to Spangenberg instead. Terence Prittie believed strongly that the Germans would not simply abandon their prisoners, 'That many officers still resolutely believed that the Germans would leave us to take our chances in Spangenberg was an amazing tribute to the myopic futility of war-weary minds.' Prittie wrote a series of articles for the *Cricketer* magazine whilst at Spangenberg that were posted back to London. Each article was written, as Prittie remarks, without access to Wisden and yet they are packed with statistics and team details.

It was possible to let off steam playing sport. Spangenberg had a sports field that men from Upper and Lower Camp were allowed to use under parole but not at the same time. Contact between the two sites were very limited. It was therefore very unusual in December 1944 when the pantomimes from Lower and Upper Camp were performed at both sites. Ted Beckwith was allowed to visit Upper Camp to collect contributions for the *Quill*.

Cricket was possible within Lower Camp, but sport within the Schloß was limited to using the moat for cricket, football and hockey, on a very small pitch. Flooded and frozen, it was used for curling in the winter. Rotenburg had to make do with its small parade ground for most sporting activity, but the men were allowed access to what John Logan called a 'rough mossy piece of course pasture', where occasional team games could be

The parade ground at Rotenburg was not large, but during the winter months it became traditional to surround part of it with low snow banks and then flood the interior to create a rink for skating and ice hockey. International matches were held, usually featuring a Canadian team. (Otago Settlers' Museum, New Zealand)

Gambling was a major activity in the camps. 'Race meetings' were popular: model horses were moved by a throw of the dice around a course. The meeting drawn by McIndoe on 29 May was threatened with cancellation when Oberstleutnant Brix learnt that one of the horses had been christened 'New Commandant – By Little Adolf out of What's Left'. John Logan's diary for 22–28 May 1944 records that two prisoners had been marched before the Commandant as a result. (Otago Settlers' Museum, New Zealand)

played. It had been an athletics track. More regular sport was to be had on the camp's skating rink each winter. Half of the parade ground was flooded within snow banks. Once the water froze there was space for skating and ice hockey. In January 1945 a Canadian hockey team drew with England 4-4.

Most of the Canadians had arrived in the camps after Dieppe, but the Arnhem operation brought 'CANLOAN' officers; subalterns, of whom the Canadian Army had a surplus, who served with British regiments. The unusual regimental affiliation made many existing prisoners suspicious of the newcomers until news of the scheme spread through the camps.

There was of course no opportunity to play polo, nor the other favourite activity of former cavalry regiments, hunting. Major Bruce Middleton Hope Shand, 12th Lancers, the father of the Duchess of Cornwall, felt the loss. Shand had been captured in the confusion of the Eighth Army's pursuit of the Afrika

Korps after El Alamein. Shand was able to get into the surrounding country on parole walks and in parties to cut wood for the castle's central heating boiler. It is unlikely that 'Gone away or the Harkaway Hunt', a board game for two players devised by Ted Beckwith, fulfilled Shand's fox hunting desires. Ted Beckwith also did some yacht racing at Spangenberg, but again sadly it was one of his board games.

Captain Ian Reid, Black Watch, was another horse-lover and like Shand was unfortunate to have been captured as the Allies were in the ascendancy in North Africa. His account of time in and out of Italian camps and his final escape was published in 1947 by Gollanz as *Prisoners at Large; the Story of Five Escapes*. Reid was an inveterate escapee and was one of the first to part company with Oflag IX A/Z, on 29 March 1945. In 1970 he achieved a life-long ambition by becoming the Point-to-Point correspondent on *The Times*.

The Canadians introduced baseball and softball to Rotenburg. One game is described in a poem written in the camp, a match between the 'Mandarines' and the 'Tomcats', on which men had 'pledged their pants and their back pay'. A chaplain describes there being three 'firms' of bookmakers at Rotenburg. Bets were made on almost anything, including the next day's weather. Favourite bets were on the date of their liberation or the end of the war.

Escape attempts occurred at both camps. The only successful one from Rotenburg was in early 1943 by two Indian Army officers who reached Switzerland. Unfortunately, the British official histories of the camps do not explain how they got out of the camp. Spangenberg Upper Camp in the Schloß and sitting on its rocky promontory was not an easy place to escape from. For almost a year from July 1942 there was work on a tunnel, before the Germans discovered it. The other route out of Upper Camp was by variations on booms and aerial runways to cross the moat. Two men did get across the moat in October 1943 and reached Darmstadt before being recaptured. A tunnel at Lower Camp that was planned to go 40 yards collapsed after 19 yards.

Bill Edwards, who collaborated with Terence Prittie on an account of his time in camps and their escape attempts, was also a pretty regular escapee. He had been captured whilst serving with 7th Battalion Royal West Kent Regiment. His penultimate escape attempt was from Obermaßfeld prison hospital in 1943, where he had been temporarily transferred from Spangenberg. He was within 15 miles of the Swiss border when he was recaptured.

The War Office history of Rotenburg rather oddly omits the last escape from the camp, made in September 1944. Seven men, disguised as orderlies under the supervision of two other prisoners disguised as German guards, walked out of the main gate having made a copy of the key to the gate. Lieutenant Hamish Forbes, Welsh Guards, describes the key being dropped accidentally by a guard, found, copied and returned to the Germans, in the hope that its loss would not be reported and new locks fitted. The 'guards' had wooden rifles and uniforms made by the prisoners. The men were all back in the camp in October. Whilst in police hands, they were threatened with being handed over to the Gestapo, as a result of the hardening of German attitudes to escape following the breakout from Stalag Luft III. Forbes had been captured in France near Dunkirk in 1940 and in all made an impressive 10 escape attempts.

One of the oddest escape attempts was a tunnel at Rotenburg that started above ground, on the first floor. The tunnel went into an outside wall in an upstairs toilet and then down inside the rubble-filled core of the wall. It was to have then gone under the surrounding concrete and asphalt, and out beyond the perimeter wire. The Germans discovered the spoil from the tunnel dumped in the roof space in June 1944, but it took them a month to find the tunnel. When the Jakob-Grimm-Schule was renovated in the 1980s there was still rubble from the tunnel lying on the rafters in the roof.

The most senior officer at Rotenburg to record his experiences was a member of the escape committee. Major Edward James Augustus Howard 'Peter' Brush, Rifle Brigade. Peter Brush was Security Officer at Rotenburg. He had been captured like Rupert Holland and Terence Prittie at Calais in 1940. He was 44 in 1945. His diary shows him as a blunt, no-nonsense man. An Ulsterman, in the 1970s he confided to friends that he could sort out the IRA very quickly if he and his old regiment were given a free hand. Brush's account includes this exchange concerning the end:

> I remember a very decent officer, a man older than myself, saying at one of our meals, 'Well, anyway, it couldn't make much difference to us because I think Hitler will make certain we're all killed before any relieving army gets us.' I remember afterwards saying 'I don't think that as a First World War Officer someone like you should make a remark like that. I know we all had it in our hearts, but for God's sake, let's keep it there and not start spouting defeatism.'

One man's account, unsurprisingly, includes more spiritual reflections on life in the camp and beyond the wire. The Reverend George William Forster was a Roman Catholic Chaplain. Forster had joined the army as a chaplain in 1940. He was in his mid-thirties in 1945. After the war he returned to the North East as a parish priest. George Forster was captured at Tobruk in 1942. He was a good natured man who found the occasional confusion caused amongst young women by his being a young soldier, but also a priest, very amusing. He seems to have found his time in prison camp in Roman Catholic Italy more spiritually uplifting than being in German hands later in the war. Christmas was of course important: 'Our Midnight Mass by dim candle-light, so redolent of that stable in Bethlehem, in the heart of hostile Germany, gave balm to our souls. Peace within us, peace with our German captors. Alas, 24 hours later

Marcus Edwards, Royal Australian Artillery, was captured in Crete in 1941. His diary consists of pithy comments usually with a strong anti-German bias. He personifies what Reverend George Forster called the 'hard nuts' amongst the prisoners: men who never had a good word for anyone or thing German. He was a very competent violinist, and his widow, the composer Miriam Hyde, created the Marcus Edwards Violin Prize for young violinists in his memory. (Green Collection)

Lieutenant Frank Slater, Queen's Own Cameron Highlanders. Slater was captured along with the rest of 51st Highland Division in June 1940. In 1947 Hutchinson published a collection of his drawings in *As You Were: A Book of Caricatures*. Many of the drawings depict men playing musical instruments or in costume for plays – a reminder of the important role of music and drama in the prisoners' lives. (Green Collection)

we would exult at the sound of Allied planes dealing destruction and death to German cities, but at least for Christmas Day we were at peace with ourselves and our guards.'

George Forster refers in his account of prison life to 'hard nuts' amongst the prisoners, who had a hatred of all Germans and things German. The hard nuts were usually also regular escapees. One was Lieutenant Marcus Edwards, Australian

Artillery. Marcus is shown in a caricature drawn by Lieutenant Frank Slater, Queen's Own Cameron Highlanders, as a maniacal violinist. His love of music was matched in its intensity by his dislike of the Germans. His diary has terse entries that include 'Hatred of Germans rising'. Edwards had been captured in Crete in 1941. Forster's hard nuts included Hamish Forbes and Captain David 'Moose' Maud, Somerset Light Infantry. Maud had led the September 1944 escape attempt from Rotenburg.

All the liberated men should have completed a liberation questionnaire once they were back in Allied hands. Sadly, only 50 per cent of the documents have survived for the two Oflags. The questionnaire asked where the men had been captured, had they been ill treated and had they experienced any evidence of treachery by fellow prisoners. Amongst the questionnaires that have survived are those of Bombardier G. Buchan and Gunner F. Buckland, both Royal Artillery and both having given their ranks on the form as 'General'; their army numbers gave them away. It is hard not to sympathise with them: they are finally liberated, back in British hands, and the army gives them forms to fill in.

Lieutenant Frank Slater, Queen's Own Cameron Highlanders, drew many of the men in the camps. He like many others had been captured when the 51st Highland Division surrendered. They had been left isolated by the surrender of French troops around them. His progression like the other prisoners around German camps brought him into contact with many men who would end the war in Spangenberg or Rotenburg. His drawing of Marcus Edwards and his violin is one of many showing prisoners with musical instruments. The YMCA provided many of the instruments. Rotenburg had both a classical and a jazz orchestra and on Christmas night 1944 there was a recital of music composed in the camp.

Music was one of the things that help keep the men sane. Under the Geneva Convention as officers they were not allowed to work. Music, along with painting, theatrical performances

Lieutenant Desmond Llewelyn as Theseus in a production of *A Midsummer Night's Dream*, directed by Michael Langham, Rotenburg, October 1944. This was the last major production at Rotenburg. The costumes were provided by a theatrical costumiers in Frankfurt. Llewelyn had been captured in France in 1940 whilst serving with the Royal Welch Fusiliers. He had been an actor before the war and returned to the stage afterwards. His best known role was as 'Q' in the James Bond films. (Green Collection)

and education filled the void for many. Rotenburg housed two men who would become well-known in the theatre and cinema after the war. Michael Langham had been a solicitor's clerk before joining the Gordon Highlanders as a Lieutenant alongside his brother Geoffrey. Both were captured at St Valéry-en-Caux in June 1940 when 51st Highland Division surrendered and both were in Oflag IX A/Z in 1945. Michael discovered his love – and more significantly, his talent – for the theatre whilst a prisoner. Logan commented after Langham transferred to the 'theatrical mess' – a cubicle with other prisoners interested in the theatre – that he was 'too pre-occupied with one thing, that boy'. After the war Langham managed theatres in Coventry, Birmingham and Glasgow, and directed at the Old Vic and Stratford. He spent ever more time in North America directing at Stratford Ontario and on Broadway. He and his wife spent time in the 1950s with Picasso. When interviewed for this book a few years before his death an American theatre award had just been named after him. Michael Langham died in 2011 aged 91. Whilst Langham became a well-known figure in theatrical circles, his fellow prisoner, Desmond Llewellyn, Lieutenant Royal Welch Fusiliers, achieved global stardom playing 'Q' in the James Bond films. His camp nickname was 'Ham', a little unfair given that he was a professional actor before the war. He had appeared on the infant BBC Television in January 1939 in a one-act play about Bonnie Prince Charlie. Llewelyn had been captured in May 1940 during the retreat to Dunkirk.

The theatrical presentations at Rotenburg were not only serious plays. The orderlies put on a revue in November 1944, 'Rise and Shine', that included an item 'The Old School Tie – a Borstalian broadside'. Alan Green's strong chapel background left him with some qualms over the content, despite his being a member of the 'Black Gang' that built the stage sets, 'A fairly good show, ' he wrote about 'Rise and Shine'. 'But the emphasis seems to be on smut, and especially on women and good food.'

The *Quill* included several cartoons based on longing for female company. At Rotenburg the men found the parade of young women from the town by the camp on Sunday afternoons of such interest that it was reported in both German and British magazines.

Educational activities in the camps included professional legal and accountancy qualifications, with examination papers posted back to the UK for marking. Captain Patrick Corfield, Royal Artillery, also a member of the ill-fated 51st Highland Division, gained his law qualifications as a prisoner. After the war he became an MP and served as Minister for Aerospace in an early Thatcher government. Captain Baldwin Wilson, 1 Border, had been a bank clerk before the war. He took, and passed, his Part II Associate Examinations of Banking in the seven months he was in the camp, although he did not get notice of his success until after his release in June 1945. Formal educational activities were led by Captain Charles 'Prof' Hamson. Hamson had been born in Constantinople, as he insisted on calling Istanbul, and was a fluent Greek speaker. He had been working with Cretan guerrillas when he was captured. After the war he returned to Cambridge and became an authority on international and comparative law.

There were less formal educational activities. Harry Roberts, for example, gave two talks on the REME and his diary includes other talks he attended, on Hadrian's Wall, soil erosion and Cardinal Wolsey. John Sewell chaired a Shakespeare Society at Spangeberg that met to read through plays. At least one man did not believe that he benefited from his incarceration, despite the educative efforts made. Lieutenant Harold Ashton, Royal Engineers, captured near Arras in May 1940, described his time

Lieutenant Ken White's notes written after the war identifies the group from left as 'Padre; believed [Captain] Charles Hamson; Doctor; nurse.' Captain Charles John 'Jack' Hamson was involved in educational activities in the camp. He had been captured whilst working with the resistance in Crete. Stabsarzt Dr Hehenkampf was the German doctor at Rotenburg. The woman with him was one of two who accompanied the column and were described variously as 'nurse', 'interpreter', 'secretary', or 'the Doctor's sister'. Some accounts refer to Hauptmann Weigands's wife accompanying them and she could have been the interpreter. Apart from Lieutenant Ken White, the prisoners refer to the Doctor as being helpful. White had no time for him. (Marion Gerritsen-Teunissen Collection)

A drawing class at Rotenburg. It was through a window in this room that Hauptmann Heyl put a warning shot as prisoners cheered Allied aircraft attacking trains on the railway the other side of the Fulda. Heyl's actions led to one of the two war crimes trials that he was subjected to in 1946. (Otago Settlers' Museum, New Zealand)

as a prisoner in articles for the Royal Engineer's magazine entitled 'Wasted Years'.

Although life in the Oflags was not physically demanding in the way that it was for NCOs and other ranks, who were expected to work, it was mentally hard. At Rotenburg two men committed suicide. Brigadier Nicholson had been the senior officer of the Calais garrison in 1940. Nicholson's death affected the camp greatly and the men agreed not to talk about it after the war. He had been a popular SBO, but the isolation that came with the job had led him to worry needlessly about his compromising the code used by SBOs to communicate with the UK. The Germans involved him in a propaganda visit to the site of the Russian massacre of Polish prisoners at Katyn, which must have also tormented him. The other man to take his own life was an Australian, Lieutenant John Learmouth, who was tipped over the edge by news of his brother being killed in action in New Guinea. Being a prisoner of war could feel like a life sentence. The men served their imprisonment with no release date. Until 1943 there was little hope of any release unless it came as a result of a German victory. Guilt over being captured or of still being alive whilst others had died around you, being apart from loved ones, the complete

Life in the Oflags was physically better than that in Stalags or Arbeitskommandos, but emotionally it was very tough. Boredom and feelings of guilt that somehow they had survived when comrades had died preyed on men's' minds, to the extent that there were two suicides at Rotenburg. (Otago Settlers' Museum, New Zealand)

This photograph of Leighton 'Lee' Hill and his YMCA mobile cinema in North Africa was sent as a New Year's card in late 1941. Lee was captured in the aftermath of the Battle of Sidi Azeiz in December 1941, so 1942 was not a good year for him. After liberation he became a war correspondent with the rank of 2nd Lieutenant and went back to Belgium. He took more still shots and some ciné footage of former prisoners being processed in Brussels. (New Zealand Film Archive Stills Collection)

lack of privacy, the cold, the poor food – they all added up to a recipe for depression.

As well as giving themselves a purpose through education, the men countered depression through humour. The Geneva Convention required that prisoners obey the orders of their captors. On one occasion the Commandant at Rotenburg decided that the men's slovenly dress at roll call was to much and he ordered them to wear hats. Accordingly, all the prisoners paraded bareheaded. Dismissed to get their hats, they reassembled with no hats. After several attempts the men finally paraded wearing any head gear they could find, including paper hats.

Leighton 'Lee' McLeod Hill took photographs of the march. In 1945 Lee was 38 and undeniably a character; a larger than life entrepreneur. According to his New Zealand Army records he was a Lance-Corporal. On the Rotenburg nominal roll he is listed as a Lieutenant. Changing ranks and identities was not unheard of in the camps. It was a way of confusing and hence annoying the Germans. It was also a way for NCOs and other ranks to receive the better treatment that came with being an officer prisoner. In Hill's case he was a non-combatant like the medical staff and padres. He was employed by the YMCA and led, or was part of, a unit that showed films to the troops in North Africa.

Before the war Lee had worked in the New Zealand film industry. He had co-produced the country's first talkie in 1936, *Down on the Farm*. After the war Lee formed Television Films Ltd many years before TV reached New Zealand. It was a common joke amongst the prisoners that no one who had been captured in North Africa would admit to having been caught by the Italians. Lee Hill went further. He had not just been captured by the Africa Korps, his YMCA film trailer had been captured personally by Rommel at Tobruk in late 1941. Although none of the other accounts refer to Lee by name, he was well known in the camp for the film shows that he presented in the evenings using British, American and German feature films and German documentaries.

Where Lee got his camera and film from is a mystery. In a later magazine article he promised to describe everything 'except for the incidental circumstances under which I "acquired" the camera and the films which enabled me to accompany my story with a pictorial record of events'. Hill's diary for the period from 27 March until 5 April is missing. Having a camera in the camp would have been difficult. Cameras were crucial to creating false passes and identity cards for escapees, and were therefore one of the items that the regular German searches were designed to find. Lee makes no reference to the photographs taken in the camp. There were, for example, photographs of the 'Midsummer Night's Dream' production. Presumably these were taken by an authorised German photographer. 'Acquired' suggests that Hill did not buy it with chocolate or cigarettes, so we are left with found, which is unlikely, or stole. The first photograph that has come to light dates from Easter Sunday morning at the Kalkhof. If he 'acquired' it there, photographing the yard with people watching from the windows of the overlooking house would have been risky. By the process of elimination the most likely source was Rockensuß or the billet near Oetmannshausen. The story of Lee and his camera is complicated by the fact that he had taken pictures whilst in an Italian camp. These include a shot taken inside a railway wagon whilst the prisoners were being moved to Germany in 1943.

George Forster mentions watching the films that Hill presented. Rita Hayworth in *You Were Never Lovelier* made a big impact and was shown several times due to popular demand. Harry Roberts wrote of seeing Roy Rogers in *Silver Spurs* in January. He also records watching seven silent German documentaries – ant life, glass-making, elephants and the life of a pea, hooded crows, glassmaking and the 1914–1918 War. Lee called the documentaries 'Lee Hills Film Factualities'. He noted that he had 'found' around 200, but where and how he does not say.

The silent films had commentaries. These were given by a prisoner whose stories were not believed in the camp. They earned him the nick-name 'Bullshit'. His stories were true. 'Bullshit' Smith was listed in the camp records as Captain Keith A. Smith, Royal Artillery. But was in fact Captain A Quas-Cohen, 9 Commando. Concerned how he would be treated as a Jewish Commando, Quas-Cohen had adopted a false identity. He had originally served with the Royal Artillery, but had volunteered for special operations. He had been captured during Operation *Sunstar*, a canoe reconnaissance of the French coast near Le Havre.

Two prisoners in Rotenburg had been sentenced to death after capture whilst on reconnaissance missions to the Channel Islands. Lieutenant John Symes and Lieutenant Hubert Nicolle, both originally Hampshire Regiment, were captured whilst in the Commandos on Guernsey in 1940 and convicted of spying. They were taken to France and imprisoned in Paris, where their POW status was recognised and their sentences were commuted.

From 1 April 1945 Lee Hill compiled a photographic record of Oflag IX A/Z, but if he took photographs before then, they have disappeared. Lee played up the mystery of how he obtained the camera and film, but it is clear that he was taking photographs quite openly. He records discussing with one of the German officers excursions from the column to get more film and a ciné camera. Lieutenant Kenneth White, Royal Artillery, believed that Hill had bribed a Corporal in the guard to get him a Leica camera and film before they left the camp. If Lee did take photographs earlier or in the camp he makes no comment about them. Few of Hill's photographs have captions and most have had to be identified from clues in the men's diaries or from John McIndoe's drawings, which are captioned and dated.

Captain John Leslie McIndoe recorded all aspects of camp life and many of his drawings and paintings have survived. This was helped by the fact that some were sent back to the UK for exhibition whilst he was still a prisoner. The notes for his last

Captain John McIndoe, New Zealand Expeditionary Force. McIndoe had always regretted not serving in the First World War and was determined to see action in 1939. He was captured in Crete in May 1941. As a prisoner he produced over 300 pieces of work including many portraits of his fellow prisoners. The wet road suggests that Lee Hill took this photograph on 3/4 April. McIndoe is loaded down with the box that had his sketchbooks and no doubt some of his pictures painted whilst in the camp, and a pack on his back. (Otago Settlers' Museum, New Zealand)

exhibition, which opened immediately after his return from Germany at Simpsons of Piccadilly, describe three other exhibitions of his work, including pictures accepted by the annual Royal Institute of Water Colours at the Royal Academy. In all, the notes mention 'more than 300 pictures and portraits' made by McIndoe whilst a prisoner.

John McIndoe, in contrast to Lee Hill, had a more reflective personality. A self portrait shows him in his great coat with the collar turned up and a knitted woollen hat. He is evidently cold and not very happy. A photograph taken by Lee Hill in April shows McIndoe as a tired, slightly haunted man, with his drawing equipment and pictures in a former Red Cross parcel box hanging from his neck and with a pack on his back.

He was nearly 47 when the camp was evacuated. McIndoe's pictures include drawings of men creating the ice rink from part of the camp parade ground and then using it in February 1944, and of them unloading Red Cross parcels from a horse-drawn cart in the snow. The drawings capture the cold and, in the case of the skating, the unease of men not at home on the ice with great economy. He also drew a typical small dormitory. At Rotenburg they were known as cubicles or 'cubes'. McIndoe's drawing shows four bunks and one man sitting reading, who is taking up most of the space. Most of the men describe the cubes having eight residents, for example George Forster, who gave the size of his room as 12 feet by 14 feet, 'shared this with seven

Lieutenant-Colonel Clay and his deputy Lieutenant-Colonel Kennedy, the senior British officers. (SBOs) at Rotenburg. Lee Hill may have taken this picture during the rest day at Nohra in early April. Basil Clay, 7th Battalion Royal West Kent Regiment, was captured in Belgium in 1940. Lieutenant-Colonel Geoffrey Kennedy, East Surrey Regiment, was captured outside Dunkirk in May 1940, whilst commanding the 4th Battalion of the Oxfordshire and Buckinghamshire Light Infantry. Kennedy was awarded the OBE after the war for his work in prison camps. (Green Collection)

Medical orderlies, Nohra, 5 April 1945. First aid during the march was provided by two New Zealand medical orderlies, Don and Jack Fraser (unrelated). Lee Hill's diary includes a description of men on the march that suggests it was almost a pleasant outing, 'Don & Jack Frazer of Nelson are doing grand job as R.A.P. on the trip. They get time to have a lot of fun cooking great meals on the camp fire.' (Green Collection)

others'. Perhaps McIndoe was showing only half of the room. At Spangenberg the men's rooms were known as Messes. John Sewell, the former railwayman, was the grandly titled President of his Mess.

There were other men who left little or no record, but who are central to the story of the Oflags. On the British side the role of Senior British Officer at Rotenburg was shared between Lieutenant-Colonel Basil Laing Clay, Royal West Kent Regiment and Lieutenant-Colonel Geoffrey Welshman 'Bart' Kennedy MC, East Surrey Regiment. Only Clay left any record and that was in a report to the War Office on the help that the camp had received from the Swedish YMCA and Red Cross. 'Bart' Kennedy had won his Military Cross in 1918. In 1945 he was 50 years old. Frank Slater's cartoon shows a smallish, energetic man, marching across the page. And in a Lee Hill photograph taken in April 1945, although Basil Clay is a few inches taller than Kennedy, more patrician with a pipe confidently clenched in his teeth, it is Kennedy who appears the more alert. One can imagine him muttering under his breath that Lee Hill should hurry up, take his blasted picture and go away. Kennedy had been captured near Dunkirk on 30 May 1940 whilst on secondment to lead the 4th Battalion the Ox and Bucks. In his papers at the Imperial War Museum is the nominal roll for Rotenburg at January 1945, along with camp Christmas dinner menus. Once the camp had been liberated Clay became Commanding Officer.

The prisoners naturally organised the camps along military lines. Spangenberg's Upper and Lower Camps were treated as separate battalions, with Colonel Holland as the most senior British Officer and also commander of Lower Camp. Upper Camp was commanded by Lieutenant-Colonel E.A.B. Miller, King's Royal Rifle Corps. At Rotenburg battalions were split into companies, platoons and sections. At Spangenberg the only grouping was into the Upper and Lower Camp battalions of around 200 men each.

Although the camps were for officers, there were also NCOs and other ranks serving as orderlies. Of the 40-odd accounts by prisoners only two are by orderlies. One covers the final period of the men's captivity in outline, whilst the other is primarily a collection of verse describing incidents in prison life. The poetry was written by Sapper Les Robertson, New Zealand Expeditionary Force. He had been captured in Crete.

Four jolly gardeners are we
Gardening in the heart of Germany,
Arriving at work half an hour late,
After cursing children guarding the Commandantur gate.
We hoe and plant day by day,
Dig and rake for 70 pfennig pay,

Watch the women walking by
And look for welcome visitors from the sky.

The 'Commandantur' or more correctly *Kommandtur,* was the camp headquarters. Les Robertson spent time in several working parties, arbeitskommando, and as an orderly at the other hospital in Wehrkreis IX at Haina 50 miles west of the Fulda. Reserve Lazarett Haina specialised in eye problems and housed many blind prisoners. Robertson and the other prisoners would not have been aware that the State Asylum at Haina was part of the Third Reich's euthanasia programme established to murder those not able to contribute to the state.

The biggest omission is a German commentary. Captain John Kennedy, RAMC, provides the only estimate of the size of the guard for one of the camps. He wrote of '80 German guards and most of the officers on the staff of the camp' accompanying Oflag IX A/Z during their evacuation. The guards for both camps came from *Landesschützenbataillon* 631, a Territorial Army

Captain John James Kennedy, RAMC was an eye specialist but was pressed into service as a generalist during Oflag IX A/Z's evacuation. Lee Hill's diary records him photographing the medical staff during the rest day on Friday 6 April 1945 at Nohra. None of his patients have been identified. (Green Collection)

Oberfeldwebel Heinrich Sultan had been the caretaker of the Jakob-Grimm-Schule before the war and became an Oberfeldwebel in the guard once the school became a prison camp. Sultan had been wounded whilst serving in the German Army in the First World War. He returned to the school in 1945 and once more became caretaker in the US hospitals that occupied the building and then with the school once it returned. (Noll Collection)

unit. Sadly, of these only three men left fragmentary notes and just one refers to the whole march.

Oberfeldwebel Heinrich Sultan was the caretaker of the school that housed Oflag IX A/Z. In 1966 he wrote an account of his life at the camp for the school magazine. There are also statements made to British military tribunals by the *Abwehroffizier* – Security Officer – of Oflag IX A/Z, Hauptmann Prosper Heyl and by *Obergefreiter* Martin Christian Erhard, both from Rotenburg, but these are limited. No camp papers survive. Ted Beckwith at Spangenberg saw the Germans burning their records in late March. Hauptmann Heyl in a statement to the British after the war claimed to have burnt records at Rotenburg in March 1945.

This makes Heinrich Sultan's memoir significant. In 1939 the school had been selected as a military hospital and in August 1939, in pouring rain and using open farm wagons to carry books and equipment, Sultan organised the school's move to the centre of Rotenburg. With the school gone, 500 beds were set up under the direction of a fierce German matron from the *Reichsarbeitsdienst* – German Labour Service. The beds were never used. They were removed four weeks later when the buildings became a prison camp. The first inmates were Polish officers and 68 Polish priests. The SS moved the priests to Dachau, where 66 died. Sultan was warned not to watch their removal too closely. The Polish officers were transferred to a camp in northern Germany. If the British prisoners knew of Rotenburg's terrible history they never mention it.

Sultan's only son was killed at Stalingrad. Sultan's personal tragedy and that of Prosper Heyl were known in some detail to the men. John Logan's diary for week beginning 22 May 1944: 'The new guard commander in the camp served 6 ½ years [sic] in the last War, lost the use of his left arm and was blown up in both legs, had a son wounded at Stalingrad in this War and has lost his house in Dortmund in an air raid.'

The German Commandants set the tone for camp life and they would direct the men's final weeks as prisoners. Sadly they have left no record of their time as Commandants or of the evacuations. Both were serving in the prisoner of war service – the *Kriegsgefangenenwesen* – having offended the Party in one way or another.

In 1945 the overall commander of both camps was *Oberst* Kurt Schrader. He was 51 in 1945. His papers show that he was a respected and well liked officer. But he was separated from his wife and in Nazi Germany this was a bar to further promotion, even when it was fully accepted by his superiors that he was in no way to blame for his marital situation. His personal records show that he could never expect any post in the field army. So despite good reports, he spent time in the backwaters of the staff of Wehrkreis IX at Meiningen, before becoming Commandant at Spangenberg in October 1942. He spoke Russian and French, and no doubt his English was more than passable. He had been on the staff of the joint German-Soviet Commission established during the occupation of Poland.

His army reports describe him as good at building relationships and dealing with work efficiently; ideal qualities for a man who had to cope with two camps holding almost 60 British colonels, who as events proved were not going to let the small matter of being POWs curb their behaviour. Schrader had little to do with the day-to-day operation of the camps and Robert Montgomery remembered *Hauptmann* Roth, the *Lageroffizier* at Upper Camp, as the most senior German officer seen at the Schloß.

Schrader's deputy was *Oberstleutnant* Rudolf Carl Otto Franz Brix. Brix was also Commandant of Oflag IX A/Z. In the turmoil at the end of the war, only part of Brix's early military records survived. He was a year younger than Schrader. He had been born in Hannover, but his family had connections with Nordhausen and Wimmelburg. He had joined the cavalry in August 1914. After the First World War he transferred to the police and eventually reached the rank of Hauptmann. He managed the German equestrian team at the 1936 Olympics. Brix rejoined the army in 1936 as a Major during Hitler's expansion of the army. During the war he served with 510 Infantry Regiment in the 293rd Infantry Division in France and on the Eastern Front. The Division suffered heavy casualties during the Battle of Kursk. He was promoted to Oberstleutnant in 1942.

Brix's previous police experience was known to some prisoners, including Captain John Logan Argyll & Sutherland Highlanders, the latter describing him as an 'SS appointee'. In fact at the time Brix arrived at Rotenburg the SS had no connection with the camps. Himmler was appointed to lead the Reserve Army, responsible for prisoner of war camps, after the bomb attack on Hitler in June 1944. The police connection was not particularly significant, as many former soldiers joined the police after the First World War and returned to the military under Hitler. Brix's military correctness earned him the dislike of the prisoners and the suspicion of the regime. Lee Hill, for example, described him as a 'tiger' for sticking to his duties during the evacuation and questioning possible deserters, whilst Germany crumbled around him.

Brix had succeeded Major Herman Bormann as Commandant. Dr Bormann had been the school's headmaster and went back to teaching when Brix arrived. Major Bormann was liked by the prisoners – who nicknamed him 'Daddy Bormann'. After the war, Brix moved to Rotenburg from Potsdam. In the early 1970s he was teaching at a riding school. He was known as a very correct man, still kissing the hands of ladies decades after the war. For Brix, as with Schrader, his posting to an Oflag was a demotion. Brix was not enthusiastic about the Nazi Party. He believed that the traditions and good name of the German Army were more important than the Party and it was this that led to him being transferred to Oflag IX A/Z at Rotenburg.

Hauptmann August Seybold led Oflag IX A/H for most of its evacuation. He was the Abwehroffizier, the security officer. Unlike his opposite number at Rotenburg, Seybold was liked. 'He had a sense of humour,' was Robert Montgomery's comment. William Watson thought that Seybold had been a school teacher before the war. Hauptmann Prosper Heyl at Rotenburg was tried for war crimes in 1946, though these were minor and he was acquitted on one charge and though found guilty of the second, the sentence was not confirmed.

One German who was living alongside the prisoners at Rotenburg has contributed his recollections as a schoolboy to this story. Björn Ulf Noll's father taught German, Latin and Theology at the Jakob-Grimm-Schule. During the war the family continued to live in the school house that was attached to the main building. He was possibly one of the children that Les Robertson saw guarding the gate. Björn's memories include the unofficial 'apology parade' that followed a failed escape attempt by Hamish Forbes, Rupert Lubbock and others. The party having broken down a door in the former school building found themselves, not as they hoped, in an empty corridor in the Commandant's house, but in the bedroom of Frau Schmoll, the elderly wife of a retired forester who was one of several people sharing the house. Frau Bormann was so outraged that the bedroom of a German lady could be violated in this way that she insisted her husband instigate an apology parade. Since the British side could not allow the event to reflect badly on the British Army, the members of the apology party wore civilian clothes. It thus became a purely unofficial, personal, event.

Björn Ulf Noll's memories are matched to an extent by those of Harald Schlanstedt, who was a 16-year-old in 1945 from Wimmelburg, a copper mining village on the edge of the Harz Mountains. He would witness the eventual liberation of Oflag IX A/Z.

There was a neutral witness. The Reverend Gunner Celander was a Swede and the YMCA representative for Hesse and Thuringia. His job was to alleviate suffering, whether it was that of German civilians under Allied bombing, or of the prisoners of war. His account of this period is in the Swedish National Archives. Gunnar Celander was born to Swedish parents in New York in 1894. The family returned to Sweden in 1905. Gunnar graduated from Lund University with a degree in theology and was ordained in 1920. In 1943 his office and home in Kassel were destroyed in an air raid. He first rented a flat in a Kassel suburb, spending nights in the country under trees or bridges. Eventually he decided the safest place to be during air raids was near an Allied POW camp, so he set about building a house at Rotenburg. 'The Schwedenheim' was built with volunteers from Oflag IX A/Z on the high ground east of the River Fulda and close to the Lutheran cemetery.

Celander was known and respected by men from both Oflags, but at the war's end spent more time with the Rotenburg prisoners. Intriguingly, on 10 March Celander and his boss went to Oflag IX A/Z with a 16mm ciné camera. Lee Hill recorded their activities: 'On Saturday Mr Berg & Father Celander the Swedish YMCA arrived, and with Berg's films, shot 300 feet of 16mm

Technician Charles Sumners was a photographer and a driver with the US Army's 166th Signal Company, US Army photographers being part of the Signal Corps. He spent most of early April with 6th Armored, from crossing the Fulda till the capture of Mühlhausen. (Sumners Collection)

film, but light & enthusiasm were poor.' Sadly there is no further reference to the film and it doe not seem to have survived.

There was another photographer who would witness the end of the war in Germany and events around the two camps. Charles Eugene Sumners, Technician 5th Grade, 166th Signal Company, served with the US Army in Europe and was attached to Patton's 3rd Army in March and April 1945. He photographed US Engineers repairing the bridge across the Fulda and some of 6th Armored Division's advance towards Mühlhausen. Many of his negatives from this period have disappeared, but the images remain in books published at the end of the war.

Another American wrote an account of his part in the eventual liberation of the prisoners. Corporal John Irwin, 33rd Armored Regiment, 3rd Armored Division, served with 1st Army in the US 12th Army Group. Irwin was 18 when he joined the US Army and served as a tank gunner, first in Shermans and latterly in one of the new, more powerful Pershings. Irwin was part of the Task Force that eventually liberated Oflag IX A/Z. After the war Irwin gained his doctorate in Philosophy. Irwin described his wartime experiences in *Another River, Another Town*, published in 2002.

Accounts of the men's captivity naturally tend to give more prominence to memorable events. For most of the time the men faced sheer grinding boredom and hunger, made worse in the earliest years of captivity by the hopelessness of their position. It was a better life physically than many NCOs and other ranks experienced in their working parties but like all prisoners in Germany it was a miserable experience. By March 1945 there was at last hope that the ordeal would soon be over, even if the fear of massacre still hung over the camps.

2

LIBERATION ON THE FULDA?

Suddenly, after March 8th 1945, we were astonished to read that the Americans had captured the Rhine Bridge at Remagen – intact! As the crow flies, Remagen is about 18 kilometres from Rotenburg on the Fulda – under 120 miles.

Lieutenant 'Butch' Laing, Sherwood Foresters, Oflag IX A/Z, captured Norway April 1940.

On 11 March the German daily radio bulletin reported, with no preamble of any kind, the news that there was an enemy bridgehead across the Rhine, at Remagen. The item presupposed that the listener already knew of the capture of the Ludendorff bridge: 'The enemy have, despite strong resistance, managed to expand their foothold on the east bank of the Rhine.' The Americans had in fact captured the railway bridge three days earlier, but it was not until 11 March that the Germans released the news. That day, Lee Hill wrote in his diary '...we had a Rhine bash! Quite the best meal I've had for some time, with tea good & strong for breakfast, good coffee & milk and sugar at 11.15, "Winnie" salmon & potatoes a la Bradley for lunch, tea at 3.30 and at supper we had toad in the hole, potatoes a la Montgomery, peas a l'Anglaise & Remagen Rice Pudding!'

Other men recorded similar bashes created in their own messes. Whilst the capture of the Remagen bridge meant that there would be no stalemate on the Rhine, freedom for the men in the Oflags was to be delayed. The road network from Remagen was not suited to a major advance eastwards and although the bridgehead was gradually expanded the Allies stuck to their original plans for the main assault across the Rhine to be by Montgomery's 21st Army Group north of the Ruhr on 23 March. In the event, Patton's 3rd Army beat Montgomery across by a day and managed to bounce the Rhine at Oppenheim south-west of Frankfurt on 22 March. By 24 March with the successful crossing by 21st Army Group there were three Allied bridgeheads across the Rhine.

The Allies' plan was for the 21st Army Group to push across the north German plain with Hamburg, the Baltic and possibly Berlin as its objective. Its southernmost unit, US 9th Army under General Simpson, would form one arm of a pincer around the German Army Group B in the Ruhr. The other pincer would come from US 1st Army, under General Hodges, breaking out of the Remagen bridgehead. To protect 1st Army's flank, Patton's 3rd Army would move north-east from Oppenheim via Frankfurt towards Kassel. Once Kassel and the Ruhr were secured the American armies would turn eastwards and advance in line, with 1st Army along the southern flank of the Harz Mountains to the Elbe north of Leipzig and 3rd Army to the Czech border via Erfurt and Weimer. The factor therefore that would have most impact on the timing of the American advance eastwards was the speed with which they could close the Ruhr pocket and eliminate resistance at Kassel.

The German forces that should have opposed the Americans had been badly cut up even before they withdrew behind the Rhine. In the north, Army Group H was soon to be confined to the Netherlands. South of them in the Ruhr was Army

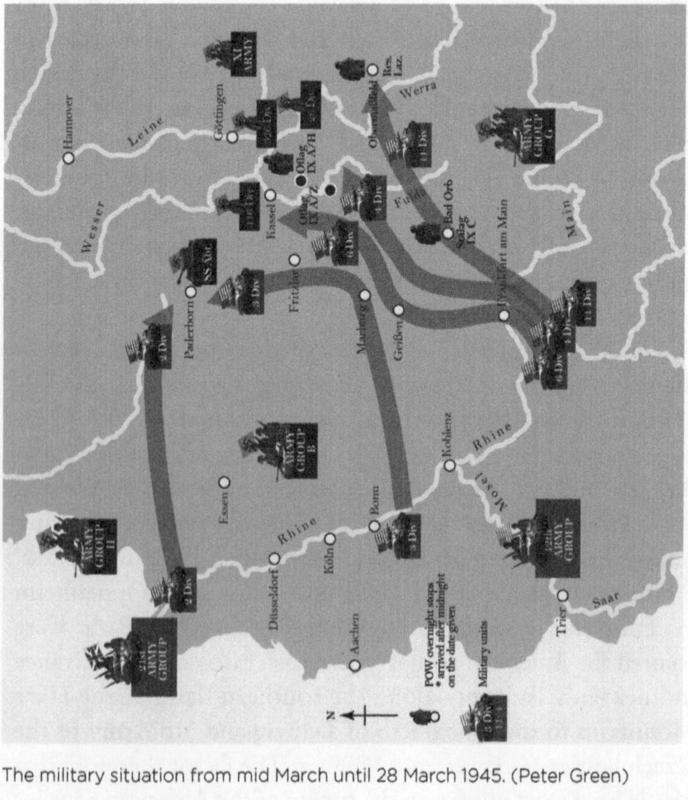

The military situation from mid March until 28 March 1945. (Peter Green)

Group B, further south was Army Group G. The American advances from Remagen and from Frankfurt pinned a large part of Army Group G against the Rhine. Thereafter there was little that German commanders could do to prevent 1st and 3rd Army advancing at will. On 28 March, 3rd Armored Division, part of 1st Army, had reached Marburg, 50 miles from the Oflags. But the next day they turned 90 degrees northwards towards the Ruhr. That day the Division covered almost 100 miles before reaching Paderborn. Here, finally, its advance shuddered to a halt. Paderborn was at the centre of a military training area and the training units had been organised as SS Brigade *Westfalen*. The Brigade included part of Heavy Panzer Battalion 507 that was re-equipping with Tiger II tanks at Sennelager. Brigade Westfalen had been tasked to cut across the line of the American advance from the south. They and 3rd Armored met outside of Paderborn. For the next five days 1st Army had a severe fight on its hands trying to eliminate the SS's Tigers, before it could link up with 9th Army coming from the north.

South of them, 3rd Army had cleared Frankfort by 28 March and was advancing north-eastwards towards Kassel. Its lead unit, 6th Armored, would pass 20 miles to the west of the high ground behind Rotenburg. But of more immediate concern to the Germans, and the best hope of liberation for the prisoners, was the next American unit to the south, 4th Armored. They would reach Bad Hersfeld 10 miles south of Rotenburg on 30 March and if they maintained their direction of advance would be east of the camps the following day.

Taking Kassel was originally intended to be 1st Army's responsibility, but as they remained heavily engaged around Paderborn, it became a task for 3rd Army. This change of plan, brought about largely by the Germans demonstrating the superiority of Tiger tanks over 3rd Armored's Shermans, would affect the men at Spangenberg and Rotenburg over the coming weeks. Instead of advancing on a broad front with 1st Army, Patton's units would begin to push farther and faster east than other American units. This created an American salient around Erfurt.

With all hope of holding the Americans on the Rhine gone, the Germans began to plug the gap between Army Group B in the Ruhr and Army Group G in the south. Eleventh Army, a new army, was created from training groups and stragglers. General Fretter-Pico, a veteran of the Eastern Front, took command of one of its corps east of Kassel in early April. He was shocked to find no coherent front line nor any complete German units. His Corps had two newly formed *Volksgrenadier* Divisions, 26 and 326, and detachments and brigades scraped together from wherever men and equipment could be found. Both Volksgrenadier Divisions were considerably under strength. Hitler demanded that Kassel was to be held at all costs and the city was declared a fortress – 'Festung Kassel'. The 166th Reserve Infantry Division from Denmark was rushed to bolster its defence. South of Kassel, Fretter-Pico began to create a defensive line along the Fulda. At Rotenburg the SS organised a collecting point for stragglers who were then allocated to ad hoc units. Although less than 100 feet wide south of Kassel, the Fulda does have high ground on its eastern bank that provided some basis for defence. Spangenberg, six miles east of the Fulda and Rotenburg, 500 yards to the west of the river, would lie on the new front line.

Kassel was also significant for the part it played in the administration of the Oflags. It was where the headquarters for Wehrkreis IX, including the prisoner of war administration, was based. If Kassel were to be lost to the Germans it would complicate matters for Oberst Schrader. His primary concern during the seven days before Easter would be how quickly the Americans moved. By 28 March he had the answer. At the speed that their armoured divisions were moving the Americans could arrive at the camps in two or at the most three days.

There had been some signs that the guards at both camps had become demoralised since the Allied landings in Normandy in 1944. In August 1944 a guard at Spangenberg had commented on news of the Allied advances through France that it was fine,

Oflag IX A/Z's guard detachment. The guards for both camps were provided by Landesschützenbataillon 631, a Territorial Army unit with its headquarters in the former castle of the Princes of Hesse at Rotenburg. According to the senior British camp medical officer, Captain John Kennedy RAMC, 80 officers and men of the guard accompanied them on their evacuation. The man giving instructions here is Unteroffizier Altmann. (Green Collection)

Lee Hill took few photographs of Oflag IX A/Z's guards. This blurred image shows one of two dog handlers, either Obergefreiter Martin Christian Erhard or Alois Schleicher. Erhard was a witness at the Rockensuß war crime trial; he was a farmer from the village of Oberthalhausen, about six miles west of Rotenburg. Either before the march began or on the first day of the march he gave his home address to Captain Quas-Cohen and Lieutenant Smith and offered to shelter them if they escaped. (Marion Gerritsen-Teunissen Collection)

Captain John Logan, Argyll & Sutherland Highlanders, who was captured on the Somme in June 1940. Collins published his diary in 1948. It provides a detailed account of his life as a prisoner from 1940 until Wednesday 28 March 1945. His last entry describes men still convinced that the Germans would not evacuate the camps. (Green Collection)

but that they needed to go faster. Hauptmann Roth was overheard in late March saying, 'It's all up with Germany now.' In January 1945 John Logan recorded one of the dog handlers at Rotenburg being carried out of the guard's quarters drunk, singing the Internationale.

Spangenberg now saw a new source of income for the prisoners: the provision of 'Holdentod' – notes written in English that affirmed that the German holder had treated his English captives well. It was hoped these would bring better treatment if the guard was himself captured. At Rotenburg, Reverend George Forster remembered, 'An Austrian officer, who had recently arrived, used to greet us when no Germans were present with two salutes. First he gave the normal "Heil Hitler",

Oberst Kurt Schrader, the Commandant of Oflag IX A/H and its sub camp A/Z. His career was blighted by his separation from his wife that went against Nazi social mores regarding the family. He survived the war and according to British records he was living in Spangenberg in 1946. (Bundesarchive)

Oberstleutnant Rudolf Brix took over as Commandant at Rotenburg and Oberst Schrader's deputy after service in France and on the Eastern Front. He was not liked by the prisoners, but this seems to have been influenced largely by his succeeding the more easygoing Major Bormann, the Jakob-Grimm-Schule's headmaster, and Brix's very correct Prussian manner, rather than any specific incidents. Major Bormann was known to the prisoners as 'Daddy Bormann'. (Bundesarchiv)

then followed it with a sarcastic "Heil blutig Hitler".' In January 1945 Hauptmann Heyl was believed to have confessed to a senior British officer that Germany had lost the war.

The guards may have been showing signs of demoralisation, but senior officers at both camps would do everything, within the Geneva Convention, to keep their prisoners from being liberated. The option that the prisoners would have preferred was that they be left alone to be liberated or moved into nearby woods to shelter. However, the Geneva Convention was clear that prisoners should not be exposed to danger and removed from the battlefield quickly. Besides which the Germans had already decided that the men were too valuable a military resource to be abandoned. Given Germany's situation, with hindsight this appears crazy, but the Third Reich was determined that the war would not end as it had in 1918. Whether from fear of the regime or from the hope of new wonder weapons, Germany would continue to fight.

Once on the road the two Oflags would continue to be managed together. Their initial objective was the same, their routes were similar and usually they were billeted within a few miles of each other. The exception was the first night, when the two camps were 10 miles apart. The guards were aware that the camps would march near to each other. 'The Germans told us that they would be near us on the march. Later we found this was a lie,' wrote Edward Baxter. Baxter's interpretation of 'near' was too literal. The camps were close, but the men from either column could not be aware of it. When both camps were billeted at Wanfried they were on either side of the town. Men from A/H were allowed to enter the town under parole: prisoners from A/Z were not. In fact to have marched alongside or close together would have contravened standing German orders not to combine marching columns.

The German plan was for Oflag A/H to take three days to reach Mühlhausen. The Rotenburg column had a delayed start on its second day that may have meant it needed four days. None of the Rotenburg men mention how long they expected to be walking, but some of the Spangenberg men did. They were issued with three days of German rations, with the remaining tea, porridge and Red Cross tins distributed amongst the columns. The Rotenburg men were also issued with the camp reserves of dry rations, such as powdered milk, biscuits and cocoa. Men from both camps carried chocolate, sugar, soap and cigarettes that they had been able to save to trade with German civilians. No instructions have survived for either camp. But post-war interrogations of two commandants of camps in the east suggest that Schrader would have drawn up plans to move his prisoners in 1944. The trigger for this was the order issued by Field Marshal Keitel of 19 July for the defence of Germany. Task 6 of this dealt with planning for evacuations. Prisoners of war came first: '(a) Preparations, in cooperation with Reich Commissioners for Defence, for moving prisoners of war to the rear.' This was followed by instructions regarding moving foreign labour to the rear and finally, measures for evacuating the German civilian population. The Order concludes by saying that these instructions are to be used only as a guide and that they should be kept secret so as to avoid 'unnecessary commotion among the civilian population'.

The evacuation plans would then have been modified in February 1945 when the German military High Command (OKW) issued instructions for marches of POWs '*Merkblatt über Vorbereitung und Durchführung von Marschbewegungen (aus den Erfahrungen über Gebietsräumen und Ausweichbewegungen von Kriegsgefangenen*' – 'on the preparation and execution of evacuations of camps on foot based on earlier experiences'. The 'earlier experiences' is a reference to the sudden evacuations from the East in the vicious winter that were underway as the instructions were circulated. Some of those marches would continue until the end of April, with the men having covered 500 miles or more.

The instructions specified, 'Directions are to be prepared for the head guards, showing the route, the stopovers and the destination assembly space. These directions are to be locked up together with secret written instructions for the head guards.'

The OKW instructions required that camp staff were trained so as to make their own preparations for evacuating their camp. The head guard of a unit was to be energetic, able to think independently and if necessary to act independently. From the little that is known of other evacuations in Wehrkreis IX it does not appear that there was a single order for camps to move on a specific date. Details of the route of a small working party, Arbeitskommando 1249 from Stalag IX C, has survived. The kommando was based in Lohra near Marburg and west of the Oflags. The kommando left on 28 March after 3rd Armored had already reached Marburg. Their objective appears to have been Stalag IX C near Weimar, but with American troops already north-east of them the priority for their guard was to reach the east bank of the Fulda. Another kommando from Stalag IX C, kommando 106, left the potassium mines where it had been working on 1 April. They too had an American unit north-east of them by the time that they moved.

Early in March survivors of the evacuation marches from camps in the east arrived in Spangenberg and Rotenburg. The stories they told of sudden evacuation, atrocious weather, the brutality of their guards and the lack of food, appalled the men. Prisoners from Stalag VIII A Gorlitz, Stalag 344 (formerly Stalag VIII B) Lamsdorf and Stalag Luft III Sagan are recorded in men's diaries as arriving at the two Oflags. Some were only passing through, like the two stretcher cases from Sagan seen by Ted Beckwith in early March and possibly travelling to Obermaßfeld hospital. Their story of 19 days continuously walking, 20 kilometres a day through the snow and sleeping in open fields, leaves Beckwith unable to comment. At this point his diary trails off, the sentence incomplete. Later that month a Padre who had marched from Stalag 344 to Stalag IX A at Ziegenhain provides more evidence of atrocities in the East. Beckwith's 'C of E Padre' is possibly the same man who gave a talk at Rotenburg on the eastern marches.

Harry Roberts records Reverend W.V. Wrigley, a South African Padre, giving a lecture on the forced marches from the eastern camps on Sunday March 18. Lee Hill describes him as coming from Gorlitz. A South African doctor is said to have talked to the men in Upper Camp. Padres, doctors and medical orderlies were the men most commonly moved by the Germans to meet the physical and spiritual needs of prisoners. Stalag IX A had become grossly overcrowded with Americans captured in the Ardennes and men marched from the east. On 25 March, Beckwith describes a padre and a doctor from Spangenberg going to assist at Zeigenhain and notes that the camp now had priority for Red Cross parcels.

Concern over the fitness of some of the older prisoners to cope with an evacuation march feature in the accounts from Spangenberg. Terence Prittie noted that '…such a march would be tough, possibly too tough for men whose muscles were weak and limbs lax after months of under-nourishment and years of sedentary existence.' He decided that if the camp was evacuated he would leave the column at the earliest opportunity to avoid the ordeal of a long journey on foot.

At Rotenburg, whilst being appalled at the details of the eastern marches, the men learned from them. The most important thing was to have a kit bag or rucksack packed and ready to go at a moment's notice. The pack should have, along with clothes and food, if at all possible cigarettes, soap and chocolate to use to barter with the civilian population.

Some of the men made rucksacks from shirts or coats sewn along the bottom and with the arms adapted as straps, or from kitbags with braces sewn on as straps. Harry Roberts made a kitbag in an afternoon 'from old trousers'. Others had bags and cases. John McIndoe converted a Red Cross box into a carrier for his pictures and sketchbook. He carried this on his chest, suspended from the straps of his rucksack on his back. Terence Prittie at Spangenberg described men recovering hidden stocks of food from chimneys or under floorboards and distributing it amongst themselves; the making of packs and water bottles; and men copying maps of the area.

Lee Hill's later pictures show men with bedrolls, improvised rucksacks and bags hanging on their chests to counterbalance bags carried on their backs. Others travelled light. Harold Ashton wrote that he carried 'nothing much more than a toothbrush and a safety razor'. In a Lee Hill photograph of a group of New Zealand and Canadian prisoners, one of the Canadians appear to be carrying only a mug and small bag, whilst the New Zealanders are more heavily loaded. Was this because the Canadian had been a prisoner for only a short period? Perhaps a CANLOAN officer captured at Arnhem, whereas the longer term prisoners had amassed more possessions? Surprisingly only Harry Roberts refers to boots or shoes. He had tried unsuccessfully on 22 March to get his boots repaired but 'there were no vacancies.' Presumably he was able to get them fixed before he left because they stood up to the coming weeks on the road without any further comment.

Both camps had a news system that combined information from their secret radios, news from German communiqués and the German newspapers. A daily news report was then circulated to news readers who disseminated the information room by room. The news of front lines that could be attributed to German sources was entered on maps; the one at Rotenburg being in the main lobby of the building. In this way the men could get a reasonably accurate picture of the military situation and make judgements about their own situation. By the beginning of the week before Easter it was clear to the men that if the Americans continued to advance at their current rate they could be liberated by the end of the week.

Whilst evacuation became more possible, no formal notice was given to the prisoners until the following day. On Tuesday 27 March, Colonel Holland had an interview with Oberst Schrader who told Holland that he had not received an order to evacuate but stressed that if Spangenberg were to become

Sketches drawn whilst Oflag IX A/Z was at Diedorf. Captain Neil Canavan, New Zealand Expeditionary Force, prepares for the day's walk to Lengefeld with his pipe clenched between his teeth. (Otago Settlers' Museum, New Zealand)

John McIndoe (far left) sits drawing. The photograph appears to show men waiting to move, which suggests it is a temporary stop, whilst the high ground behind the houses and the dry weather place them on the road to Nohra. McIndoe could therefore be drawing the lunch stop at Großwenden. The men's kit demonstrates the range of ways they carried their rations and change of clothes. (Green Collection)

a battlefield it was best if the prisoners were moved. Holland agreed but suggested that the preferable option was for the Commandant, the German Security and Medical Officers to remain with the men and await the arrival of the Americans. He reminded the commandant that there were a large number of men over 40 years old in the camp who would find an evacuation on foot very difficult. Schrader's response was that this would require him to 'depart from his duty as a German officer'. Colonel Holland's news was passed on by a meeting of representatives of messes in Upper and Lower Camps. They were told that they should be prepared to move at two hours' notice. On the same day Gunnar Celander was told by Brix that Rotenberg camp would move the next day, Wednesday 28 March. In fact it would be Thursday before the camps left. On the Wednesday, Harry Roberts' diary records a 'terrific flap re packing', but even so he finished off planting cucumber seeds in the camp gardens.

After so long in captivity many men had accumulated large numbers of books, letters and photographs from home. The OKW instructions for camp evacuations made specific reference to the amount of baggage prisoners could take with them.

> **Inspection of POW baggage**
> The POWs are only allowed the amount of baggage in their quarters that they are able to carry themselves during the march without impeding their ability to walk.

Possessions that they could not carry were nailed into crates and placed in what they hoped would be secure storage. Sewell left behind one wooden box with its lid nailed on and two kit bags. At Rotenburg possessions that could not be carried went into a store room. The key was given to Major Bormann, the previous commandant and now back in his pre-war job as headmaster of the school, for safe keeping. Harold Ashton noted that he left in the camp all that he valued, 'scores of drawings and sketches in a wooden box marked with my mother's address in Staffordshire,

Kr.-Gef. Offizierlager IX A Ausgestellt: Rotenburg/Fulda.
Hauptlager
Zweiglager am 23. SEPT 1943 194..

Kennkarte für Kriegsgefangene

Nur gültig für den Lagerbetrieb und in Verbindung mit der Erk.-Marke Nr. 220

Dienstgrad: Oblt.
Name: Laing
Vorname: Walter Kenneth

23. OKT. 1943

Zur Beachtung!
Die Kennkarte dient als Ausweis der Krf. gegenüber den Organen der deutschen Lagerkommandantur. Sie ist wie die Erk.-Marke stets mitzuführen u. mit dieser auf Verlangen bei namentlichen Appells und beim Verlassen des Lagers vorzuweisen.
Verlust ist sofort zu melden.

Der Kommandant

Lieutenant Walter Kenneth 'Butch' Laing, Sherwood Foresters, was a school teacher who joined the Territorial Army in January 1939. He was called up in September. In April 1940 the regiment formed part of the Allied Expeditionary Force to Norway. Laing was captured at the end of the month. He spent time in several camps before arriving at Rotenburg in July 1943. (Imperial War Museum)

hoping that one day they would reach me'. George Forster had a a portable altar set with silk vestments that had been given to him by Archbishop Borgongini Duca, Papal Nuncio to Italy on behalf of Pope Pius XII, when he was in an Italian camp in 1942. Far too heavy to carry, this too went into the store room.

Butch Laing could only remember having the morning for packing. His account includes a reference to what would quickly prove a crucial addition to the Rotenburg men's baggage. 'At Oflag IX A/Z we had received one coarse white bed sheet. Someone had the bright idea of packing these to show if fighter-planes swooped down to investigate.' The sheets were used to spell out 'P W'. Edward Baxter: carried the vertical stroke of the letter 'P'. Company Commanders would order the sheet carriers to rush into the nearest field at the side of the road and spread out the white sheets to form the letters PW. The system worked. The Rotenburg column was never attacked. The Spangenberg column had no such identification but it travelled by night. Ralph Wilbraham described them as lying up 'all day, the

Germans agreeing it is not safe in the daytime with Allied bombers overhead'. Arbeitskommando 1249 walking behind the two Oflags also travelled by night, often leaving around midnight and arriving at their billet just after dawn, again presumably to avoid air attack.

RAF Typhoons rocketed and machine-gunned a column from Stalag XI B at Fallingbostel, and Oflag VII B from Eichstatt was attacked by USAAF Mustangs during their evacuation on 14 April 1945. Four American Mustangs had been shooting up a nearby railway station, when they spotted the column of prisoners. The men failed to realise the danger they were in until the very last minute and many were caught in the open by the machine guns. Ten men were killed and more than 40 wounded. Rotenburg's bed sheets would prove to be a vital piece of kit.

With the likelihood that they would soon be outside the wire the thoughts of many prisoners turned to escape. Peter Brush, the security officer at Rotenburg, was asked for his advice on escaping. He acknowledged that there would be little difficulty. There were not enough guards to cover all of the men. He didn't even think that they wanted to. The guards' priority was to act correctly so that when the Americans overtook the column, they would be told that the prisoners had been treated well.

The real threat to the men's safety that Brush could foresee were the SS or rogue elements of the regime, who were unlikely to play by the rules if they recaptured an escapee. For Brush it was a balancing act between short-term security and the chance that they might all be shot at the end of the march.

Escape briefings were also held at Spangenberg Upper Camp, a few hours before the march began. According to Bill Edwards, Lieutenant-Colonel Miller's assessment was that escape could not now assist the Allied war effort, however a successful escape would still be regarded as a 'good show', and he ordered any officer who might get away to contact the Americans, and give them the positions of the marching columns. Colonel Miller also made it clear that an attempt was to be made only in circumstances which would not endanger the lives of other officers, the main duty of an officer at that stage of the war being to get himself home alive. Colonel Holland gave a similar briefing to men in the Lower Camp. The briefings at all the camps concluded with the latest assessment of the position of American units based on the last BBC broadcast received on the camps' secret radios.

The prisoners at both camps had been paired in a 'buddy system' to provide support for each other, especially if an opportunity to escape occurred. The system allowed that if they did make a break, one would sleep whilst the other could keep watch. At Spangenberg, Terence Prittie was paired with Major Walter Clough-Taylor, Royal Welch Fusiliers; both were determined to escape as soon as possible. In practice the men from Spangenberg found the numbers of Germans with them, especially on the first night, too many.

It became apparent as the evacuations wore on that the POWs and their guards were in a similar position, bound together for mutual protection as Germany crumbled around them. In the long term the Germans had to balance doing their duty whilst ensuring that they could in time hand their prisoners over the Allies safe and well. By the fourth day, many of the Spangenberg column, guards included, felt that the march had now gone on for too long.

The evacuations of the camps were not in any way comparable with the death marches of concentration camp prisoners or the forced marches through the snow of Allied prisoners away from the Russians. They were also more benign than those of three arbeitskommando from the Wehrkreis whose records of evacuation have survived. But they did form a tiny part of the wider dislocation of German society that led millions to take to the roads. They included civilian refugees from bombed cities and from former German territories in the East; French and Belgian POWs who had slipped away from the farms or factories were they had been working as forced labour; and German soldiers trying to get back to their homes without meeting the

SS or any of the mobile courts that were hanging deserters from street lamps.

In their handling of the Oflags the Germans followed most of the OKW instructions. For example these specified that, 'The daily walking distances should not exceed 20–25 kilometres.' The Geneva Convention also had daily distances of 20 kilometres per day for moving prisoners on foot: 'The evacuation of prisoners on foot shall in normal circumstances be effected by stages of not more than 20 kilometres per day, unless the necessity for reaching water and food depôts requires longer stages.'

The longest distance Oflag IX A/H walked was just under 25km; on its final leg it covered 12km. Oflag IX A/Z's longest stage was 18km. Arbeitskommando 1249's journey lasted almost a month and they often walked 20–25km each day. The kommando was small, around 20 men, but collected more men as it marched. It had originated at Obermaßfeld hospital. Post-War German records have this kommando providing 'general labour' to the community of Lohra near Marburg, west of the Fulda. Since the kommando was led by Captain Bruce Jeffrey, 18th Airlanding Field Ambulance, it may have been providing basic medical assistance to other prisoners in the area. Jeffrey's papers include a note of the daily stages and comments on their journey. The data on Kommando 106's march is more superficial, limited to a series of places through which the group travelled, with no dates or comments. It was compiled by Private Ronald Cheetham, 9 Sherwood Foresters. Their evacuation last 12 days, starting on 1 April. They too appear to have regularly walked around 20km a day. Finally, the experience of a sub-camp of Stalag IX C at Pfafferode to the west of Mühlhausen was recorded by Robert Prouse, Canadian Provost Corps. His group also made 25km-plus each day from 2 April to 7 April. The OKW stipulated rest periods and where rests could be taken. 'During the march, rests have to be taken as follows: (a) after the first half hour a rest of 5 minutes (for toilet break and for organising footwear); (b) after every 2 hours a rest of 15 minutes. The rests may not be taken in or near inhabited places because of the risk of escape. After three days of walking a day of rest is to be observed.'

There is little information on the kommando's marches, but the Oflags did get their regular rests, but often in or near villages. Kommando 1249 and Oflags did have rest days, but it appears that these were not regularly every four days, though there were some very short walks on some days for Oflag IX A/Z.

The difference between the treatment of the Oflags and the kommandos is best accounted for by the fact that the men in the Oflags were senior officers, who were able to assert themselves over their guards. Even so, many officers found their daily stages difficult. And on at least one day a young man, Lieutenant Harry Roberts, also felt the strain. Harry Roberts had been paralysed at Arnhem and had only recovered the use of his legs

Reverend Gunnar Celander, YMCA. Lee Hill took this picture in Windeberg on the morning of 4 April. Celander is standing by the YMCA lorry, with his own car in the distance by the church. As well as helping Allied prisoners, Gunnar provided support to German civilians and he received several awards for his work in Germany, including the British King's Medal for Service in the Cause of Freedom in 1948. The medal was introduced in August 1945 to mark acts of courage by foreign civilians, primarily those who had assisted British escapees in enemy occupied territory. There are no records of Celander specifically helping escapers. (Green Collection)

Björn Ulf Noll spent the war years living in the house built for teachers alongside the school buildings that had become a prisoner of war camp. His father taught German, Latin and Theology at the Jakob-Grimm-Schule. Björn was 13 when the war ended. His memories and those of his network of friends have provided an added dimension to the history of life at Oflag IX A/Z. (Noll Collection)

in prison camp. He wrote of a 'Hellish morning, no reasonable rests. Stopped at 4–5 for lunch. Tea supplied. Felt absolutely buggered. Writing this after eating. Just wondering if I can complete the remainder.'

The OKW instructions suggested that vehicles be hired to carry the camp equipment. Sick prisoners were to be moved by train. Rotenburg had two carts provided by Gustav Dörr, a carrier in Rotenburg. Along with the wagons he also supplied sixteen horses and two Russian POWs as drivers. Gustav Dörr joined the evacuation. Perhaps not just to look after his property; did he feel safer surrounded by Allied prisoners? As well as Dörr's carts, the Reverend Gunnar Celander would join the column with his Opel car and trailer, and the Red Cross lorry with its Danish driver, Jörgensen. At Spangenberg two horse-drawn carts each were provided for Upper and Lower Camps. These too were presumably provided by a civilian contractor. So both camps had four vehicles.

In his post-war report, Celander described his role as more than a provider of physical support to the men. It is clear from the diary of Oflag IX A/H's Senior Officer, Colonel Holland, that he had a good appreciation of the relative position of his column and the Americans, better than could have been provided by talking to German civilians. Gunnar Celander described himself '... as a kind of liaison officer between the German and the English staff and attached to the English staff as a kind of secret service man'. Perhaps if the SBOs from Rotenburg had left accounts, Celander's role would be clearer. Celander is mentioned only once during

Captain Ralph Wilbraham, Pioneer Corps, had served with the Cheshire Yeomanry in Palestine during the First World War, and won the Military Cross. He was called up in 1939 and went to France as a Captain in the Auxiliary Military Pioneers. He was captured near Rouen in June 1940. After the war he was Director of the Cheshire Red Cross. Wilbraham was 52 years old and one of the oldest prisoners in either camp. (Wilbraham Collection)

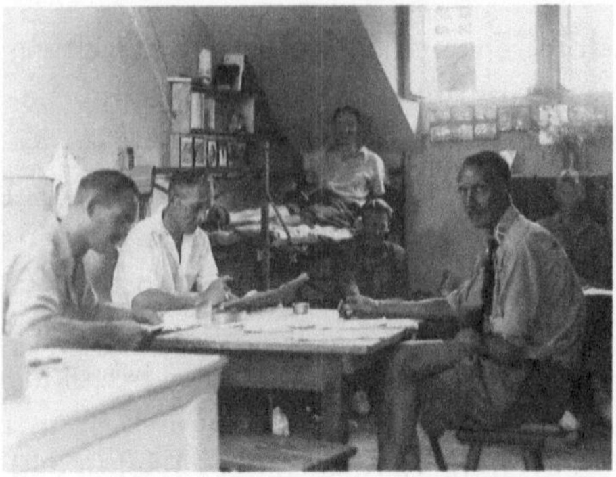

A mess at Oflag IX A/H Lower Camp, Elbersdorf. This photograph was taken in the summer of 1941 by John Mansel, before all British and Commonwealth officers were moved to the 'super camp' at Oflag VI B, at Warburg, north of Kassel, in 1941. By March 1945 only Ted Beckwith (right) from this group had returned to Elbersdorf. (Mansell Collection)

the evacuation in an account by a man from Spangenberg, but he did play his part in Oflag IX A/H's evacuation.

It was not just the prisoners who had possessions to be sorted and stored. Unteroffizier Altman put his spare belongings into store at Oberfeldwebel Heinrich Sultan's house in Rotenburg. Björn Ulf-Noll was volunteered by his father to take Altman's heavy trunk on the family wheeled trolley into Rotenburg. Celander too prepared to leave his new home on the east bank of the Fulda. Ten prisoners cleaned up around Celander's home and office and painted 'YMCA' on the roof and the walls 'to notify bombers, thunderbolts and artillery fire'.

The Germans would be taking their prisoners into an increasingly confused countryside. The OKW instructions assumed that communication could be difficult once a column was on the road. 'Since in most cases destroyed telephone connections are to be expected, motorcycles or bicycles have to be used to guarantee the transmission of the order for withdrawal.' Lee Hill's photographs include one of a German NCO pushing his bicycle across a field track and the men's accounts include messages being sent by cyclists.

Ted Beckwith at Spangenberg learned from some of the guards that they too were concerned about their departure and the walking that it would entail. Ralph Wilbraham noted that the guards 'view the prospect of a long walk with considerable misgivings'. The guards were men considered unfit for front line army service. *Oberfeldwebel* Heinrich Sultan was blind in one eye, as a result of a wound suffered during the 1914–1918 war. *Obergefreiter* Martin Christian Erhard, one of the two dog handlers, *Hundeführer*, had a deformed hand. Ted Beckwith at Spangenberg noted the fitter men from the guard being weeded out for active service during 1944. In March he learned that one of the former guards, a translator, had been killed on the Western Front. As previously mentioned, the Guards came from Landesschützenbataillon 631, a territorial unit, with its Kommandtur in the former palace of the Landgrave's of Hesse-Rotenburg in the centre of Rotenburg. Although some Landesschützenbataillonen were pressed into front-line service towards the end of the war, 631 was not. It had been raised in June 1940 and by 1945 had six companies. As well as providing guards for the Oflags it also guarded French and Belgian POWs working on farms, bridges and railways.

Nazi propaganda had emphasised the possible arrival of African American troops. Ted Beckwith heard that the talk in Elbersdorf village was that any Allied troops would be welcome apart from black ones.

The immediate concern for the prisoners was the weather. It was good for the start of their journey. Harry Roberts had described Wednesday 14 March as the first real summer's day, and he had sat outside until the afternoon. By the start of the following week the men were able to sit outside and listen to the distant roar of battle, what the Germans had grown accustomed to call '*Donner ohne Regen*' – thunder without rain. There would be rainy days, even some sleet, during the camps' journeys but on the whole the men were blessed with good spring weather.

The formal order that they were to leave was given to both camps on the morning of Thursday 29 March. John Sewell learnt the news just after breakfast. In his usual diary style he immediately follows the alarming news with details of his

Harry Roberts, REME, was severely wounded and paralysed on landing at Arnhem. Taken prisoner his wounds recovered to such an extent that he was fully mobile by the time Rotenburg was evacuated six months later. Harry retained the diary that he kept throughout his captivity and also wrote a post-war memoir in the 1990s. (Muriel Roberts Collection)

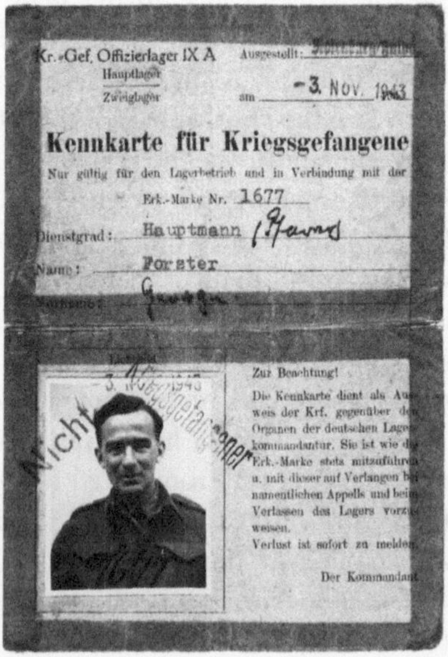

Kr.-Gef. Offizierlager IX A Ausgestellt: [illegible]
Hauptlager
Zweiglager am -3. Nov. 1943

Kennkarte für Kriegsgefangene

Nur gültig für den Lagerbetrieb und in Verbindung mit der Erk.-Marke Nr. 1677

Dienstgrad: Hauptmann / Pfarrer
Name: Forster
Vorname: George

Nicht Kriegsgefangener

Zur Beachtung!
Die Kennkarte dient als Ausweis der Krf. gegenüber den Organen der deutschen Lagerkommandantur. Sie ist wie die Erk.-Marke stets mitzuführen u. mit dieser auf Verlangen bei namentlichen Appells und beim Verlassen des Lagers vorzuweisen.
Verlust ist sofort zu melden.
Der Kommandant

Reverend George Forster, Royal Army Chaplains' Department, was a Roman Catholic chaplain who had been captured in North Africa. His innate sense of humour surfaces in his diary when he refers to nurses and young women being nonplussed to discover that their young and lively colleague was a priest. (Ushaw College Collection)

breakfast. Reverend Forster was told as he came from celebrating mass for Holy Thursday. He described it as 'bad news' and that the mood in the camp was sombre. Rotenburg was told that they would leave around noon; Spangenberg that they would march no earlier than 1400hrs.

For many it was a great disappointment. Terence Prittie on the previous night had heard some of his fellow prisoners talking of American tanks arriving at the camp gates in the morning. It was not an unreasonable expectation. Stalag IX A's crowded main camp at Ziegenhain, with its undernourished inmates

– Americans and survivors of the winter marches from the East – was liberated in this way by units of the 6th Armored the following day, Good Friday.

The last hours at the Oflags were spent disposing of possessions that could not be carried, including food. John Sewell recorded a meal provided for the whole of Upper Camp before they left. He described it as a 'real bash meal'. It included a pudding, some of which was Christmas pudding. Lower camp at Spangenberg was closer to local settlements than the other two. Ralph Wilbraham noted that his fellow prisoners spent much of the morning of 29 March throwing socks, soap and clothing over the wire to the villagers, who 'scramble like animals for the booty, not even hesitating to jump into the creek for any articles that fall short of the roadway'. Ted Beckwith gave his two canaries and their cage to Herr Schanze, whose farmhouse was opposite the main gate at Elbersdorf.

At Rotenburg, George Forster and his comrades in his 'cube' had an unexpected bonus. One of their number, Major Mervyn Bull, Australian Army Service Corps, had been hoarding his weekly ration of a bar of chocolate. Now he insisted on sharing this equally with his seven roommates. Each received six bars. Forster commented, 'It was a noble act of charity, particularly in view of the great scarcity of food over the last few months.' In the coming days chocolate, along with soap and cigarettes, would pay for food.

Before the camps could leave, the sick from both camp hospitals were moved to Spangenberg to travel by train to Mühlhausen. There were 49 men from Spangenberg and 10 from Rotenburg considered too ill to walk. The Rotenburg men were driven to Spangenberg. The combined party left by train at 1900hrs. The relative numbers are further evidence that Rotenburg's prisoners were younger and fitter. Although Rotenburg's hospital was considered the better one of the two camps and Spangenberg men were normally transferred to it as appropriate, the railway at Spangenberg was not threatened by the American advance. Two other men, too ill to be moved, were left at the Spangenberg hospital. The men sent to Mühlhausen by train were liberated by the Americans on 5 April. Men already at the main Wehrkreis hospital at Obermaßfeld were not moved.

Records compiled after the war by German civil authorities for the Allies show that the destination for all the men was Mühlhausen in Thuringia. Both camps were faced with a 45-mile walk. But Mühlhausen was probably only a rail head for travel south to Bavaria. By the end of the war the Germans had two main concentrations of Western POWs: at Moosburg near Munich in Bavaria and at Fallingbostel, between Hannover and Hamburg in the north. At several points later in the evacuations, travel by train does form part of the German plans. In the confusion of the German retreat, accommodation on a train for 59 sick was achievable: a train to carry 900 was not. Using the classic European railway vans able to hold '40 hommes et 8 cheveaux',

McIndoe's crowded mess at Rotenburg, 1942. Many Rotenburg prisoners describe there being eight men to a room, so perhaps this drawing is of only half the room shared by McIndoe. (Otago Settlers' Museum, New Zealand)

the Germans would have needed almost 25 vans to take the camps to Mühlhausen. Though when some prisoners were sent to Rotenburg in 1943, they travelled in 3rd class carriages.

Those prisoners who thought that the Germans would find moving the camps difficult were half right. In the past, when moving large numbers of men to both camps, the Germans had used trains. Now with the Americans about to cut the railway line north and south of Rotenburg, the only operational line was that through Spangenberg. This was part of the '*Kanonenbahn*', a strategic military railway that linked Berlin with Alsace and which passed through no major settlements so as to provide for the speedy movement of men and equipment. The sick men would use the Kanonenbahn to travel in a roundabout route to Mühlhausen and their journey would have taken all of the night. However getting sufficient vans to Spangenberg for both camps was evidently not possible. Perhaps Mühlhausen had them sitting in its railway yards waiting for the columns to arrive? Ted Beckwith still thought being moved by train directly from Spangenberg was an option. He divided his packing in three categories: 'Heavy', to be left no matter what; 'Train', if they are to be moved by rail; and lightest of all 'Walk'.

Rotenburg eventually emptied at 1400hrs and Spangenberg at dusk, 1700. At Rotenburg their departure was significant enough for Harry Roberts to give a precise time, '2.20 pm'. Only one prisoner's account gives the correct destination. Lieutenant James Symes, formerly Hampshire Regiment, but captured whilst a Commando on the Channel Islands, has Mühlhausen. However Symes' account may have been edited after the war. None of the Spangeberg men even speculate about their destination. Others at Rotenburg believed they were going to a camp at Nordhausen on the edge of the Harz Mountains or to the Bavarian redoubt. Lieutenant Harold Ashton, Royal Engineers, Oflag IX A/Z, thought that 'by special order of Hitler we were to be moved to Berlin for some reason I shall never know.' Heinrich Sultan's memoirs just give a direction,

'East'. Obergefreiter Martin Erhard, one of the guards, in a statement to the British after the war said their orders were to go to Thuringia.

On the afternoon of Thursday 29 March the nearest Allied troops were US 4th Armored Division at Bad Hersfeld, 11 miles south of Rotenburg. If the Division continued to advance in the same direction as they had in previous days, they could be at Rotenburg and Spangenberg within a day and at Mühlhausen within two days.

3

EASTWARDS

> The prisoners had to be evacuated. Everything had to be prepared. Bacon and bread were procured by us, as we had to take food supplies along for 600 men. Then we went eastwards.
>
> Oberfeldwebel Heinrich Sultan, Landesschützenbataillon 631, Oflag IX A/Z, Rotenburg an der Fulda.

The country around Spangenberg and Rotenburg is similar to the Scottish Borders. Rich green rolling fields rising to dark beech and conifer woods along the hills. The men from both camps had been allowed parole walks in the immediate countryside, so the early stages of their journeys were along relatively familiar routes. Many prisoners decided that they would never see anything they left at the camps, and because they could not carry all their possessions, they were dressed in their best uniforms. Not parade ground standard certainly, but unlike in the summer of 1940, they were not a beaten army. Alan Green wrote in his diary, 'There is one thing though, I've not yet fallen into the rut of being improperly dressed. I feel that to be dressed as the CO of the Btn … helps to keep morale up.' In contrast, John Sewell, ever practical, lists the items of clothing

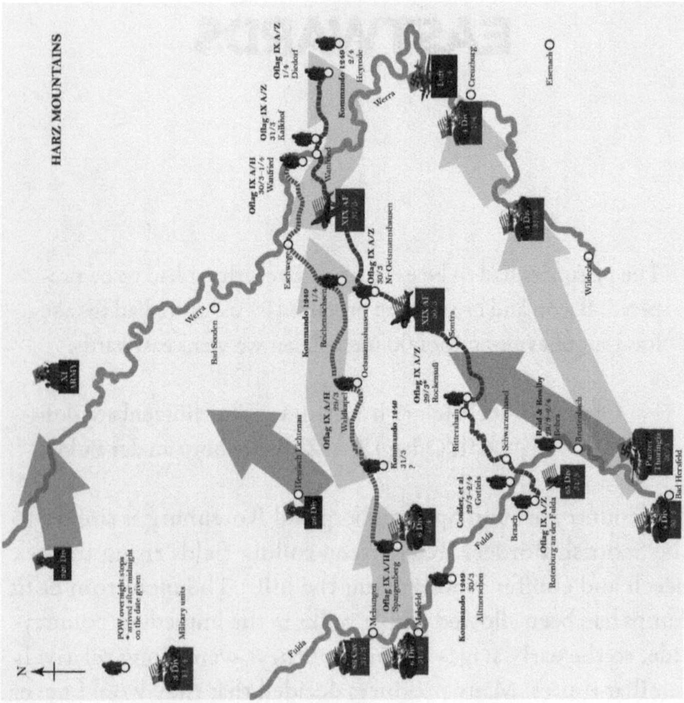

The camps are evacuated. (Peter Green)

he was wearing as he left Spangenberg: 'Two thin vests, one thin pants and KD [khaki drill] shorts under my SD [service dress] uniform.' Lieutenant Hubert Nicolle, Hampshire Regiment and Commandos describes a motley crew, 'Festooned with pots and pans, old tins, water bottles and blankets, our haversacks bulging with food and other necessities, we looked more like refugees than British officers.'

Bill Edwards recalled looking back as they left the castle at Spangenberg and seeing cheerful, smiling faces behind him, but within an hour at least one officer, Major E. Jones, RASC, captured in France in 1940, had been unable to continue and been placed on one of the carts. Inadequate food and no exercise was no preparation for a long hike, despite the early euphoria of leaving the wire behind. Most of the men appear not to have known how long they would be walking; where they would be stopping or even if they were stopping that night. It would have been a daunting prospect; but the presence of their equally suffering and familiar guards would have provided some encouragement that their journey would not end in disaster. Major Shand, Oflag IX A/H: 'Although few of us were in much shape physically, everyone was in the highest spirits knowing that the American troops were not far away and we were in sound of perpetual gunfire.'

The men were walking in far better conditions than those of the winter marches from the east and they were better prepared. They did not know it, but they were also better off than some of the arbeitskommando which were also beginning to be moved away from the Americans. Lieutenant Bruce Jeffrey RAMC, captured at Arnhem, was serving as a doctor with Arbeitskommando 1249 at Lohra 30 miles west of Rotenburg. The kommando had been providing labour for the town council. His group left at 0800hrs on 29 March to walk the 150 miles to their base, Stalag IX C, at Bad Sulza. After two days walking they crossed the River Fulda at Altmorschen 4 miles west of Spangenberg. Liberation for the prisoners had been very close;

by that evening American patrols were searching for bridges to cross the Fulda around Altmorschen. The kommando was about to start a marathon journey that would eventually take them to northern Bavaria. Jeffrey told his family that his evacuation march was a 'worse ordeal than Arnhem'. Unlike the two Oflags, he would be on the road for almost a month

Both Oflags started their journeys under the command of their Abwehroffiziers, Hauptmann August Seybold at Spangenberg and Hauptmann Prosper Heyl at Rotenburg. Oberst Schrader had moved his headquarters to Mühlhausen and initially Oberstleutnant Brix was also there. He returned to the Rotenburg column during the first day and then stayed with it. Seybold commanded the Spangenberg column for the first three days of its evacuation, until the arrival of a Major Fleischmann from Oberst Schrader's headquarters. The intention to move the sick to Mühlhausen rather than the more usual hospital at Obermaßfeld should have given the men clues as to their destination, but it appears not to have. The men already transferred to the hospital at Obermaßfeld were not evacuated.

Although the prisoners and some of the guard walked, there are intermittent references in the men's accounts of German vehicles: Brix using a 'staff' car and Hauptmann Hofmann being driven from the Spangeberg column to the Rotenburg one by an RASC Corporal. And of course IX A/Z had Gunner Celander's car and the YMCA lorry. Tractors and trailers to carry sick prisoners also appear.

Only some of the prisoners mention the risk that their march might end in disaster with them being shot or retained as hostages. During the march the presence of their normal guards was reassuring. Nevertheless, there were prisoners who were suspicious of all German motives; Forster's 'hard-nuts' who were keen to escape. The would-be escapees were in a minority in both Oflags as most prisoners saw little point in taking the risk of leaving the column. Had their guards been replaced by the SS they might have changed their minds. Terence Prittie was one who dreaded 'the possibility that special SS guards would take charge of us and make certain that at least [only a] few of us would live to see relieving Allied troops or their homes again.' As they left the camps the guards were accompanied by some of the camp staff – doctors from both camps and with the Rotenburg column two German women. Lee Hill identified one as the doctor's sister, the other as a translator. One may in fact have been Hauptmann Heyl's secretary, Frau Weigand, the sister or wife of Rotenburg's *Lageroffizier* Hauptmann Weigand.

It is customary to describe camp evacuations as forced marches. In the case of the two Oflags the prisoners' accounts make it clear that they did not march. They ambled or plodded. Lieutenant Michael Langham, Gordon Highlanders, remembered just 'trudging'. Captain Ian Reid, Black Watch, described Oflag IX A/Z as 'a long and straggling, slow-moving column that eventually plodded out through the barbed-wire gates.' Björn Ulf Noll, returning to the school house with the family trolley, with Unteroffizier Altman's belongings safely lodged at Heinrich Sultan's house, also remembered them walking with less than military precision. 'They were all making up a very poor body of men which might be only called a column by those who knew what was happening,' he remembered. One of the prisoners spotted Björn and the very desirable trolley he was pulling. A tall young man left the column and spoke to him in English. 'From the little I understood in combination with the officer's gestures was that he had offered me 4000 cigarettes for the empty trolley I was pulling.' Björn was not to be bought. The issue was not the number of cigarettes, simply the reception he would get at home if he did not get the family trolley back. In 1945 Germany the family trolley was, in practical terms, the equivalent of a family car.

The first stages of Oflag IX A/Z's route were straightforward. It was the route that Celander's volunteer helpers had taken to the Schwedenheim: right out of the main gate and south into the centre of Rotenburg and then across the town bridge to reach the Kassel-Bebra road on the east bank. The prisoners' presence on the streets of Rotenburg would have signified to the inhabitants that great changes were on the way. But as it was the Americans and not the Russians who were approaching the town, there was no immediate move to leave. Later in the march John Logan noted that the civilians expected, '... black men in tanks, gangsters, sadists and every other kind of fiend are expected to appear and wreak their vengeance. Suicide is in the air.' Once over the bridge the Rotenburg column turned south towards Bebra and Bad Hersfeld, walking alongside the railway from Kassel. They saw German troops preparing to defend the Fulda. At Rotenburg this was Panzer *Abteilung* 44, 'Detachment 44'. It was an ad hoc unit – one of several 11th Army units attempting to hold a line between the Ruhr, Kassel and the south. Edward Baxter described seeing a Tiger tank, but in reality it would have been an assault gun, one of 20 *Sturmgeschütz* IIIs sent by train from the Fallingbostel training area After walking along the main road southwards for a short distance, Oflag IX A/Z turned east on a minor road across the flank of the wooded hills above Rotenburg towards the village of Schwarzenhasel. Harry Roberts' diary with its precise timings gives the column's average speed at just over 1 mile an hour. In an uncharacteristic downbeat tone Edlmann noted that everyone was 'tired and weak'. They reached the wooded stretch of road in the late afternoon, just as Oflag IX A/H was leaving Spangenberg. The gloom of the woods offered the first opportunities for escape and several got away. Edlmann names five – Lieutenant Peter Conder, Royal Signals, Lieutenant John Cripps, King's Royal Rifle Corps, Lieutenant Ralph Pilcher, Welsh Guards, Lieutenant Basil Rought-Rought, Royal Norfolk Regiment and Henry Morgan. John Cripps was a distant relative of Sir Stafford Cripps, at the time the British Ambassador to Russia. 'Henry' must have been a nickname, there were two Morgans at Rotenburg, neither has the initial 'H'. Eventually Conder and his comrades reached a farm that they had visited on parole walks. This was possibly the farm at Guttels that was a regular destination on parole walks for Oflag IX A/Z. Wherever the farm was, the farmer had anti-Nazi sympathies and was already sheltering around 20 fugitives, including political prisoners.

Once the column had passed Schwarzenhasel it was completely dark, although there was a full moon. Their route began to climb towards Rockensüß, zigzagging in almost Alpine fashion, up through the dark beech woods. The bends in the road now provided an opportunity for Ian Reid and Lieutenant George Bowlby, Royal Scots Fusiliers, to get away, unrecorded by Edlmann. Ian Reid heard the guard shout halt and fire, but the bullets missed by a wide margin. Later escapees thought that the guards would not have shot to kill. Their shots were to prevent accusations of dereliction of duty. No attempt was made to pursue any of the escapees. There were no men to spare

BRITISH PRISONERS WERE MARCHED INLAND BY GERMAN CAPTORS AS ADVANCING ALLIED ARMIES APPROACHED. BUT AS OUR TROOPS OVERTOOK THE WEHRMACHT THESE FORCED MARCHES LED TO FREEDOM

FORCED MARCH TO—FREEDOM

This is the first picture story of a forced march through Germany by British and Dominion prisoners-of-war. Pictures were taken behind the Nazi guards' backs by Lee Hill, New Zealand Army Film Cameraman, who describes the dramatic events below

This is the story of a *forced* march which I recently made as a prisoner of the Germans. They had dragged me and hundreds of British officers from a prisoner-of-war camp at Rotenburg on the River Fulda towards the interior of Germany, in the vain hope that they could prevent our liberation by the advancing Allied armies and could themselves escape capture and defeat.

It is a story symbolic of the experiences of tens of thousands of Allied war prisoners who were liberated by the victorious drive of our armies. It ended in—freedom: and in that respect, I guess, it is also symbolic of the travail of war through which our people went on the arduous road to victory.

Freedom came to us in the form of the most beautiful American tanks that I have ever seen. It was in the little village of Wimmelburg, near Eisleben—"Luther's Town" as the Germans call it—where they caught up with our marching column just as our guards had completed their plan to move us by rail into the Southern Redoubt, to hold us as hostages or, perhaps, to kill us off.

Originally we were four hundred officers, mostly British, but our party eventually grew to over 1,400 as "other ranks" from various camps joined us, Australians, Canadians, Gurkhas among them. Now they are all safely back home with their families.

I shall be frank in telling their story—and mine—except for the incidental circumstances under which I "acquired" the camera and the films which enabled me to accompany my story with a pictorial record of events. It is, I believe, the only one so far in existence depicting experiences which I shared with almost 50,000 liberated British prisoners-of-war.

Let me mention, only in passing, that I was captured while taking photographs of the battle of Sidi Aziz in Cyrenaica. After two years' captivity in Italy we were moved to Germany, and I eventually landed in Oflag IX A.Z. at Rotenburg, which was as good—or as bad—as most German prison camps. The Kommandant, a German "Oberst" (Colonel), ex-police officer, was a typical Nazi brute, ignorant, unpleasant, although the firmness of our own senior officers often frustrated his nastiest designs.

Years of captivity, years of boredom and frustration! But the great days came when we knew which way the wind was blowing, when we sensed and felt that liberation was at hand. We talked, thought, dreamed about it. The month of March arrived.

Prison camp communications, secret, surreptitious, functioned excellently. Our guards talked; we

OVER

The title page of an article in the *Illustrated*, 12 May 1945, words and pictures by Lee Hill describing Oflag IX A/Z's experience. It contains two obvious lies and other statements that are perhaps not totally compatible with the truth. The slant of the article is virulently anti-German. Presumably it was editorial pressure that caused Lee Hill to accept statements that he knew were wrong. (Green Collection)

The farm has become a hotel, Hof Kuttels. (Peter Green)

from the guard to form a search party. Heinrich Sultan confirms that seven escaped on the first night. Edward Baxter wrote later that he heard shots and was told '… that these were the German farewell to Peter Conder and Cripps, who had decided that if they had to walk around Germany they could do it without German supervision.'

For most men being in the column was safer than being outside it. Remembering their briefings before the camps emptied, most prisoners thought the primary role of the guard was to protect the men from elements in Germany wanting to end the war in a Nazi *Götterdämerung*. Some prisoners might not have accepted this, but the senior officers clearly did. Whilst individual German guards might on occasions have been willing to look the other way during escapes, their officers were not.

Ian Reid's account is the only one to describe an escape made on the first day in detail. Once clear of the column, Reid and

Bowlby stopped and ate some of their black bread and Red Cross cheese, which they washed down with cold tea. They then set off westwards back towards the Fulda. When they arrived on high ground overlooking the valley it was after midnight. The main road south from Rotenburg to Bebra was busy with German transport moving south towards Bad Hersfeld and the main road eastwards. The escapees managed to slip across the road and reach the river, but there were no bridges and the river was too wide and fast flowing for them to swim. They returned across the main road and found a wood where they could lie up and wait for the Americans.

Oflag IX A/Z had stopped for food just before midnight in a large clearing, the 'Knight's Grove', two miles from the village of Rockensüß. Here the Germans provided a very welcome hot meal of ersatz coffee, sausages and bread. They eventually reached Rockensüß in the early hours of Saturday. Here they were billeted in a large barn at a farm belonging to Wilhelm

An overnight billet at an unknown location, but the photograph was probably taken during the rest day at Nohra on Friday 6 April. It is typical of the men's descriptions of the barns they slept in during the march. The prisoner on the right displays some potatoes he has bartered for soap or cigarettes. Later in the march central food stocks had declined to such an extent that the men were almost totally reliant on what they could obtain through barter. (Green Collection)

Grossgur. The villagers were friendly. The arrival of Allied POWs eager to trade their chocolate, soap and cigarettes for eggs and milk was greatly appreciated. The Rotenburg men had walked around 11 miles. According to Harry Roberts' records, they had taken almost 10 hours to cover 11 miles; spectacularly slow, although the last few miles of the route climbed quite severely. The War Office report on Oflag IX A/Z has the Senior British Officer from Oflag IX A/Z slowing their march and their being liberated after only a short journey. This was partly true. The column walked slowly, but they still reached each pre-planned overnight billet, day after day. The men at this stage might have no knowledge of what schedule they were meant to keep to, but they realised that it was in their interest to travel slowly. Edward Baxter: 'The company of old men and cripples marched in front with a strong hint that they were not to distress themselves unduly by racing.' Slowed down in this way Oflag IX A/Z hoped to be overtaken by the Americans quickly.

Upper Camp of Oflag IX A/H left around 1700hrs and Lower camp at 1730. They were soon walking in the dark. Spangenberg is on one of the main west-east routes across the Fulda into Thuringia. In their last days in camp the prisoners had seen camouflaged staff cars, lorry-loads of engineers and flak companies in the village. Many of their occupants were dirty, unshaven and dispirited. Their German civilian neighbours were unhappy to see the prisoners leave. Ralph Wilbraham shook the hands of many of the locals who had come to watch the camp empty. Many of them were in tears, for fear of what was to come and the hope lost that the prisoners would have stayed and safeguarded them from the Americans.

Surprisingly, nobody from Oflag IX A/H records that it was dangerous walking at night along roads also being used by German military transport. John Sewell counted 150 military vehicles all heading in the same direction as the prisoners, eastwards. After a few miles an extra cart with two horses was added to the column. Many of the men from Lower Camp were grateful to be able to transfer their packs to it. Like Oflag IX A/Z the column stopped once an hour for a 10-minute rest.

Terence Prittie and his escape partner Major Walter Clough-Taylor, Royal Welch Fusiliers, had decided to leave the column as early as possible into the march. Knowing the immediate area from parole walks and believing that the Americans were about 15 miles behind them it made perfect sense to escape now, rather than wait till they reached unknown parts of Germany. Prittie and Clough-Taylor made several attempts to slip away, but they were never successful. Their final attempt was foiled by an unexpected German Army lorry which picked them out in its headlights 30 yards from the road. When they returned to the column one of the guards greeted them with, '*Aber mein, lieber Freund! Was wollen Sie denn machen*?' – But, my *dear* friend! What *are* you up to? Another sentry told them that they were foolish to try and escape when the war was practically over.

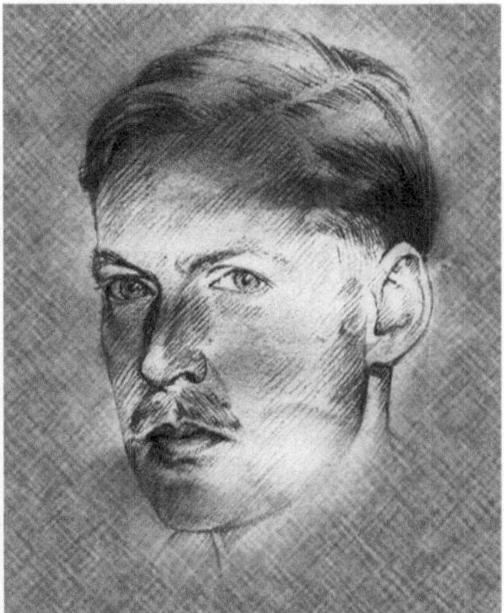

Captain Ernest Edlmann, Royal East Kent Regiment (The Buffs), was a career soldier who went on to command his regiment in Aden in the 1960s. This drawing was made by fellow prisoner Aubrey Davidson-Houston. He was also a career soldier, captured whilst serving with the Royal Sussex Regiment at Dunkirk. He began to paint portraits whilst a POW and became a full-time portrait painter after the war. On his return from Oflag VII B he was offered the command of a battalion or a place at the Slade School of Art. He chose the Slade. His later subjects included the Queen and the Duke of Edinburgh. (Edlmann Collection)

Ralph Wilbrahams thought that the guards were 'just amused' and they made no attempt to stop escapes or to shoot. Even so Terrance Prittie estimated that only two men get away on the first night. Major Mervyn Dennison and Lieutenant Tony Baxter, both younger men from 3 Parachute Regiment and recently captured at Arnhem, escaped after other men distracted a German guard's dog by blowing cigarette smoke in its face. Colonel Holland eventually counted 22 escapees in total from the Spangenberg column by the end of their journey. He provides no breakdown by date or place of escape.

That evening was the first night after the full moon and though, according to RAF reports of the period, there was almost complete cloud cover over Germany, it was still light enough for the men to see something of their surroundings. It was also dry. They were passed by an odd mix of traffic, military and civilian. The lack of petrol meant many vehicles were towed by others. The risk of accidents was presumably reduced by the slow speed of the vehicles, which were in any case also going east. Eventually around 0100hrs on 30 March, Oflag IX A/H reached the village of Waldkappel. The Germans had prepared soup for them, so that they also got a hot meal before turning in. Both Upper and Lower Camp were billeted in one crowded barn. Just as the men from Rotenburg had found, the German civilians were friendly, happy to trade or boil water for washing or cooking.

Oflag IX A/H had marched 15 miles at a speed of 2.5 miles an hour, including their 10 minute stops each hour. The Spangenberg men would stay in their billet all the following day and march again in the late evening of 30 March. Although the German standing orders stressed that night marches should be avoided wherever possible, they had been written without the need to take Allied air supremacy into account. That morning, the men settled down to trade. Some gave chocolates to the village children. Lunch was a stew prepared by Andy Newman though potatoes promised by the Germans failed to arrive. The men got large amounts of ersatz coffee from the villagers.

An air attack on the railway station during the afternoon resulted in all the lights going out in the barn so that by 1900hrs it was pitch black inside. John Sewell preparing for the next stage decided to prepare for the coming nights' walk by 'bashing a tin of pilchards'. Their guards continued to treat them with respect. Sewell was the recipient of a kind gesture. Too late to get his pack on the cart for prisoners' kit, he was offered space on the guards' cart. He found the guards being very decent, 'a very different matter to those earlier marches – all shouting, all prodding – when the Germans thought they were winning.'

Despite the friendly reception that Oflag IX A/Z had received whilst in Rockensüß, the fears that Peter Brush had expressed about the dangers of escaping were forcibly brought home after breakfast on Good Friday 30 March. Frau Grossgur had obligingly boiled water and cooked eggs for almost the whole camp. 'Butch' Laing remembered the local population as 'friendly, tired of their government and the war, and very disposed to barter for soap and cigarettes.' George Forster even remembered a sing-song round a piano in the morning before they left and most prisoners mention exchanging cigarettes and chocolate for food. Breakfast was a wonderful experience with fresh eggs for the first time in five years of captivity. Ernest Edlmann described his as the first big breakfast he had eaten since 1940. It was made up of eggs and porridge. He also records that Captain Jim Symonds, Northamptonshire Regiment, ate 20 eggs. The impact of these on Symonds' body can only be shuddered at. Captain Kennedy, the British medical officer at Rotenburg, noted after the war that 'Besides blistered feet, the only other cause of sickness was diarrhoea, which was fairly common.' References to upset stomachs and 'squitters' occur in most men's diaries.

Confused by the ease in which some escapes had been made the previous evening and by the friendly reception given to them by the villagers, some of the men decided that this was the time to escape by hiding in the barn whilst the column departed without them. Captain Quass-Cohn 9 Commando suggested that the escape came about 'on the advice of a Polish farm worker'.

The escapees failed to appreciate that there was a difference between POWs with soap, chocolates and cigarettes to barter, under German Army control, and escaped prisoners that could get the villagers accused of collaborating with the enemy. Nor could Oberstleutnant Brix ignore the escape of several men at one go from the first overnight stop. There is some confusion on numbers of escapees and their names. Obergefreiter Martin Christian Erhard describes the roll being taken on Friday morning and eight men being missing. Presumably the first-day escapees had already been noticed on arrival at Rockensuß. Reverend Forster has six escapees, as does Ernest Edlmann. Marcus Edwards entry for 30 March reads: 'Onwards via Sontra to Oetmannshausen, nr Hoheneiche. Saw a train shot up. David, Maude & Brooke escaped but recaptured & beaten up.' Lieutenant A.G. Smith, York and Lancaster Regiment, in his deposition to the post-war trial, refers to six definite escapees and possibly one or two others, but was not sure because he was dazed at the time. The names he gives are Captain J.K. Smith, Royal Artillery (aka Quass-Cohn, aka 'Bullshit' Smith), Captain David 'Moose' Maud, Captain Somerset Light Infantry, Captain W.J. Wood, Royal Army Service Corps, Lieutenant Rynkiewiez, 3 Carpathian Brigade and Captain P.N. McDonald, New Zealand Forces. At a postwar trial the defendants were accused of assaulting three men: Smith, Maude and Quass-Cohn.

Not everyone was focussed on the march. Michael Langham, for example, recalls little of the march except it being an annoying interruption to the discussions he was having with his friends on politics and the theatre. Harry Roberts' diary for 30 March lists his breakfast, 'more milk – eggs – onions', then their departure time of 11.50 and the 'good marching on the road' to Sontra for a lunch halt.

Nazi philosophy had always emphasised competition between political and military groups to achieve Party objectives. Now that German society was coming apart, the reaction of the different factions to defeat varied enormously; some towns surrendered, others had to be bombed and shelled into rubble and submission. Depending on which representatives of the Party or armed forces found an escapee, chances of survival could be poor or excellent. Although Allied POWs were generally treated correctly, some were badly treated. Of all the regime's captives, Allied prisoners of war and in particular officers were at the most acceptable end of the spectrum of captivity, hunger, ill treatment and murder. For Russian POWs and those in concentration camps the reality was continued and hellish suffering. The countryside could be just as deadly for German troops or civilians suspected of desertion or surrender. The imminent arrival of the front line brought loyalty to the regime to the forefront of people's minds.

Oberstleutnant Brix called out the Volkssturm to assist a few of his men searching the farm, so that the main body could march on. By the time the Volkssturm arrived the column had left. Harry Roberts has the column leaving at 11.30. Lieutenant A.G. Smith in his pre-trial statement recorded that he noticed men with dogs at 12.00, but it was not until around 1300hrs that the search really started.

The Volkssturm had been planned as a citizen militia, evidence of the National Socialist will and a step towards a completely militarised society, but concerns over their legal status under the Geneva Convention had led to their becoming auxiliary units under Wehrmacht command. At least one of the guards, Obergefreiter Martin Erhard, equated membership of the Party and the Volkssturm with an unsympathetic view of the Wehrmacht. This may be a grass-roots reflection on the power shifts at the top following the bomb plot on Hitler's life, which led the Party to rely more on Himmler and the SS instead of the regular army.

Erhard claimed to have used his dog in the search and that he found several men, but did not alert anyone to his discoveries and the men remained hidden. Then the Volkssturm arrived. Martin Erhard told British investigators later, 'Some of the members of the Volkssturm stabbed with their pitchforks on the hiding places to force the British soldiers to come out. In this way three or four Englishmen and later, all eight were found.'

The events at Rockensuß became the basis for a trial after the war. The accounts of Erhard and the members of the Volkssturm come from the records of the war crime trial. Herr Adam Diegel, Rockensüß Volkssturm, in his statement to the British investigators said that he was annoyed at being got out again to search for prisoners. Wild goose chases for escaped prisoners and airmen from downed aircraft must have occupied much of the Volkssturm's time. It should have not come as a surprise to the prisoners that a particularly hot-headed member of the Volkssturm was not willing to treat war as a game or respect the Geneva Convention, whilst round-the-clock bombing wrecked the cities around them and their country was being overrun by Allied armies.

All the prisoners' statements from the war crimes proceedings describe them being thrown to the lower floors of the barn and then being beaten with heavy sticks. Quass-Cohen understood German and he heard the mob being incited to further violence. The would-be escapees feared that they would be shot. Quass-Cohen was identified as a Jew, and he and Rynkiwiez, a Polish officer, received most of the mob's attention. The Guards and Volkssturm interrogated at the British trial describe similar events. The Volkssturm leader, Herr Rudolph Karl Funck, has Diegel hitting men, but denied that they had been thrown or pushed; they had jumped down to escape the blows. Rudolph Funck:

> The Wehrmacht gave me the order to turn over the hay, whereupon the Volkssturm took some hay forks. The hay was thoroughly turned over and I heard cries: 'There they are.' I then went to the hayloft and saw there a British officer with

> glasses. Diegel hit him several times with its oak would stick across the back and on his behind. The stick broke in two. I shouted: 'Stop.' I wanted to prevent the man from falling down 2.5m on to the floor. To avoid Diegel's blows, however, the man jumped on to a beam, broke his glasses and fell, hitting my automatic pistol, which I was carrying on my left shoulder. The man climbed down the ladder into the yard.

This nasty situation that was only defused by the return of Hauptmann Heyl and Gunnar Celander. The crowd was dispersed, Rynkiewiez released from the chair to which he had been tied and the prisoners taken into the farmhouse for first aid. David Maude was the most seriously beaten and he was taken away in Celander's car. The others were marched off and eventually rejoined the column that night. Contrary to the description of the incident in the article in *Illustrated* magazine article by Lee Hill – 'They were ferreted out by Volkssturm and SS Black Guards, beaten with rifle butts, hit with whips, threatened with death'– there was no SS involved in the search, nor were any whips used.

Further westwards, Reid and Bowlby were also about to be recaptured. On the morning of 30 March they were discovered by a party of German gunners collecting brushwood to camouflage their guns. Their captors were friendly. As at Rockensüß cigarettes were exchanged for bread. The men washed. And at 14.00hrs they were marched down the Rotenburg road to Bebra. On the road they passed elements of Panzer Abteilung 44, the battle group, preparing to defend the Fulda around Rotenburg. Disturbingly, an SS motorcyclist tried to run them over. But at Bebra, Reid and Bowlby were placed in the town prison. The Germans attempted to contact Oflag IX A/Z, but now that it had gone from Rotenburg there is no one who could be found who knew where it was going. Over the next few days Reid and Bowlby found their lives at risk from SS units in the town convinced that they were commandos, and therefore on their wanted list, along with German deserters. For the time being, on Saturday 30 March, in the town prison with a regular army officer in command, they were safe.

Ten miles to the northeast the rest of Oflag IX A/Z stopped for lunch at Sontra. They were now on the main road to Göttingen, potentially directly in the path of the tanks of 4th Armored. The column had to avoid trees being felled across the road as road blocks and saw troops with panzerfausts in place to protect them. The inadequacy of the defenders boosted morale. 'Our spirits rise,' noted Ernest Edlmann. The prisoners' morale is further raised by an increase in American air activity, though walking along the road with its parallel railway line was potentially dangerous. 'Butch' Laing recorded fighters attacking a train on the line alongside the road. The men's white PW signs were displayed and they escaped the attention of the American aircraft. Further from the column Lieutenant-Colonel Clay and Gunnar Celander narrowly missed being machine-gunned by aircraft as they travelled ahead of the column to make arrangements for the column's arrival at their next billet. Harry Roberts described the different reactions to air attack. At the first low-level pass '...there was a flash of red berets as the "airborne" hit the ditch at the side of the road – to the derision of the older prisoners, who had a childlike faith in the large PW recognition signs which we pegged out in the hope that Allied planes would not mistake us for a German column.' A little later as the column passed some railway sidings and more American fighter-bombers appeared, although the members of 1st Airborne reached the ditch first, it was a close thing and they were flattened by the rest of the column jumping on top of them.

As the day progressed there was rain, but the weather had cleared by the time Oflag IX A/Z reached its overnight billet close to Oetmannshausen, a small village where the military railway through Spangenberg crossed the railway heading north from Bebra towards Göttingen. In addition to the railway junction the village was at a crossroads between roads running north-south and west-east again from Spangenberg. With American aircraft roaming the areas close behind the front line searching for any movement of German troops by rail or road, Oetmannshausen was a risky place for Oflag IX A/Z.

As they settled in, Oflag IX A/H were four miles away at Waldkappel on the road to Oetmannshausen. Prisoners' accounts from Oflag IX A/Z mention several locations for their second night stop: some say Oetmannshausen, others Hoheneiche and some Reichensachsen. Ernest Edlmann's precise military-style notes indicate a farm between Hoheneiche and Reichensachsen, which would indeed be close to Oetmannshausen. Since the men had no sources for place names apart from what German civilians told them, the multiplicity of names should not surprise. Had they been in a farm in Oetmannshausen itself, then surely men in both camps would have seen each other and recorded the fact. None do. Wherever he was, Harry Roberts was certainly not impressed by his billet. He describes it as chaos, with men unwilling to open their kit for fear of losing things in the crowded and no doubt straw-covered barn. Reverend Forster was able to spend the night with local people, who at great risk allowed him to listen to the BBC radio news. Like the other prisoners he was realising that compared to ordinary Germans, or their guards, he was rich. His trade goods where in greater demand than the guards' marks.

That evening Ernest Edlmann reflected on the beatings at Rockensüß. He was suspicious of the claims by the failed escapees that Hauptmann Heyl had saved their lives. He preferred to believe that it was a 'stunt' by Heyl. That night from his bed on dry straw he could hear German armour on the road going north.

West of the prisoners on 30 March the 6th Armored had motored to the outskirts of Kassel, but its advance was about to come to a halt. The Kassel garrison, reinforced by the 166 Reserve Infantry Division, together with the city's anti-aircraft batteries firing as ground support, plus the final Tiger IIs from the city's

Henschel tank factory, were able to halt the Americans. Unlike Frankfurt, Kassel was to be strongly defended as the hinge connecting German armies in the Ruhr with those farther south. Since armoured units were not the best units to capture cities street by street, 6th Armored's orders were that if they were prevented from occupying Kassel quickly, they were to leave the city to the following infantry divisions, turn east, cross the Fulda and then head via Mühlhausen-Erfurt in the direction of Czechoslovakia. Once across the Fulda, 6th Armored would be following directly in the footsteps of the Oflags.

Also on 30 March, at Bad Hersfeld, 4th Armored had prevented a German attempt to cut the US Army's advance northwards. This was 12 miles from Rotenburg. Panzer Brigade Thüringia, the ad hoc battle group made up of a training unit with a tank battalion, an assault gun battalion, a Panzer Grenadier regiment and a reconnaissance battalion, was to attack the flank of the American advance. All the component units of the Brigade were well under strength, but they should have been

A train under air attack; the target appears to be in at least two sections and was more probably wagons in sidings than a train underway. The picture best fits descriptions in the men's accounts of 10 April as they walked from Uftrungen to Dittichenrode. This took them along the main Kassel-Nordhausen-Halle railway line, but it is unlikely that any trains were running at the time; passenger trains had not run for several weeks. (Green Collection)

reinforced by 40 assault guns delivered by rail directly to Bad Hersfeld along the railway that the Rotenburg men had walked alongside in the morning. Few of the guns made it into action. They and 4th Armored arrived almost simultaneously at the rail head and the Germans came off worst. The Americans were now 20 miles south of Sontra and given the speed of their advance, if they continued northeast up the main road from Bad Hersfeld towards Göttingen they would easily overtake both columns next day. In the meantime, the German defeat contributed to the streams of vehicles that passed Oflag IX A/Z in the night.

For the first two nights of the evacuation Celander had left Oflag IX A/Z and returned to Rotenburg, but on Saturday 31 March he had to leave the Schwedenheim as fighting erupted along the Fulda. Now the inhabitants of Rotenburg did leave their homes for the safety of the woods on the surrounding hills. Björn Ulf Noll's family and the rest of the inhabitants of the school house on Braacher Straße went to a wooded valley, the 'Eulersgrund' at the back of the school to shelter from the shelling. Celander hung a large Swedish flag from an upper window, nailed a certificate from the Swedish Embassy on the garage door proclaiming that the house was Swedish property and left to accompany Oflag IX A/Z.

Two US divisions, 6th Armored in the north and 65th Infantry a little to their south, had begun searching for crossing points on the Fulda. Until the Americans found a way over the river they were of no immediate concern tor Oberst Schrader and the other German commanders; it was the activities of the 4th Armored that were the most worrying. By the evening of 30 March it was evident that although they were not going to follow the road to Sontra, Oetmannshausen and on to Eschwege, the Americans were still travelling in the direction of Mühlhausen. If they wished, the Americans would be able to reach the town well before the two camps. In fact, 4th Armored's orders were to move around the south of Mühlhausen and on eastwards towards Weimar. Schrader's two columns were travelling at under 2 miles an hour and covering no more 10 miles a day. The American tanks were in some periods covering four times that distance.

It was not only the Germans who were concerned about the speed of some of the units from US 3rd Army. American commanders were also unhappy with the eastward salient that was developing around 4th Armored as it pushed forward. For the time being, the area north and south of the Division was empty of Allied troops. North of the 4th the Americans were still on the west bank of the Fulda. Fortunately for 3rd Army, there were only scattered German units on its northern flank. Warfare at this stage involved frantic German attempts to create defensive positions with road blocks and blown bridges at key points, supported by rare air attacks. The troops holding the positions could be SS or Wehrmacht or the Volkssturm, or even teenagers from the *Reichsarbeitsdienst* – German Labour Service – manning anti-aircraft guns. American units would push on each day, sometimes into a void with no German units for several miles, at other times into heavy fire-fights that required the destruction of an entire village by air support.

Hauptmann Seybold held Oflag IX A/H at Waldkappel until two hours past sunset before setting off on the second stage of their journey eastwards. They left in two groups, Lower Camp at 21.30 and Upper Camp at 21.45. There was still German transport sharing the road: in one instance horse-drawn carts mixed in with two light tanks. Their route took them through Oetmannshausen around midnight. Oflag IX A/Z had reached the area at 19.00 hrs the previous evening. Neither Oflag refers to meeting the other. The Spangenberg column crossed the north–south road and then went northeast through Reichensachsen where they stopped for half an hour, giving John Sewell time to eat 'a massive würst sandwich' that he had prepared at Waldkappel. Lieutenant Jeffrey and Arbeitskommando 1249 would spend the night at Reichensachsen the following evening, 31 March.

Terence Prittie and Walter Clough-Taylor had, despite the good natured response of the guards, decided that escaping at this stage of the war was foolhardy. They and Bill Edwards agreed that they would not make an attempt to get away during that night. The euphoria of the opportunity to escape the night before had evaporated. All three would change their minds again in the coming days.

Six hours after starting out Oflag IX A/H had reached Eschwege, 10 miles from Waldkappel. Their average speed had dropped to 1.5 miles an hour. Eschwege appeared untouched by air raids and the column marched directly through the town centre. Walking at night suited John Sewell. He found the first part of the journey in the moonlight and the comparative warmth of late March pleasant. The final stretch was less enjoyable. The last six miles from Eschwege to Wanfried, took it out of him. By the time he arrived at their billet for the night Sewell was not feeling quite so happy. The journey was now having a serious effect on the older men and many had to have periodic lifts on the carts. Ralph Wilbraham says they straggled through Eschwege and then had a 'longish hill' to climb before dropping back into the valley of the Werra. They crossed the river at Wanfried and turned left to a large barn west of the town. Beckwith notes that the bridge was prepared for demolition and had two Volkssturm guards. Their journey ended at 07.30. The men were exhausted. They had covered about 16 miles. Colonel Holland recorded them having short stops every half hour and two longer halts. The barn had no water or electricity, but the men were relieved to halt. The Germans brought bread, sausage, soup and ersatz coffee, which the men supplemented with tea and porridge. They had been on the road for ten hours. There was no announcement, but Saturday would be a rest day.

Behind them the Rotenburg column was waking. Harry Roberts was feeling the effects of the rich food. He couldn't face breakfast. It was a problem that would get worse for Oflag IX A/Z. The unusual food they were now getting through barter

Prisoners holding their 'PW' sheet signs, one of the improvised methods of preventing USAAF bombers mistaking the column for a German military column. These are being used at Hain on Saturday 7 April 1945. The men stopped for lunch here in an orchard at the back of the village. (Green Collection)

was having an increasing disastrous effect on their stomachs. There was also considerable air activity and their position that morning was uncomfortable, at a junction of two main roads and two railway lines. Roberts' diary notes 'Enormous air activity & shelling'. Butch Laing describes them moving along the road in small parties holding their PW signs. Lieutenant James Symes wrote that one American pilot flew over them at about 100 feet and waved.

At one stage Oberstleutnant Brix and Hauptmann Heyl discussed moving off the road into the woods and waiting for the Americans to arrive, but in the end they continued to walk on. Colonels Clay and Kennedy supported the idea of moving the column into the woods, but had they done so, it would have been almost 48 hours before the Americans arrived. Although they could hear American artillery firing across the Fulda, the Germans had blown all the bridges, and it would take time for them to be repaired. They would not reach Oetmannshausen until 2 April. Around the Rotenburg column American fighter bombers were attacking anything that moved, providing additional support to the artillery. Oberstleutnant Brix was under stress. He interrogated German stragglers, suspicious that they were deserters. He grabbed a guard's rifle and took one or two shots at aircraft as prisoners shouted their disapproval. If there was anything likely to get them attacked by US aircraft, it was the Germans using the column's 'PW' signs as cover to fire at aircraft.

The natural route from Oetmannshausen towards Mühlhausen was the one taken during the previous night by Oflag IX A/H through Eschwege. But now in daylight Brix, seeing the town as a likely target for air attack, led Oflag IX A/Z directly east across the valley and then contoured along small roads around the dramatic hills south of Eschwege. Bridges across the Werra, especially at Eschwege, were German choke points as they struggled to cross to the eastern bank of the River Werra and regroup. They made easy targets for American fighter-bombers. 'Butch' Laing described a particularly anxious moment, when a German armoured fighting vehicle came down the road followed by an American fighter. The vehicle stopped immediately in front of Laing's party, and the occupants got out very hastily. The prisoners expected the worst and put out their PW signs. Thankfully after a low level check the fighter flew off and left them in peace.

Rotenburg's route often had them walking with forest on either side of the road, which provided some cover from aircraft. Eventually after stopping for a meal break at 16.00hrs, they dropped into the valley of the Werra and, like Oflag IX A/H 12 hours before them, crossed the river at Wanfried. In a few months Wanfried would lie on the border between the Russian and US zones. The Rotenburg column turned right, away from Oflag IX A/H's barn, and walked through the town until they reached The Kalkhof farm, a mile or so to the east. Behind them a Volkssturm unit was guarding the Wanfried bridge. By 2 April all the bridges across the Werra south of Eschwege had been destroyed. The railway bridge at Eschwege and those north of the town went the next day.

Ernest Edlmann's account of the afternoon of 31 March describes the noise of fighting behind the column gradually dying down until there was a dramatic explosion from the area around Eschwege later in the day. Like their comrades in Oflag IX A/H many of the Rotenburg men found the day extremely tiring. Ernest Edlmann described it as 'the longest and most tiring march yet', with many men ill from the food. The column had walked 12 miles. Like the Spangenberg men earlier that day, Edlmann was not impressed with their billet, '...pitch dark, and awful job to see where to sleep. Absolute hell. Stew ran out before we got it!' Wanfried with its undamaged and picturesque half-timbered houses had been a pleasant interlude for the men as they tramped through it. The Kalkhof was less attractive. It had a large detached house with a courtyard lined at three sides with barns and stables.

The Kalkhof, Easter Sunday morning. Dörr's carts in the foreground with either guards or, given the absence of rifles, the carts' Russian POW drivers. McIndoe's caption is 'The barn where 450 officers were quartered at Wanfried.'. (Otago Settlers' Museum, New Zealand)

The Kalkhof, Easter Sunday morning, 1 April 1945. This is the earliest surviving example of the photographs taken by Lee Hill of the march of Oflag IX A/Z. The pile of split logs will provide fuel for cooking and heating in the houses and barns that form the Kalkhof. Many of the outbuildings in this part of the Kalkhof have now been demolished, but the archway and the house to the left of it remain. The vehicle is the YMCA lorry usually driven by Niels Jörgensen, the Danish YMCA worker. From the windows of the house in the background people watch the prisoners wash, shave and cook breakfast. This was not the only house at the Kalkhof. Between the road and the yards seen here, is a rather finer detached house that was used by the Americans and Russians to negotiate a modification to the boundaries of their respective occupation zones in September 1945. (Marion Gerritsen-Teunissen Collection)

Today the Kalkhof is a riding stables, but it is still very much as it was in 1945. From their billet the men could easily see the main road to Mühlhausen 100 yards away. It was from the Kalkhof that Edward Baxter saw a party of POWs marching past on the main road and was told by a guard that they were from Oflag IX A/H. Baxter's informant was wrong, no doubt the guard was guessing. But there were other groups of POWs from arbeitskommandos travelling east at the same time. Kommando 1249 would pass the Kalkhof during the early hours of 2 April. They reached Reichensachsen just past Oetmannshausen on the day before. Lieutenant Jeffrey's diary has 'Reichensachsen ++ strafe', so they too were seeing demonstrations of American airpower.

For most of Oflag IX A/Z the priority was a warm and dry place to sleep after the day's ordeal. At 12 miles it was to be the longest stage of the Rotenburg men's march. For many the day was made worse by stomach complaints. Harry Roberts felt weak and described the morning as 'hellish'. Roberts noted troops and vehicles passing the Kalkhof on the main road all night. But his concern was whether he would be able to keep going and complete the rest of the journey. Despite the risks of air attack or an encounter with the SS, the thing that gave the men most problems was diarrhoea.

On both sides of Wanfried the Oflags were billeted in very cramped conditions. Oflag IX A/H were crowded into a barn that was about half the size of the previous night's. It had no water and no lighting. John Sewell noted that Oberst Schrader inspected the billet and that this led to a water cart being provided, along with some soup. With the water cart come four nervous young Germans who had been told that the Americans would shoot them if they were captured.

At Bebra, now 30 miles behind them and directly on the new front line, it was Lieutenants Reid and Bowlby who had reason to be nervous. On the morning of 31 March they had found there were two other prisoners of war in Bebra jail. One was a Royal Air Force officer; the other was an American sergeant from an unnamed armoured division. The American was convinced that the arrival of the Americans would be heralded by an artillery bombardment that would flatten the town, killing them all. It was not the Americans that would be the threat. In the afternoon fighting began around the prison. There was an SS unit in the building next door. Sheltering in the prison cellars the POWs were found by the SS and taken outside to be shot as spies. At the last minute their lives were saved by the prison commandant, but they remained in the prison and at risk from the SS until the Americans seized the town.

The other group of early escapees were still in hiding at a farm above Rotenburg. They had insufficient food and were anxiously waiting for signs that the artillery bombardment they could hear was the preamble to Americans appearing on the east bank of the Fulda. At Ober Melsungen, a railway bridge was repaired by 25th Armored Engineer Battalion and the 86th Cavalry were able to get their light vehicles across the river. It was no use for the rest of the Division. The next road bridge south at Malsfeld, close to Spangenberg, had lost one span but it was repairable. Starting work at 2000hrs on 31 March, the engineers had the bridge ready for use by 0930hrs the next day. Farther south, 65th Infantry Division found the small bridge at Braach north of Rotenburg still standing but in need of repair. Rotenburg town bridge was blown, as were the bridges near Bebra. In the next few days the Americans would build a pontoon bridge there.

By early Easter Sunday, 1 April, the Germans apparently had two American armoured thrusts to worry about. In fact,

Men from 1st Platoon, 25 Engineer Company (US Army) working in the late afternoon of 31 March 1945 to replace the destroyed span of the Malsfeld road bridge across the River Fulda. As a temporary repair to get the vehicles of 6th Armored across, the engineers used treadway road sections more normally used on pontoons. The bridge was ready for use in less than 12 hours and the 6th Armored were across and east of Spangenberg by the end of 1 April. The photograph is taken from the eastern side of the bridge. (Sumners' Family Collection)

Braach Bridge, December 1943. From time to time prisoners were allowed to walk in the neighbourhood with a guard and under parole. Braach was a popular destination for the men from Rotenburg. The small village with its bridge over the Fulda was less than 2 miles north of Rotenburg. In April 1945 this bridge would be captured intact by the Americans, but was not sufficiently strong to carry their tanks or other heavy vehicles. (Otago Settlers' Museum, New Zealand)

4th Armored in the south was no longer a threat. Despite worries over their exposed left flank, the Americans had decided to follow up rumours of a major German communications centre at Ohrdruf 30 miles south-east of Mühlhausen. One of the rumours was that Hitler had moved there from Berlin. In fact, it was close to Field Marshal Kesselring's headquarters. From his command train near the town he controlled all German armies in the West. Kesselring's train left Ohrdruf for Blankenburg in the Harz Mountains on 3 April, the day before the Americans arrived.

Oflag IX A/H were told by Hauptmann Seybold that they should be prepared to move again in the evening, which would have given them 24 hours rest. But Colonel Holland objected to any move. The Geneva Convention required prisoners to obey the orders of their captors. Holland therefore did not explicitly refuse. Instead he protested that the column was not in a fit state to continue. Terence Prittie realised that some of the older officers 'had taken virtually no exercise for three years. They might be 45 or 50 years of age, and had been forced to make two desperately wearing marches on which they carried a fast quantity of kit. Many of them were incapable of going on.' Colonel Holland told the Germans that the column should not travel under any circumstances. Instead, they should be moved to a quiet village off the main roads and to wait there until the Allies arrived.

At this moment the German plans for both camps are difficult to determine. The facts come from the prisoners' accounts, most of whom were not directly involved in the discussions. Both of the Oflags could reach Mühlhausen in one stage. The Spangenberg column would need to walk another 14 miles, Rotenburg around 12. Whilst Colonels Kennedy and Clay with Oflag IX A/Z did not object to their moving, neither camp moved at what had become their usual time.

Oberst Schrader had visited Oflag IX A/H at their barn outside Wanfried early in the morning on Easter Sunday, possibly whilst it was still dark. Once he had finished his inspection and left, Colonel Holland gave his objections to moving to Seybold. Objecting to Seybold and not to Schrader gave Holland two advantages. He was a Colonel, the German a Captain, and more importantly, Schrader was out of reach, in his car somewhere on the road back to Mühlhausen. If Seybold could be browbeaten into consulting his senior officer, which would take several hours, then the Americans got closer. Holland was playing for time.

Seybold eventually decided to consult Schrader. Sewell believed that the messages were sent by bicycle and that they to took 2½ hours each way. Earlier on his way back to his headquarters, Schrader had visited the Rotenburg column at the Kalkhof. John McIndoe drew a conference at the Kalkhof between the SBOs of Oflag IX A/Z and at least three senior German officers, one of whom could have been Schrader. His caption says only 'G. Commandant'. Had the messenger reached him at the Kalkhof, the restated order to Seybold to march that evening could have reached Oflag IX A/H in under an hour. But it was late afternoon before Schrader underlined the importance of moving by sending a more senior officer, Major Fleischmann, to take over command from Seybold. The discussions between Holland and Seybold reach the rest of the prisoners and from Easter afternoon onwards there were rumours that they would be walking to Mühlhausen that night. Eventually it was agreed that they would move on, but not until the next day and with a tractor and trailer to carry those unable to walk.

The men of Oflag IX A/H in the meantime were enjoying the delay. They were allowed to leave the immediate vicinity of the barn under parole. There had been an Easter Communion at 07.30hrs, with an altar improvised from a field gate lifted off its hinges and a wooden cross. Sewell followed Communion with a breakfast of half a tin of bacon, with mustard, and a cup of tea, and then took advantage of the parole to sit on the hillside in the sun. Above him the Luftwaffe put in a rare appearance and around midday there was half an hour of air battles. The cause of all this air activity was 4th Armored's attempts to cross the Werra at Creuzburg, 10 miles to the south of Wanfried. Their pontoon bridges were continually wrecked by the Luftwaffe and it took 4th Armored until 3 April to secure the bridgehead.

Sewell meanwhile was in a 'state of comparative bliss': soup in his belly and a pipe in the sun. There was another food issue in the mid-afternoon, this time of pea soup. Nevertheless Sewell was beginning to be worried about his own rations. There had been no German issue of dry foods since they left Spangenberg. He was particularly keen to get some bread, since his own stock was down to:

1 tin meat roll (unopened)
1 tin peas (unopened)
¾ tin margarine
4 oz tobacco tin ¾ full of sugar

2 Red X biscuits
¾ biscuit tin containing mixture of cocoa milk powder and sugar and supply of salt

The only disturbance to the men's rest was the continual sound of shellfire or bombing. Around him the prisoners spread out from the barn to shelters made in haystacks, under carts or against walls, anywhere to be away from the barn that was an obvious target. Even the arrival of Major Fleischmann from Schrader's headquarters to replace Hauptmann Seybold as the Senior German Officer had done little to disturb the men's rest. Fleischman had orders to move to Mühlhausen, but like Brix his orders changed in the afternoon.

Oflag IX A/Z also had a late start, which was much appreciated. There was Easter Communion. Harry Roberts breakfasted on egg, bacon, bread and onions, washed down with cocoa – and then remarked that he felt fairly fit although his stomach wasn't too settled'. Oddly, whilst Sewell four miles away talks of aerial battles and shellfire, Ernest Edlmann describes the day as 'Peaceful, no sign of battle'. The downside to the absence of aerial activity and the noise of shellfire is that it meant there were no American troops nearby. No liberation today. The contrast between Sewell's air activity and shellfire and the peace at Rotenburg is difficult to reconcile, until it is remembered that the men's diaries were personal accounts and not official logs. There had been so many periods of aircraft noise and gunfire, presumably for some it no longer registered.

When the Rotenburg column does leave the Kalkhof, Edlmann describes a route lined with the debris of war. Lorries with charred bodies, the victims of American air attacks and Russian prisoners, 'columns of Asiatic slaves under swine of German NCO who kept beating them.' The contrast between their own treatment and that of the Russian prisoners could not have been more stark. Hugh Cartwright: '...passed by a long column of Russian prisoners being beaten along by their guards.

Senior German and British Officers at the Kalkhof Conference, 1 April 1945. John McIndoe's caption reads 'Col Clay and Kennedy [SBOs] in conference with G. Commandant + staff Easter Sunday, Wanfried.' If the German group included Oberst Schrader then this drawing shows him inspecting Oflag IX A/Z, and briefing Oberstleutnant Brix, after his earlier inspection of the Spangenberg column and meeting with Colonel Holland, at which Holland tried to stop Oflag IX A/H moving again. The tentative identification of the officers is, from left to right: Heyl, Brix, Schrader, Clay and Kennedy. (Otago Settlers' Museum, New Zealand)

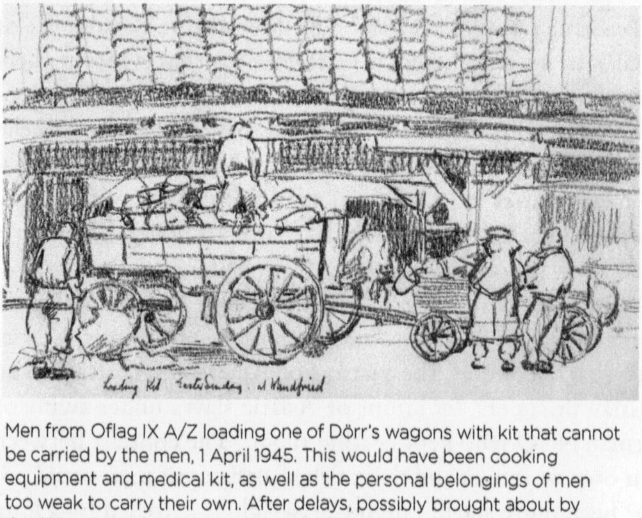

Men from Oflag IX A/Z loading one of Dörr's wagons with kit that cannot be carried by the men, 1 April 1945. This would have been cooking equipment and medical kit, as well as the personal belongings of men too weak to carry their own. After delays, possibly brought about by the objections of Colonel Holland with the Spangenberg column, the Rotenburg men eventually left in the afternoon, but only got as far as Diedorf. (Otago Settlers' Museum, New Zealand)

The Kalkhof in Thuringia is still a farm, as it was in 1945. (Peter Green)

Our guards were still addressing us as "Meine Herrn" as they urged us along.'

Oflag IX A/Z arrived at Diedorf after a couple of hours and took their normal hourly rest. The weather was good and on another occasion the ramble would have been quite pleasant. As they sat in the sun on the wide grassy verge outside the village, the men were in for a surprise. What they assumed was only a rest was about to become an overnight stop. Baxter describes another conference between the Germans and the SBOs that leads to Major Chillingworth returning to tell them the 'astonishing news' that they were staying at Diedorf and that they would be billeted in the village under parole. The men would be free to go where they liked within a small radius of their billets, and to do as much trading with the inhabitants as they wished. The prisoners did not know it but the Germans had changed their plans. Neither column was going to Mühlhausen.

Diedorf was Oflag IX A/Z's best billet of the march so far. Reverend Forster who had not been able to celebrate Easter Mass at the Kalkhof was finally able to say Mass at Diedorf. His billet was opposite a convent. Reverend Forster was able to persuade Hauptmann Heyl that he and a Canadian priest, Father Desnoyer, could visit the convent, where the Sisters gave the two priests a warm welcome. After Mass the men were given coffee and cake before they returned to their billet in a barn.

'Butch' Laing slept on the cobbled floor of a coach house, but his attempts to trade for some fresh bread failed. He was the only prisoner who records being rebuffed. Despite the agreement that the men could trade, Laing was refused by a villager who was more concerned what the Gestapo would do to him: 'He told me that ... the security-police would have the right to shoot him.'

Ernest Edlmann was able to get two loaves of bread from a villager and met some German paratroops. In Edlmann's opinion they had no idea of the gravity of the situation facing Germany. Belief in the Führer, miracle weapons, fear of the Party or in the

Prisoners in their overnight billet; McIndoe's caption has 'in the barn during air raid Easter Sunday', which makes the location either Kalkhof in the morning or Diedorf that evening. (Otago Settlers' Museum, New Zealand)

last resort fear of the Russians and the dreaded American gangsters would keep Germany fighting. Later that day Edlmann met a Dutch farm worker, Henrik-Gerrit Moen, who offered to arrange an escape for the next day. Moen offered to provide Ernest and his partner Frederick Corfield with civilian clothes. The Dutchman would follow the column and then hand over the clothes once the prisoners had slipped away somewhere outside the village. 'He gave me his blessing, and a rosary!' Edlmann later gave the rosary to his mother.

Arbeitskommando 1249 were beginning to catch up with the two Oflags. By Easter Day they had reached Reichensachsen after walking from midnight to midday. Next day they would continue eastwards past Diedorf, where they would leave behind a sick prisoner, before arriving at their billet for the night at Heyrode at midday. It was 2 miles past Diedorf on the road to Mühlhausen and they missed the Rotenburg men by a couple of hours. The kommando's immediate objective was their base Stalag, 60 miles due east. As their commandant was not able to communicate with the many working parties that would also be trudging eastwards, there was no way that they could be diverted away from possible American advances. Arbeitskommando 106 had left the potassium mines at Dorndorf that day and would spend the night at Bad Liebenstein, as far east as Diedorf but 30 miles south of Eisenach. Stalag IX C's sub-camp at Pfafferode would not be evacuated until 0800hrs on 2 April, when it began to walk to Ebeleben, north-east of Mühlhausen.

Farther west, Sixth Armored crossed the Fulda at Malsfeld on 1 April. Unlike in other towns nearby that had peacefully surrendered as the Americans arrived, the Germans defended Spangenberg. Fighting went on into the late afternoon, when the German Army retreated, but by then the schloß, former home of Upper Camp, had been attacked by the USAAF and destroyed with napalm. (Napalm incendiary bombs were first dropped in France in July 1944.)

By the evening of Easter Sunday, 6th Armored was bivouacked in an arc around Spangenberg. To their south 65th Infantry had reached the Fulda from Braach through Rotenburg to Bebra. Rotenburg escaped the fate of Spangenberg, despite the SS's original intention to defend the town. A few American shells were dropped near the former camp buildings, damaging the roof. Björn Ulf Noll's family believed the Americans knew the buildings were empty and the shelling was a warning to the town. In the end, the only damage to Rotenburg was to the town bridge and two houses close to it.

The Americans would reached the outskirts of Eschwege on 2 April and by the next day they would be over the Werra south of Wanfried. Prisoners from Oflag IX A/H who went to collect water from Wanfried learned from civilians that the Americans were 12 miles away to the south. This was 4th Armored. Crossing the Werra would be more difficult than the Fulda. But on Easter Sunday the Germans could still plausibly expect American tanks to arrive at Mühlhausen from the south within 24 hours.

4

THE GERMAN PLAN B

> Seybold has given up any idea of counting us and there are several officers missing. I myself have come to the conclusion that it is better to stick to the main body.
>
> Captain Ralph Wilbraham MC, Pioneer Corps, Oflag IX A/H, Upper Camp, captured France June 1940.

Colonel Holland's objections to Oflag IX A/H moving were finally overcome in the late evening of Easter Sunday. The men were warned to be ready to move early the next day, Monday 2 April. Major Fleischmann had finally got a grip on the column and the prisoners noted an improvement in the guard's discipline; but it was only superficial. Bill Edwards noticed that when Major Fleischmann asked one German officer had he counted his prisoners the man said that he had, when in fact, Edwards knew that he had not. The guards were also in some confusion, with sentries around the barn missing as they struggled to collect their kit. They too had not been expecting to leave in the dark. There was no concerted effort to ensure that all the prisoners were present before they left the field at 0500hrs. It was just after dawn. With men lying under carts and in haystacks, some many yards from the barn – what Ted Beckwith described as the 'suburbs' – the opportunities for escape had multiplied.

Three groups at least escaped by climbing a gulley at rear of the barn and into the woods on the hillside. Although the escapees made quite a din as they struggled up the slope, the rest of the column made even more noise as they got their kit together in the dark and re-joined their walking groups. The largest group of escapees consisted of Major Richard Barclay, Royal Artillery, Major Clough-Taylor, Royal Welch Fusiliers, Lieutenant Kane, Terence Prittie, Lieutenant Rose and Lieutenant Acton, Rifle Brigade. There were also two separate pairs of escapees: Major Bill Shand, 12 Lancers and Lieutenant Ronnie Swayne, Herefordshire Regiment; and Major Bill Arnold, Royal Artillery, and Captain Thomas Cleasby, Border Regiment, both from the Air Landing Brigade of 1st Airborne Division who had been captured at Arnhem. The escapees managed to reach the cover of the hill top shrubs and trees before it was completely light. The groups would spend the next few days together.

Major Fleischmann had promised Colonel Holland a short walk to their next billet. It would be only 10 kilometres, but there was understandable suspicion that the Germans planned to march them farther once they had the column on the move. The prisoners' suspicions were not borne out by events. Despite the disorganisation around them, the weaker prisoners were not forgotten by the Germans. A tractor and trailer was produced to carry them. The short distance proved to be correct, it was only 7 miles to their next billet at Lengenfeld unterm Stein.

The village was in the next valley to Wanfried, less than 5 miles in a straight line to the north. Oflag IX A/H's route took them through Wanfried and past the Kalkhof, abandoned by their Rotenburg comrades the previous afternoon. After a steep climb out of the valley of the Werra, they looped back on themselves and went down the next valley to Lengenfeld. It was a large village of half-timbered houses with red tile roofs, overlooked by a schloß, but dominated by the 80-foot tall viaduct

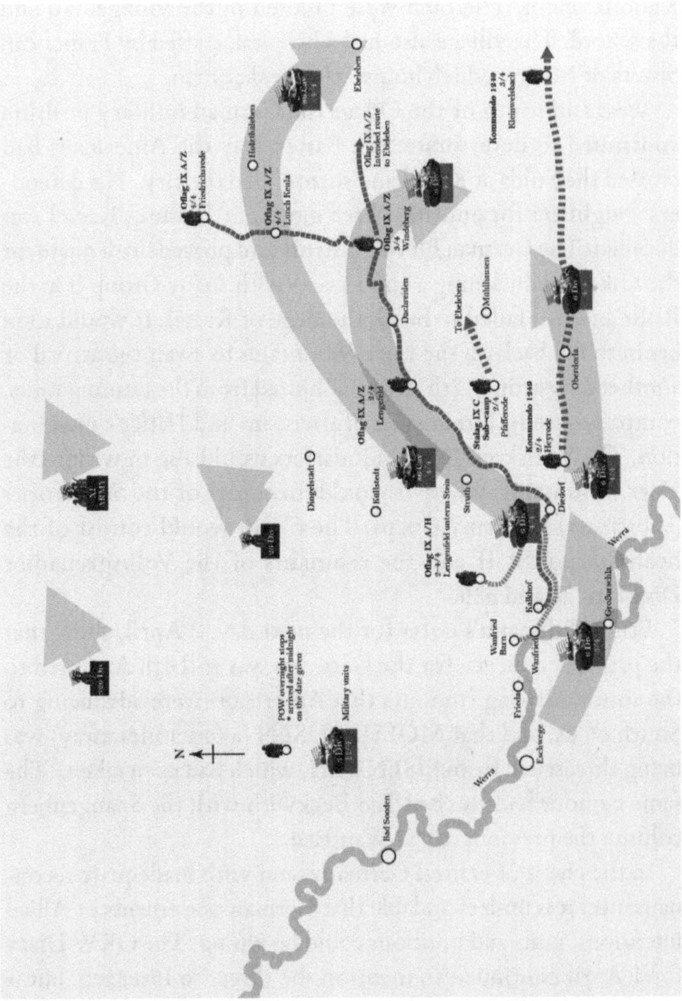

The Americans capture Mühlhausen, 3–8 April 1945. (Peter Green)

that took the railway across the valley and directly over village. It was the same railway that passed through Spangenberg, the Kanonenbahn. The men were billeted in the village hall and the school. The village also had a hospital, staffed by Franciscan Sisters of Mercy, which housed the weaker men.

West and south of the Oflags the German military position continued to deteriorate. On Easter Day the Americans had crossed the Fulda at Kassel and surrounded the city. The defenders fought on for another three days, but Festung Kassel was doomed. The German Eleventh Army had proved inadequate for the task of maintaining a connection with Army Group B in the Ruhr and had failed to break the siege of Kassel. It would soon begin to fall back on the Harz Mountains to await the arrival of another new army, 12th Army, conjured from the training units, company-strength remnants of divisions and Hitler's imagination. The Wehrkreis IX's headquarters would also move into the Harz Mountains, where it would form part of the *Stellvertreter* (substitute) IX Army Corps. The Corps would consist of the headquarters staff and the remnants of the Volksgrenadier Divisions 26 and 326.

Ernest Edlmann's notes for the next day, 2 April, show that the primary concern for the Germans was still 4th Armored to the south, 'Strong rumours that Americans were advancing to South of us, and that MÜLHLAUSEN (a few miles away) was being threatened from EISENACH, which had been taken.' The same rumour had reached Ted Beckwith with the Spangenberg column the previous day at Wanfried.

In the chaos of central Germany, and with inadequate reconnaissance, it is understandable that German assessments of Allied intentions, units and positions could be wrong. The OKW Diary for 1 April continued to mention the threat to Eisenach, but it also mentions American troops around Melsungen on the Fulda. The Military Bulletin produced for public consumption described the German counter attack at Bad Hersfeld as pushing into the American flank, whereas it had been defeated two days previously.

Oberst Schrader's new plan was for the two Oflags to walk to Ebeleben, a rail head 15 miles northeast of Mühlhausen. The plan was notified to Colonel Holland in the evening of 2 April. Presumably it was passed to Colonel Clay at the same time. In the absence of any mention of it amongst the accounts of the Rotenburg men, it must be assumed that the news did not reach any of the men. Colonels Clay and Kennedy must have kept the potentially disheartening news to themselves.

Why was Oflag IX A/H not made to walk farther? Later that day Oflag IX A/Z walked to Lengefeld, the village briefly becoming the intended next billet for Oflag A/H. If the complaints from Colonel Holland had affected the German plans, it was only temporary. The Spangenberg column would be expected to move the following day. Perhaps having changed the route at short notice the previous day the Germans could not find new billets for both camps.

Lengenfeld unterm Stein certainly had sufficient buildings to hold all the Spangenberg men. The villages beyond were smaller. But had Oflag IX A/H left overnight on 31 March–1 April they could have reached Lengefeld in one go and the distance would have matched their earlier journeys. Instead, it is the Rotenburg men who spend the night of 2 April at Lengefeld. From now on the earlier pattern of Oflag IX A/H being ahead of the Rotenburg column is reversed. The stop at Lengenfeld was not caused by low morale amongst the guard nor was it part of a personal agreement struck between Fleischmann and Holland. It was a deliberate pre-planned stop in their journey. Oflag IX A/H were expected in the village. Although the Germans had begun to implement their new plan for the Oflags' evacuation, but they did so with little urgency compared to plans affecting other prisoners. Bruce Jeffries with Arbeitskommando 1249, for example, walked 17 miles almost due east on both 2 and 3 April. Unusually, Oflag IX A/H spent most of the time walking in daylight, though they only took three hours to reach their billet. They arrived at Lengenfeld at 0700hrs.

Despite Major Fleischman's presence and the fact that the column had finally moved, the guards' morale remained low. Ralph Wilbraham: 'The Germans have given up any attempt to guard us. At least six of the postern have disappeared on their bicycles. The remainder stand about in groups clutching their hand baggage and ready to give themselves up whenever the Americans entered the town.' In contrast, the guard with the Rotenburg men were sticking to their task. Ernest Edlmann and Patrick Corfield would not be able to slip away from the column to meet their new Dutch friend with his spare civilian clothing.

Oflag IX A/Z set off at 0900hrs. The clocks had gone forward in the night, so for the men it would have felt like an early start. They headed northwards, no longer towards Mühlhausen. Some thought that they were travelling to Nordhausen. Ernest Edlmann was certainly aware, as they left, that they were walking in the direction of Nordhausen. He told the author that he knew that he didn't want to go there, but had no knowledge of the horrors of the SS slave labour camps that surrounded the town. For Edlmann it was simply a case of enough was enough: he wanted to be free of the march and free of the Germans. The early start could have allowed the column to be well on the way to Ebeleben, but like the Spangenberg column they travelled a short distance, only eight miles, from Diedorf to Lengefeld.

They were now walking though more open countryside. Apart from occasional woodlands there was little shelter from the wind or rain and the weather was about to break. It would start to rain that evening. Over the next few days there would be more rain and sometimes sleet. The weather affected the men who had escaped from Oflag IX A/H at Wanfried the most. It would have no impact on the rest of the Spangenberg men at Lengenfeld and few of the Rotenburg men make any complaints about having to walk in the wet. The main feature of the *Eichsfeld*, the area north of Mühlhausen, is a series of small north-west to south-east ridges overlain on a landscape that gradually

Men from Oflag IX A/Z washing in a farm yard in Diedorf on the morning of Easter Monday, 2 April 1945. The men are sharing the yard with a pile of logs or possibly even peat cuttings, fuel for the house. (Otago Settlers' Museum, New Zealand)

Oflag IX A/Z spent the night of 2 April in several barns amongst fields at Lengefeld. Presumably this was the view from the barn where McIndoe slept. Parked outside the barn is Celander's Opel car and the YMCA lorry. (Otago Settlers' Museum, New Zealand)

rises towards the north-east, before dropping steeply to flatter ground, the *Goldene Aue* – Golden Meadow. This stretches east-west along the southern flank of the Harz Mountains. The villages the Rotenburg men passed through in the next few days had notices from the local *Gauleiter* pasted on walls and doors, 'If any white flags are shown here, all male adults of the village will be shot. Those who refuse to build roadblocks will also be shot.' The Gauleiter of Thuringia, Herr 'Fritz' Sauckel, was also the Reich Plenipotentiary for Labour. He was condemned to death at Nuremburg for his part in creating and operating the Third Reich's slave labour system.

Despite the short distance it took Oflag IX A/Z seven hours to reach their billet. Lengefeld was 10 miles to the east of Lengenfeld and Oflag IX A/H. Compared to the Spangenberg men, Oflag IX A/Z's home for the night was poor, a group of barns in the middle of a muddy field outside the village. The rain that arrived around 19.00 would not have made their surroundings any more attractive. As Oflag IX A/H had found at Wanfried, providing water supplies to field barns could be difficult. There was none in Harry Roberts' barn, but 'Butch' Laing was luckier, he even had access to hot water. The arrival of the prisoners with their trade goods soon attracted people, especially children, from the village willing

Men washing and cleaning their teeth on the morning of 3 April by one of the field barns at Lengefeld. (Green Collection)

Men of Oflag IX A/Z wait to move off on the morning of 3 April. A German officer is in the foreground and John McIndoe sits at the corner of the barn in the centre of the picture. (Green Collection)

to barter. Harry Roberts got some bread. 'Butch' Laing found a German anti-aircraft battery whose commander wanted to exchange a radio for 150 cigarettes to 'improve his men's morale'.

Unlike Oflag IX A/H, Oberstleutnant Brix had his column well under control. Brix's achievement in maintaining discipline amongst his men was all the more commendable given the demoralised state of other German soldiers in the area. Ernest Edlmann met a lot of troops not afraid to rail against Hitler and the Nazis. Many seemed to him to be deserters. There was '…an anti-tank battery from Remagen area, good chaps, but knew they were beaten.' The Germans' frequently used their 88 mm anti-aircraft guns as anti-tank weapons, so it is likely that Ernest's unit was the same battery that Laing refers to. Ernest had a good a night in the barn. But for others stomach upsets were still a serious problem. Edlmann's escape partner Captain Frederick Corfield Royal Artillery was particularly badly smitten. The implications of 400-odd men with diarrhoea, no toilets and an already muddy field, are not to be dwelt upon.

Edward Baxter was happy with Lengefeld. He got three-quarters of a loaf and some sausage. All the prisoners were issued with a tin of meat produced by Gunnar Celander with the help of Heinrich Sultan. Baxter thought it was German Army rations, 'the German equivalent of our bully beef'. Harry Roberts cooked some bacon with his black market bread. Despite the mud, the men ate in relative comfort. They were surrounded by evidence of Germany's forced labour economy that the farms depended upon. Edward Baxter:

> At the farm where we stayed and in the villages we found quite a number of Poles and other foreign workers. As we had two Polish officers and several good French and German speakers we generally managed to get some news from them. They all said that they had been very badly treated by their German masters. The Germans appeared to have taken large numbers of young girls from Poland for farm work.

German agriculture had always depended on seasonal workers from beyond its borders, Poles in particular. Its wartime economy was critically short of labour. Conscripted labour was one response to the problem: slave labour sold as a raw material by the SS was another. There were also Allied POWs, NCOs and other ranks, in Arbeitskommandos. Their work was not meant to benefit the war effort of their captors. Many Allied prisoners, working in mines or helping repair railway track after air raids, found it hard to understand how they were not helping the German war effort.

Compared to Rotenburg's barns in a muddy field, Oflag IX A/H were in paradise. Both Upper and Lower camps had hot baths on demand. Lower Camp were in a school and the Schloß on the edge of the village, whilst Upper Camp were in the village hall. John Sewell went to the Schloß for his first hot bath for over four years. He lunched on three helpings of German stew with some bread and two potatoes. After his bath he returned to his billet and another helping of stew. Later there was cocoa and a walk around the village entirely untroubled by the attentions of the guards. Instead, prisoners exchanged waves to any guards that they met.

Bill Edwards, as he walked around the village, was cheered by the sight of the German Army in full retreat. The troops were rarely organised units, a mixture of old men and boys, with officers thin on the ground 'All their faces wore an air of bewilderment, all were tired out, and grey with fatigue.' Edwards was able to find the odd soldier who, having checked that no one could hear, told him that they were making their way home. The one organised unit he did meet was an artillery unit manned by Ukrainians, former Soviet troops, After musing on their fate once the war was over, Edwards comments that Spangenberg also had a few guards who had been formerly Polish prisoners of war, but he gives no further details. The villagers were terrified that they were to be overrun by Americans and found the presence of the British, even as prisoners, reassuring.

Oflag IX A/H was enjoying Lengenfeld. The men assumed that liberation was close. Some of the guard had deserted. Roll calls were abandoned. The Germans had apparently given up any idea of further moves. All the men need do was to enjoy their billets and wait for freedom. Ralph Wilbraham quotes Major Fleischmann and Hauptmann Seybold as saying that they could not move as the column was now surrounded.

The Rotenburg men who had escaped on the first day would finally be liberated that day. They had been waiting for six days. On Monday 2 April at Bebra, Ian Reid and George Bowlby woke to find the SS had pulled out at 0600hrs. A few hours later the Burgermaster of Bebra, wearing his smartest pinstriped suit and grey homburg, and carrying a vast white flag, tried to surrender the town to the two men. They declined his offer. Instead they took the Burgermaster by motorbike to find the American Army. They eventually found two suspicious American infantrymen on the far bank of the demolished Breitenbach bridge, just outside Bebra. They were from the

65th Infantry Division. Reid and Bowlby swam across, whilst the burgomaster waited for a boat. Once it became clear to the Americans who their wet visitors were, the men were given a wonderful reception – blankets, brandy, a change of clothes, white bread and frankfurters.

At this stage of the war the systems for repatriating former prisoners were nowhere near fully operational. Although the Americans were prepared to get Reid and Bowlby westwards, the men had promised two women, a German and a Czech who had shared their prison in Bebra that they would get them back to the German woman's home in Mannheim. In the chaos of collapsing Germany anything was possible and the two men are able to 'commandeer' or steal, a German car in Bebra and drive the women back to Mannheim. After a reunion meal with the German woman's family, Reid and Bowlby set off, still in the car, to Metz where they were finally absorbed in the Allied military system as RAMPs – Recovered Allied Military Personnel. On 7 April they were flown to Brussels, processed by the British Army and were back in the UK by 8 April.

Peter Conder and his comrades, who had been sheltering at the farm in the woods above Rotenburg, also met the Americans on 2 April. There had been shellfire in the night. The next morning there were American heavy lorries driving south along the road on the east bank of the Fulda. Unlike Reid and Bowlby, whose return to the UK was a largely freelance affair, Conder's party were evacuated via an American hospital. They had made themselves ill by eating too many US rations following several days close to starvation sheltering at the farm. This did not make them popular with the American medical staff, who had real sick and injured patients to care for, not greedy Limeys.

Peter Conder's prison diaries are devoted to records of the birds and bird behaviour he had seen. There is no mention of his escape, or his time in a US hospital, just his last bird record in March in Rotenburg; and then, as if by magic, on 6 April the birds he is noting are in Bedfordshire.

There was another group of men from Rotenburg and Spangenberg who were liberated in early April. Reserve-Lazarett at Obermaßfeld held men from all over the Wehrkreis, including several RAF and USAAF airmen with severe burn injuries. For administrative purposes the hospital was part of Stalag IX C and had its own arbeitskommando, 1249, to support the medical team. It was part of this kommando led by Captain Bruce Jeffrey RAMC that was following the two Oflags' path eastwards

Obermaßfeld hospital was 70 miles south of Mühlhausen and in the path of a third US armoured division, 11th Armored. Four men have left accounts of their liberation. Captain John Mountford, South Staffordshire Regiment, Lieutenant-Colonel John Frost MC, Parachute Regiment, Lieutenant William Watson MC, Commandos, and Private Martin, RAMC. Mountford and Frost had been captured and wounded at Arnhem. Watson had been transferred in error from Spangenberg – the Germans and the SBO at the time thinking he was a doctor. In time Watson did become a GP but in 1944 his main interest was in veterinary science. Martin was an orderly at the hospital. By early 1945 the main medical staff came from 1st Airborne Division and had been captured at Arnhem. The hospital had held a very unusual prisoner of war for a brief period from the autumn of 1944 until early 1945. Lieutenant Reba Whittle was a female nurse whose air evacuation Dakota had crash-landed in German-held territory. Though wounded herself, she worked as a nurse until she was repatriated in January 1945.

The Germans decided that evacuating the hospital was not practical and on the night of Easter Sunday, 1 April, the hospital's Lageroffizier, Major Lumpe, marched the guard away, leaving the medical staff and prisoners to their own devices. The hospital was close to a bridge over the Werra and next morning German engineers arrived to demolish it. The hospital staff persuaded them to allow time to move the patients away from the immediate blast zone and whilst this was being done the Americans arrived and the bridge was left intact. Even so, a brief fire fight developed around the hospital. At one stage Private H.L. Martin RAMC, one of the medical orderlies, placed the top of an operating table over wounded men to protect them. Colonel Frost took a more active part and went into the street outside to identify the position of snipers for the Americans. Several salvos from German *Nebelwerfer* mortar also landed in a field nearby before the area was secured. The American commander felt he was in an exposed position and should pull back towards the rest of the Division a few miles to the south. The patients able to walk left with some of the medical staff, but the more severe cases remained in no man's land until Thursday 5 April, when the Americans returned, this time for good, and were able to evacuate the rest of the hospital.

Terence Prittie and the other escapees from Oflag IX A/H at Wanfried were still some time away from liberation. They had spent the day under a patch of beech trees listening to the sound of artillery getting closer. They were able see Eschwege and the nearby village of Frieda being shelled and burning. The day was spent under cover and waiting for the Americans, but the rain that started at around 1900hrs, just as it was getting dark gradually became heavier. They passed a miserable night.

Despite the rumour that Oflag IX A/H at Lengenfeld was surrounded and the belief amongst the prisoners that their travelling days were over, the Germans did expect Oflag IX A/H to move again. That evening of 2 April Colonel Holland was given details of the new German plan. The camp was to walk to a railhead at Ebeleben, 30 miles to the north-east. The news did not reach the rest of the prisoners until the following day. In the meantime Major Fleischman, Hauptmann Seybold and Holland spent the rest of the evening arguing over the move. Oflag IX A/H and Lengenfeld were not yet surrounded. Both 6th Armored and 4th Armored were being delayed by German resistance at the River Werra. Colonel Holland eventually went beyond delaying tactics and refused to move at all. Major Fleischman's orders were that the camp would march the next day. On that Monday evening Holland handed Hauptmann Seybold a memorandum:

1. There is no object in sending us further. We should remain in some village off the main route.

2. All officers are physically and nervously exhausted. They are unfit to march, unfit to move by M.T. or rail in the existing conditions of air danger, congested traffic, etc.

3. I am not prepared to move by M.T. by day or by rail at any time without previous reference to the Protecting Power, as such action is against the Geneva Convention.

4. I have been left without orders of any sort all day. Officers cannot rest properly under these conditions. I must ask for orders to be received in time for me to discuss them with Major Fleischmann regarding the details of their execution.

5. To sum up, I consider that justice and humanity should dictate that we remain at Lengenfeld till the end.

The next morning as Colonel Holland waited for the Germans' response to his memorandum, the Rotenburg men set off from Lengefeld at around 10.00. Harry Roberts describes the morning as 'not so bad', presumably a reference to the rain having stopped. For some men from Oflag IX A/Z the walking had become too much. The Germans agreed to leave those unable to walk behind in the village of Lengefeld. One of George Forster's fellow padres, Father Desnoyer who had already endured a long march from the east, was one of the abandoned men. Lieutenant Desmond Llewelyn, Royal Welch Fusiliers, was another. He later claimed he used his acting ability to join the party of sick. They were told that the Germans would collect them by lorry later that day. Around 30 men were left at Lengefeld on Wednesday morning, 3 April. They and their small guard left the inconvenient barns and moved into the village.

The rest of Oflag IX A/Z set off across the open fields. There was a short, severe climb at the village of Dachreiden where the railway line from Mühlhausen to the north-west runs parallel with the slope. The trudge through the fields was ameliorated by the rumours gathered from people along the route and the sight of demoralised German Army units that indicated liberation was once more very close at hand.

Behind them at Lengenfeld unterm Stein, Major Fleischmann again ordered Colonel Holland and Oflag IX A/H to move. Overnight the Germans have made a concession. Once at Ebeleben, they would rest for two or three days before being moved by train to a permanent camp. This was not enough for Colonel Holland. He repeated his objections to Major Fleischmann. Holland describes how the simple instruction from Fleischman grows into a conference with both the junior SBOs, the British Medical Officer from Lower Camp, Major W.L. Kinnear, Hauptmanns Seybold and Hoffmann, and Oberstabsarzt Stenger, the German Medical Officer. During the discussion Holland asks to communicate directly with representatives of the Protecting Power. Major Fleischmann decides that Holland should take his objections in person to Oberst Schrader. So at midday on 3 April, with the Americans a few miles away on the west bank of the Werra, Holland, Fleischmann, Hauptmann Roth, the Lageroffizier, and Oberstabsarzt Stenger leave by car for Ebeleben. Given the American air activity whilst 6th Armored searched for a place to cross the Werra between Eschwege and Wanfried this was a risky excursion, but they arrive safely.

As Holland argued for time 36 men from Upper Camp did set off, under protest, on a farm cart pulled by a tractor to Lengefeld, 15 miles to the east. They were supposed to be an advance party with the rest of Oflag IX A/H following during the day.

It takes Colonel Holland almost two and a half hours to travel to Ebeleben. Once there a second conference ensues. Holland asks what difference it makes to the German Government if a few prisoners were lost. Schrader suggests that that is a question Holland should put to the German Government, but that he knows of nothing in the Geneva Convention that requires him to release his prisoners before the end of a war. Oberst Schrader agrees that Oflag IX A/H is too weak to walk to Ebeleben. He modifies his orders. The camp will be moved by motor transport directly from Lengenfeld to Ebeleben. Their new billets will be in the town school for the weaker men and a barn for the remainder. After they had rested for two or three days they would move to a permanent camp, perhaps by rail. Holland objects to the idea of being moved by rail. Schrader responds that in that case he will have to apply German military law and order their compliance. Aware that they are getting onto dangerous ground, Holland responds that he has not refused to obey, just stated the implications of the situation with sick and weak prisoners. Eventually, both men agree that they wish to preserve the lives and health of the prisoners. But although they share a common objective, they differ on how to achieve it. Out of the meeting comes a revised plan. The 40 weakest men at Lengenfeld will be moved by motor vehicle just after midnight on Wednesday 4 April. Other transport would arrive later for the remainder of the prisoners.

Holland's return to Lengenfeld had to be by a northerly route to avoid the American tanks that had now crossed the Werra. Prittie, Shand and the rest of the Wanfried escapees, though they did not know it, had witnessed part of 6th Armored's crossing of the Werra.

The previous night the escapees had become very cold and wet. Finally in the early dawn they decided they must find better shelter. They moved into a fir plantation, closer to the barn that had been their old billet. Here they were able to build small shelters from the branches, and their spirits rose a little, especially as the downpour gave way to drizzle, before clearing up completely. From their new hideout they could see across the Werra to the road along the west bank. As the morning wore on they discovered that they had neighbours: on one side German refugees, elderly people and children and at the front of the plantation the two other pairs of Spangenberg escapees. All day they could hear shellfire around Eschwege and Frieda as 6th Armored closed on the Werra.

In late afternoon American tanks arrive on road on the west bank of the river, opposite the escapees. The tanks come under artillery fire and halt. Prittie is puzzled by what he sees next. At around 1600hrs, the American tanks 'roared on past Wanfried bridge, through the western outskirts of the village and out of sight beyond.' What Prittie has witnessed is the effect on 6th Armored of the galvanising news that an intact bridge had been found upstream of Wanfried, at Großburschla, four miles south of Wanfried.

The Division's original plan had been to cross the Werra at several points before advancing on Mühlhausen. Now the whole division would cross at Großburschla. By Tuesday night parts of the Division would laager at Heyrode, east of Diedorf. Bruce Jeffrey's record of Arbeitskommando 1249's evacuation contains some confused overnight stops around this period. In it he records spending the evening of 2 April at Heyrode and walking to Kleinwelsbach, past Mühlhausen on the 3rd. They must have missed 6th Armored by a hair's breadth. However he also has them overnight at Reichensachsen on 1 April and then passing through Spangenberg on the 2nd, so his dates may be wrong.

By 1830hrs on Tuesday evening, Holland is back at Lengenfeld unterm Stein. The news of the impending move leaks out to some of the prisoners. Their safe haven is not as secure as they thought. Bill Edwards, using information from a friendly villager, plans to slip away and lie up in a nearby field barn until the Americans arrive. But the return of Major Fleischmann from Ebeleben has, as at Wanfried, led to a tightening of the guard. The previous day Edwards could wander at will in and around the village, now he is turned back by the guards when he tries to leave the village and check that the barns west of the town are a practical proposition. Claiming that he is visiting a fellow prisoner in the hospital he eventually manages to get out of the village and reaches the barn. It appears ideal for his purpose. On his way back he runs into a group of German infantrymen who ask for directions to Mühlhausen. His claim to be a British POW working on a farm is accepted by the dog-tired soldiers. That night Edwards, Lieutenant-Colonel Gamble, Sherwood Foresters, and Lieutenant Alan Leake, Royal Sussex Regiment, bribe a sentry with 50 cigarettes, a bar of chocolate, a bar of soap and half-pound packet of coffee, and leave the camp. Despite being followed out of the village by a gang of children whispering loudly that they are British officers, they reach the barns safely, make themselves comfortable and sleep. Whilst Edwards' party set off for their hideout, the rest of Oflag IX A/H turned in for the night expecting lorries to arrive after midnight. John Sewell's diary for 3 April does not refer to moving, so there were at least some men who did not get the bad news. Sewell does mention the sound of gun and small arms fire. He thought that the Americans were about 4 miles from them.

Fortunately for Oflag IX A/H, Oberst Schrader's plans go awry. No lorries appear either that night or on Wednesday morning. Already the children of the local haulier had immobilised the only lorries in the village by hiding key engine parts; Montgomery remembers the 'culprits' as being school girls. Finally, the travelling days of Oflag IX A/H are over. The speed of the American advance had overtaken German logistics. That the Germans could have considered moving the camps to Ebeleben the day before the Americans captured Mühlhausen is surely a reflection on the poor intelligence that Schrader was receiving. German knowledge of American movements was often confused and out of date. The German military bulletin for 2 April admitted to pressure on the Werra, but claimed that the defenders of Kassel had inflicted heavy losses on American tanks. The bulletin for 3 April admits that the Americans had fought their way into Kassel, but still has the defence of the Werra holding firm. It is also interesting to compare Oberst Schrader, struggling to continue to do his duty amidst the chaos, with Hauptmann Seybold, who evidently can see no point in continuing to move the unwilling column. To the west of Lengenfeld unterm Stein, the war had temporarily passed Prittie and his fellow escapees by. They would spend another night in their shelters under the trees, whilst German deserters and other refugees passed them by.

The Rotenburg men were no less fed up with their ordeal, but they continued to trudge north-eastwards. With the guards' morale higher than that of Oflag IX A/H, escaping was not easy. However around midday just before they reached Dachrieden, Ernest Edlmann and his partner Frederick Corfield got their chance. Both men were not fit. Ernest had strained a muscle in his left leg and was finding walking difficult: Frederick was suffering from very bad diarrhoea. At one of the regular 10-minute rests they tried to hide in a culvert under the road. The first attempt ended in farce and near disaster: the culvert was too small and Frederick got stuck. He had to be pulled out, but none of the guards noticed. Ernest then found them a larger culvert. Prisoners stood around them to screen them from the guards whilst others provided diversions. The escapees scrambled in; their kit was pushed in after them; and soon they heard the column moving off over their heads. The culvert was just tall enough for them to squat in the water. Ernest Edlmann: 'Freddy is frequently ill, and I help with his "toilet". He keeps saying he is certain we will succeed. I have the responsibility, and am not so certain.'

They suffered the drain and Corfield's diarrhoea for eight hours. When it was dark they emerged to find it raining again. They were stiff and tired. There was the welcome noise of gun fire and aircraft, indicators of approaching Allied troops. They crossed two ploughed fields and arrived at the village of Dachrieden. Ernest, who spoke German, intended to explain that they were two lost French workers looking for a bed for the night. But, before he got a chance to talk to anyone, one of Oflag IX A/Z's horse and carts with rations for the Rotenburg column stopped and asked the way. In his best 'colloquial German' Ernest told the driver to keep straight on. Edlmann was fortunate. Heinrich Sultan was directing the wagons that carried stores and equipment, acting as he wrote later as the 'Führer'. Had he been with the wagon, Edlmann and Corfield would have been recognised.

Ernest's first attempts to get them lodgings failed. One elderly couple he approached suggested that they should go to the police and ask for a bed. This was not an attractive option. Eventually, close to midnight, Edlmann got a response from a house and they were invited in. Once inside Edlmann abandoned his French farm worker story and admitted to their being British officers. He told a story '… of "dangerous" Americans being here soon, and we would guarantee his wife was not raped etc!' They were provided with food and dry their clothes. Sleeping in the sitting room is described as 'Paradise'.

Ahead of them the rest of the column had climbed the hill out of Dachrieden and walked alongside the now silent railway line for a short distance, before heading across the fields to Windeberg. At Windeberg they find that the Americans are also expected to arrive at any moment. A German field bakery unloaded its newly-baked bread on the villagers and prisoners and left hurriedly. Eating fresh German bread for the first time was a pleasant surprise for the men after the heavy, stale version they were normally issued with. There were wounded German soldiers in the village, who tell the POWs that Mühlhausen is expected to be captured the next day. Kenneth White noted on the back of one of his Lee Hill Windeberg pictures that the SS were burning documents and expecting the imminent arrival of the Americans. None of the other men mention the SS but there were certainly members of the Wehrmacht in the village. Lee Hill photographed what appears to be a good humoured exchange between a wounded German soldier with a splint on his broken arm and smiling prisoners. White thought Windeberg had a good black market, 'even ¼ lb of butter! No beer'. The lack of beer is significant. There was a gasthöf opposite their

Oflag IX A/Z walk down the main street of Dachrieden on 3 April. John McIndoe is in the left foreground, with his art materials and sketch book in the converted Red Cross box hanging around his neck. Behind the men the tower of St Nicholas Lutheran church is visible. (Green Collection)

The column is walking alongside the branch railway line from Mühlhausen through Dachrieden to the Kanonenbahn, on their way to Windeberg. By this date there were no trains running on the line, so the men were relatively safe from air attacks on the railway. (Green Collection)

The column is almost at its billet at Windeberg, 3 April. In the foreground a German officer pushes his bicycle. The German standing orders for marches recommended that the guard had cycles to be used by messengers if the telephone system was damaged. (Green Collection)

billet, but evidently it had run dry by early April. For Harry Roberts, Windeberg was the best billet so far His evening meal was an own cooked bread pudding with cocoa and apricots, and three lots of soup.

As the Rotenburg column trudged to Windeberg the RAF mounted the first of two massive daylight raids on Nordhausen. It was believed that the city was a significant military complex, which might also house officials and ministries evacuated from Berlin. It would also lie in the path of US 1st Army when they advanced eastwards. By the time of the second raid on the following day, most of Nordhausen had been destroyed and its inhabitants dispersed into the surrounding countryside. Nearly 9000 people died in the air raids. Amongst the victims were slave labourers at the Mittelwerk, the underground factories producing V2 rockets and jet aircraft engines, whose camps and barracks were located in and around Nordhausen. Although Oflag IX A/Z was only 25 miles from Nordhausen there is just one reference to the raids. 'Butch' Laing mentions a siren alarm that

Men from Oflag IX A/Z joking with a wounded German soldier on the main street of Windeberg. Behind and to the left of the main group a German woman and a prisoner appear unhappy to be caught in Lee Hill's picture. (Green Collection)

he believes to be for an air raid, but he is told by a senior officer that it is a Panzer alarm. Since the Americans were still some way behind them, it was more likely to have been an air raid. The raids would have considerable impact on the Rotenburg column in the coming days. The villages near the town and through which the column would march were now full of homeless refugees, taking up the available billets and potentially enraged the death and destruction wrought by the RAF. It was not the best preamble for the arrival of British POWs.

Tuesday night, 3 April, saw all the POWs once again hoping for liberation the next day. The men were now spread out over 15 miles: in woods to the west of Wanfried; around and in Lengenfeld unterm Stein; sheltering in Dachrieden; in the barn at Windeberg; and the small mixed group from both camps at Lengefeld.

5

FREEDOM FOR SOME

Major Fleishman arrived about 5.15 and said 'gentlemen you are free,' adding, 'this is the blackest day of my life.'

Captain John Sewell, Royal Engineers, Oflag IX A/H, captured in Greece in 1941.

Oflag IX A/Z had turned in earlier than usual on Tuesday night at Windeberg. Harry Roberts noted that the unusually early time, 2030hrs, was due to new parole regulations. He had recorded the next change in the German plans. Brix needed to keep a tight rein on his charges with the Americans near and an early start needed the following day. When it left, the column headed north. It was no longer heading towards Ebeleben. The early departure combined with the route change would prove crucial to the column's chances of liberation by the Americans.

During Tuesday the German plans began to unravel. In Bill Edwards' account written after the war, he says the guard at Lengefeld, where the small group of prisoners from both camps were staying, was withdrawn during the night of 3 April; the order coming via a telephone call from their headquarters.

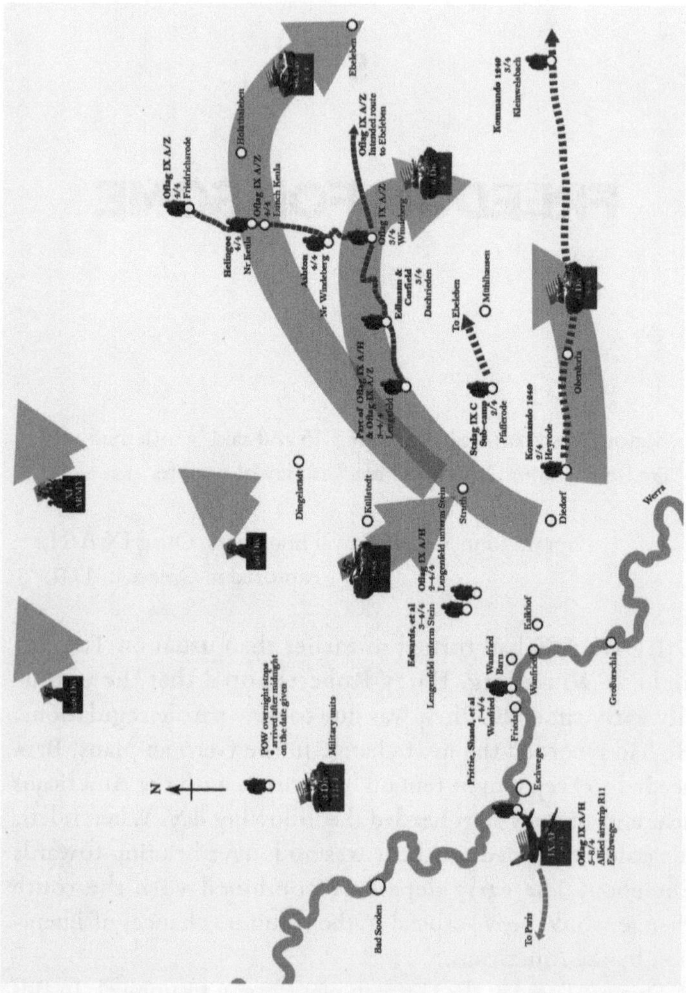

The location of men when liberated on 4 April. (Peter Green)

Their prisoners were still expecting transport to arrive to take them onto the rest of the column but it failed to arrive and the party was left marooned. The rest of Oflag IX A/H also failed to arrive at Lengefeld. The lorries promised to Colonel Holland at Lengenfeld unterm Stein had not arrived. The failure of the transport to appear was not surprising. The Americans were extremely close. Part of 6th Armored spent that night only four miles south of them.

Probably at the same time as Colonel Holland was returning from his conference with Oberst Schrader, Ebeleben was ceasing to be either column's objective. None of the Rotenburg men knew of German intentions, but their diaries and accounts are increasingly concerned about the apparently pointless rambling route. Edward Baxter wrote: 'We seemed to be doomed to walk about Germany till Germany collapsed.'

Despite the change of plan, two men did leave Oflag IX A/H to continue eastwards. Colonel Holland's account simply states that 'Hauptmann Hoffmann and Corporal Whiteley RASC (who was used by the Germans as a driver) started for Lengefeld and did not return.' Presumably this was in a vehicle of some sort. From Lengefeld, Hoffmann travels onto Brix and Oflag IX A/Z. None of the prisoners at Lengefeld refer to a visit by Hoffmann so he either must have missed them after they had moved into the village itself or he had gone straight on to catch up with the main column at Windeberg.

Holland does not explain the purpose of Hoffmann's journey. The most plausible reason was that Hofmann was a messenger, carrying the news for Brix that Oflag IX A/H was not moving and was likely to be liberated – and that Brix would soon be on his own. If Corporal Whiteley did eventually arrive with the Rotenburg column, he did not pass on the news about the likely imminent fate of Oflag IX A/H. Five days later, Lee Hill's diary includes, 'Heard today that the Spangenberg crowd are still on the road. Too bad.'

For many of the prisoners Wednesday 4 April would be their best day so far. Even Terence Prittie, Bruce Shand and the other prisoners west of Wanfried had spent a drier and quieter night in their copse near the river. The rain had slowed to a drizzle and they had not been disturbed by aircraft or gunfire. The fires at Eschwege and Frieda too had died down. The men wait in what Prittie describes as a strange stillness.

Five miles from the Wanfried escapees, outside Lengenfeld, things are noisier. Bill Edwards wakes to the noise of gunfire and aircraft. The barn had provided a comfortable night, but in the daylight he and his comrades find that the roof of the barn has a hole that makes them visible from the tall railway embankment across the valley. Fortunately, a party of German troops who appear on the railway are more concerned with the distant horizon than 50 yards in front of them and they are not discovered. Periodic bursts of small arms and shellfire confine them to their hideout into the afternoon.

In Lengenfeld village itself the atmosphere was subdued, but expectant. John Sewell recorded a few German soldiers hanging about, apparently ready to give themselves up. Two prisoners with German escorts set off at 0800 down the valley to the west to try and contact the Americans, but after a couple of miles they ran into German positions and returned. Hauptmann Seybold informed Colonel Holland they could no longer move because there was nowhere for them to go. Ralph Wilbraham also felt that the end was close: 'Four German parachutists appear and indicate that they want to give themselves up. We explained that as prisoners we are not interested in them, but they insist on dumping their weapons and make their way to the guardroom where they remain.'

At 1000hrs several aircraft, including the light reconnaissance aircraft used by the Americans, fly low over the village. The men have painted 'POW' in white paint on the roof of their billet and by digging and placing stones have spelled out the same message on the ground. The Germans want to surrender, but the only Allied troops they can surrender to are the prisoners. With nothing else for him to do, John Sewell walks round the village with a group of other prisoners trading soap and cigarettes. At one house a woman gives them schnapps, coffee and cake. Her husband is a prisoner of war in England. At another house they get a friendly reception from a woman whose husband had been killed by partisans at Turin. Sewell adds, 'It is all very sad,' even though she still had strong Nazi sympathies. Around mid-afternoon the mood in the village becomes more expectant. The men see the German rearguard withdrawing along the railway viaduct above the village. There is a short-lived moment of tension, when German troops try to force their way into the men's billet, which now has white flags hanging from it. The prisoners fear that they want to establish a defensive position, but in fact they want to surrender to the POWs. Two SS men arrive and do manage to surrender to the prisoners.

At around 1400hrs, Leutnant Glimm invites any members of the guard who wish to escape capture to leave with him. Fifteen leave. Holland's diary refers to Glimm as 'Political Officer'; the quotation marks are Holland's. This prompts the indefatigable Colonel Holland to complain to Hauptmann Seybold that withdrawing the guard is unacceptable. It was their duty to stay with the prisoners to the end and protect them from rogue German elements.

An hour later Lieutenant-Colonel Swinburne manages to speak by telephone to some surprised American troops from 65th Infantry Division in the next village. 'How do we know that this is genuine?' is the initial response. Eventually, Swinburne convinces them that there are almost 400 British prisoners in the village and that their guard wants to surrender. The waiting continues. Many have an evening meal of stew. Eventually the much anticipated moment arrives. There are American infantry in the valley! Hauptmann Seybold surrenders to Lieutenant-Colonel Miller. Colonel Holland's note of the event is written with the historical record in mind.

> At about 1600 hours I was standing outside the post office when a British officer reported that the Americans had been

> contacted at the south end of the village. I hurried up the road and met two American 2nd Lieutenants, Mark H. Schwarz and John D. Frawley of 2nd Bn. 261st Infantry Regiment of the 65th Division of the U.S. Army. These officers had come forward alone from Hildebrandshausen. Major Fleischmann with his officers and men, who (with the exception of Leutnant Glimm's small party) had conscientiously stayed with us to the end, surrendered to the American officers.

The happy coincidence of being liberated at 4pm on the 4th of the 4th was a happy mnemonic for Robert Montgomery over 60 years later.

Sewell's diary record for 1630hrs begins with the inevitable reference to food, 'another good "Andy" stew with some bread and honey (small quantity). Then at 4.42 came the great moment of the announcement "American infantry in the Valley". Hpt Seybold has handed himself over to our SBO and is now in our kitchen partaking of our stew. IT IS RELEASE DAY INDEED.'

Ralph Wilbraham had spent the early afternoon having a long hot bath, a luxury that he could only have dreamt of even a few days before. He learned of their liberation when two young people ran to the school and excitedly told them that the Americans had entered the village. The municipal diary for Lengenfeld unterm Stein – the *Ortschronik* – recorded the event:

> On 4 April, at 12.30, three of the British POWs with a white flag went to Plesse southwest of Hildebrandshausen, where there was a battle between a small German unit and a US unit. They contacted the US forces there. Around 1630hrs the three POWs returned with a small group of American infantry from Hildebrandshausen, through Heide and then down Bahnhof Straße into Lengenfeld. Five minutes later the Burgomaster

having surrendered the village, the German guards peacefully changed their role – they now became POWs.

Oflag IX A/H's liberators, the 261st Infantry Regiment from the 65th Infantry Division, were on temporary attachment to 6th Armored as it swept around the north of Mühlhausen.

Major Fleischman, was overheard saying 'This is the blackest day of my life.' The former POWs disarmed their guards, who were marched away to captivity, initially in a factory in the village. The guards were delighted that their war was over. Before they left for captivity they shook hands with their former

The negative of this Charles Sumners picture has been lost. He may have taken this picture on 5 April, the day after Oflag IX A/H was liberated, as it shows armour, in this case a Sherman with howitzer from the 15th Tank Battalion, driving through the village of Lengefeld. The caption also refers to liberating 120 POWs, far less than were at Lengefeld, but only twice the number of men from both camps liberated at Lengefeld, where there are references to US tanks. This may therefore be Lengefeld on 4 April. (Sumners Collection)

As with the previous image the negative has been lost. The caption in the history of XX Corps simply refers to this and the following picture as British POWs. It fits the description of Oflag IX A/H's liberation and is in the section covering the capture of Mühlhausen. It is also next to an image that also appears in American newsreels of the period that are very suggestive of Oflag IX A/H. It is probably of men from Spangenberg. (Sumners Collection)

Desmond Llewelyn's nickname in the camp was 'Ham'. He had been a professional actor before the war and appeared in *Campbell of Kilmhor* on BBC TV in January 1939. (Green Collection)

prisoners, almost as if it was the end of a football match. And at least one prisoner, Hugh Wilbraham gave them a present of soap. Sewell could at last believe that he was really free after 'three years, 11 months, one week of captivity'.

Bill Edwards and his party in the barn outside the village learned that they were free from one of their comrades who came to the barn shouting the good news. Oflag IX A/H may have been liberated, but with German troops still active around them the prisoners were in a dangerous position. The Americans provided a platoon of infantry and anti-tanks guns to protect them, whilst the Burgomaster provided billets for the men, most of whom slept in beds for the first time in many years.

Charles Sumners, spent early April with the 65th Infantry and 6th Armored. As well as the bridge at Malsfeld he took pictures in Waldkappel and then later of the prisoners in Lengenfeld unterm Stein after liberation. Unfortunately, most of these later negatives vanished after the war, but they feature in the official history of US XX Corps. In a posed picture cheering POWs sit on a US jeep with smiling GIs. In another, the men form a line to pass confiscated fire arms onto a heap for disposal. This picture is duplicated in a news reel of the event. Sumners' colleague in the 166th Signal Company and friend in the army was Russ Meyer, a film maker who may have shot the Lengenfeld news reel. Meyer became well-known after the war for his sexploitation films, such as *Faster, Pussycat! Kill! Kill!*

Over the hill from Lengenfeld, the Wanfried escapees had been liberated earlier that morning. Around 1000hrs as they sat under the trees, a file of armed men had come into view. Obviously they were soldiers, but whose. Once the sun broke through the clouds 'a shaft of light struck down on the little party. They wore khaki uniforms.' It suddenly dawned on the prisoners that troops walking past them are American. After a brief and somewhat crazy celebration, with hugs and shouts, during which time the Americans disappeared down the road, the prisoners grabbed their packs and rushed after them.

An American newsreel from this period, possibly shot by Russ Meyer, has extra images that show a large number of British and Commonwealth officers collecting German weapons for disposal, and as the only other large group of Allied officer POWs in the area was Oflag IX A/Z, this suggests it is Oflag IX A/H at Lengenfeld unterm Stein. (Sumners Collection)

Coming across the troops stationary by the road, one American shook Prittie's hand, but another, the Corporal, mistook them for Germans and ordered them, 'Kommen Sie mit, Kraut!' The Americans were, like those who liberated the main body of Oflag IX A/H, part of US 65th Infantry Division.

The next to be freed are those from both camps at Lengefeld. Once the main column had left, the Rotenburg men had moved from their barns to a farm house in the middle of the village. They were then joined by the party from Lengenfeld. They spent the rest of that day and much of the next morning expecting to see the rest of Oflag IX A/H arrive. Overnight their guards depart. The abandoned prisoners prepare for a siege in case hostile German troops arrive. Like the prisoners, the villagers are uncertain what to expect. During the morning odd groups of German troops, remnants of the 26th Volksgrenadier Division, pass through the village as they withdraw to the north-east. Around midday there is a sudden burst of machine-gun fire, followed by the rumble of tanks in the village. Desmond Llewelyn is puzzled by the Allied white star symbols on the tanks, '… surely they can't be Russian?' he thinks, associating any colour star with the Soviets. The prisoners emerge to find that 6th Armored has taken possession of the village. One American asks Llewelyn how long they have been prisoners. 'Five years,' they answer. 'Don't be stupid the war has not been on that long!' is the incredulous response. Their liberators are Task Force 15 of Combat Command B, 6th Armored Division. Although they press the Americans to follow the rest of Oflag IX A/Z eastwards, the task force has a route and a schedule that will take them to Dachrieden but no farther north. Their objective is to cut the main road north of Mühlhausen and then swing round to the south and isolate the town.

Meanwhile at Dachrieden, Ernest Edlmann and Freddy Corfield had moved out of Herr Langhammer's house into the loft of a barn behind the house. They had been give ersatz coffee at 0700hrs. The two men feel 'like Kings'. All they have to be concerned about is that the village might become a battlefield. They wash their kit and sort out their rations. Herr Langhammer promises to provide a bowl of soup a day and coffee for them. There is no bread, but on the whole they are sure that they can last a week if necessary. Overall they are content with their lot. Freedom cannot be far away. At 1000hrs Herr Langhammer tells them that American tanks have been reported 5 miles away, but that they have been destroyed. The message must have come via telephone somewhere in the village and was probably describing the action at Lengefeld, where the tanks had certainly not been destroyed. At lunchtime Dachrieden does indeed become a battlefield. Women and children leave the village for the relative safety of the north side of the railway embankment. It is the same embankment that Oflag IX A/Z followed the previous afternoon.

Trapped in their loft Edlmann and Corfield have only a limited view of the proceedings. When the house next door starts to burn they have a dilemma: stay put and risk burning to death or go out and possibly face German troops. Whilst they ponder their next move there is the unmistakable noise of tank tracks and the front door is kicked in. Herr Langhammer appears with two American soldiers, with Tommy guns. Ernest slides down from the loft to meet them, but is ordered to raise his hands:

> I invoke the Gods to prevent these well-trained troops from pulling the trigger. An American officer appears, questions us, believes us, and we are free. I want to kill someone, kiss someone, do something, but all we can do is shake hands with every American we see. They seem appalled to hear we had been inside for five years, but proud to have released us.

Half of Dachrieden is on fire. The road is blocked with American armour and vehicles, a temporary traffic jam caused by the fear that a German 88 mm gun is nearby. Their liberators are part of 603 Tank Destroyer Regiment commanded by Major Parks. His orders are to move directly eastwards, which prevents him following Ernest's directions to catch up with rest of Oflag IX A/Z to the north-east.

Once the Americans have moved on, Edlmann and Corfield help the inhabitants fight fires and round up escaped livestock. Leaving Dachrieden is not simple. All the American traffic is eastwards. They have been told that the US 65th Infantry Division is following the armour. It is not until the evening that they can get a lift on a lorry going west. Whilst they wait, Edlmann takes control of the village and issues orders to the Burgomaster, who behaves like an obsequious family retainer. Edlmann orders him to have the villagers take all their weapons to the police station. He recalled that 'within an hour an enormous pile of rifle, shot guns, knives, pistols, swords, and ammunition are ready for my inspection.' At the police station the four policemen formally surrender their pistols. A few hours earlier the two escapees

Windeberg main street, the same location as that used by Lee Hill to photograph Celander, by the YMCA lorry looking south towards Windeberg church. Today the scene is completely unchanged. Given the column's early start on 4 April, this picture was probably drawn on 3 April. (Otago Settlers' Museum, New Zealand)

Loading Gunnar Celander's Opel car and trailer in the farm yard at Windeberg on the morning of Wednesday 4 April, as the men prepare for the day's walk. (Green Collection)

The yard at Windeberg on 4 April, with its smelly heap of used bedding from the cattle byres. Although their diaries contain references to the smell from a similar pile in the yard at Nohra, there is no mention of it at Windeberg. (Green Collection)

had been hiding from the same men. Finally the Burgomaster's wife appears and timidly offers them a string of sausages, as a peace offering.

Eventually at 1800hrs a westward-bound American lorry arrives. It takes them first to Lengefeld and then at 2100hrs back over the Werra and on to Pfieffe, 3 miles east of Spangenberg on the Waldkapel road. They would spend the night on the floor of a signals office of 6th Armored's 'Divisional Trains' – its main supply depot. In three hours they had retraced what it had taken them almost a week to cover on foot.

The only men now under German control were those with the main body of Oflag IX A/Z. The Rotenburg column left Windeberg at 0900hrs. None of the men mention the return of the small group of guards from Lengefeld, possibly only half a dozen of them, or the arrival of Hauptmann Hoffmann. However Hoffmann is mentioned several times in Lee Hill's diary from 11 April onwards.

Instead of continuing east towards Ebeleben, as they leave Windeberg the column turns north towards Nordhausen. Brix would not have known it but he was now in a race with the 86th Cavalry, the northernmost unit of 6th Armored, who were screening the Division's northern flank. The cavalry's orders were to travel no further north than Keula and then to swing eastwards. Keula was 4.5 miles on from Windeberg. That morning as they set out Oflag IX A/Z certainly began their journey closer to Keula than the Americans, but they were on foot.

A mile or so into their journey Harold Ashton, Royal Engineers, got his chance to escape. He had tried to escape twice since being captured in France in 1940. This would be his final and successful escape attempt. Ashton wrote the account of his wartime experiences many years after the event, which presumably explains why he places Windeberg south of Mühlhausen and gives the date for Oflag IX A/Z staying at Windeberg as 2 April. These mistakes apart, his description of the spot where he left the column and the rest of his travels that morning are very clear. The beech woods that helped his escape still run alongside the road just north of Windeberg.

The morning was cold. The Easter sun shine and the drizzle had been replaced by the threat of snow. Lee Hill's pictures show roads that were still wet and muddy from the previous night's rain. But it would stay dry for Ashton to get away. Kenneth White noted on the back of his copy of Lee Hill's picture of the same beech woods that Lieutenant J.E. Helingoe, Parachute Regiment, slipped away from the column here. Ashton and Helingoe did not meet after leaving the column. Ashton got his chance when he noticed that there was no guard nearby and on the spur of the moment he ran. From the cover of the trees Harold watched the column march away. He remembered how quiet it was once they had gone. It must also have been a strange and lonely experience after five years of cramped communal existence. He walked back towards Windeberg parallel

There are two patches of woodland that match this picture south and north of Keula. It was in woodland like this that Harold Ashton and Lieutenant John Helingoe, Parachute Regiment, slipped away from the column on the morning of 4 April. (Green Collection)

One of Dörr's carts. Dörr was a carrier from Rotenburg who provided carts with Russian POW drivers to carry the column's heavy goods – initially cooking and medical gear. Later they carried some of the weaker men and their personal kit. The picture was possibly taken near Friedrichsrode on 5 or 6 April. (Marion Gerritsen-Teunissen Collection)

with the road, staying in the trees. In the distance he could see Mühlhausen being shelled.

A few fields to the west of Windeberg Ashton took cover in a hollow in a field from shelling that suddenly seemed to be aimed at him directly. A few moments later a yellow caterpillar tractor towing a gun trundled across the field, evidently an agricultural tractor pressed into military service. Ashton explained to the German gun crew that he had escaped from a column of prisoners. He then set off with them. The tone of his account shows that these are new 'friends', not captors. The Germans took him to a disused quarry between Windeberg and Kaiserhagen, the next village to the west. Sheltering from the shellfire were women and children, and groups of German soldiers, Ashton was at that point only a mile and a half from Edlmann and Corfield at Dachrieden.

Offered the chance of staying with the Germans or taking his chances in reaching the American tanks, Ashton set off westwards, half expecting to be shot at, since the gun crew had rifles. After 100 yards he turned a corner and could breathe easily. He was still the wrong side of any front line and there was still a lot of German military activity. 'There were many Germans about, motorised and on foot. You could not help admiring their steady, orderly method of retreat.' Ashton's complimentary remark about the retreating Germans is unique in the prisoners' accounts. His account also includes a description of an elderly German civilian, stick in hand, taking his morning constitutional. The chaos of Germany could encompass almost anything. Ashton eventually encountered what he describes as a platoon of Sherman tanks. Given his location they could just as easily have been light tanks from 86th Cavalry. Just as the most dangerous moment for a prisoner of war was the instant of capture, he discovered that the instant of release could be almost as dangerous; he had to walk in front of a tank to get the attention of the Americans.

Whilst Harold Ashton was meeting the Americans, the rest of Oflag IX A/Z were four miles to the north at Keula, resting by the road. It was an open exposed place for a lunch stop. Whilst they ate their lunch it hailed. They had taken three hours to reach Keula, but it was just enough to prevent their release. As he ate, Harry Roberts could hear gunfire close by and see aircraft attacking Mühlhausen. After lunch the column continued north, eventually dropping down the escarpment through the woods to Friedrichsrode.

Marcus Edwards thought Friedrichsrode a 'cowed village'. As well it might be, with what passed for the front line only 5 miles away on the edge of the escarpment. It would provide little opportunity for 400 men to trade their soap and cigarettes for food. But it offered badly needed shelter, in the afternoon the rains had returned. The hail and sleet had been replaced by a downpour as they arrived at their billet. That night there was no centrally provided evening meal. Harry Roberts was able to get some potatoes and onions, which he ate fried. He and a colleague managed another bread and butter pudding with half an egg, followed by a hot drink, from their own stocks. Despite his catering success, Harry thought it an uncomfortable billet.

None of the men's accounts refer to being so close to freedom. Had they left Windeberg at 1100 they would have been overtaken by the Americans. Ken White wrote on the back of his Lee Hill picture of Windeberg, 'Our first near miss', which suggests that he at least knew that day that the Americans were very close. Lee Hill's surviving diary which restarts the next day refers to 'waiting for the Americans at Friedrichsrode'. One might have expected that such a close encounter with the Americans would have featured in more accounts. Perhaps it was not widely known that freedom had narrowly eluded them.

Oberstleutnant Brix was either now, or would very soon be, improvising each overnight billet at the same time as the column moved. Gunner Celander's report at the end of the war includes a reference to the part he played in finding billets and in fetching food and medical supplies. This would now become a major task.

Once Mühlhausen had been captured, 6th Armored halted and with the rest of 3rd Army paused for six days before moving eastwards. Third Army were waiting for 1st and 9th Armies to complete their encirclement of the Ruhr and then come into line to the north of 3rd Army. Oflag IX A/Z would remain beyond the reach of the Americans. The uneven advance of the Americans would give Brix some breathing space. But one of the final actions of 6th Armored as it closed the trap on Mühlhausen would be more problematic for Oberst Schrader. The 86th Cavalry, screening the Division's northern flank, having reached Keula on the road to Friedrichsrode now swung eastwards at the crossroads in the village along the edge of the escarpment. Towards the end of the following day, Thursday 5 April, they reached Ebeleben. Their change of direction had prevented the Rotenberg men being liberated but it had also ensured that Oberst Schrader had to shift his headquarters once again.

The 68 men from Rotenburg and Spangenberg who had gone to a Mühlhausen hospital by train on 29 March would have been liberated on 5 April, when the Americans captured Mühlhausen.

Having just been given their freedom some men did not wish to surrender to Allied military discipline. Reid and Bowlby had evacuated themselves and their women passengers from the front. Other prisoners would join their liberators and fight their way eastwards. Readjusting to army routines and then to civilian life would take some many years. The men from Spangenberg captured at around the same time and by the same unit experienced a more disciplined and military transition from 'kriegie' to 'Recovered Allied Military Personnel'. The evening of Wednesday 4 April was spent under the protection of the 261st Infantry. Next morning Upper Camp was transported in American lorries to an abandoned Luftwaffe airfield north-west of Eschwege. The bridges across the Werra were still not repaired and like the Americans a few days before they crossed the river at Großburschla. Lower Camp joined them in the afternoon. The recently captured airfield was being restored by American engineers and was not yet operational. Despite it being south of the Werra there were still concerns over its security. There was talk of a possible German counterattack and Oflag IX A/H were organised and armed to provide for their local defence. The rumours were correct. The German Eleventh Army, unable to break the siege of the Ruhr, was preparing to make an attempt to cut the American advance by striking south-eastwards from north of Lengenfeld unterm Stein towards Eisenach.

There was another threat, this time from the rear. Most of the German units isolated between the rivers Main and Fulda by the American advances from Remagen and Frankfurt had either surrendered or their men had abandoned their weapons and were trying to return to their homes. But on 4 April elements of the 6th SS Mountain Division tried to fight their way out of the pocket. Fourth Armored's main supply route to the east was cut. For 24 hours their field hospital, 90 miles behind its lead units, was in enemy hands. 6th Armored and 65th Infantry to the north were not affected.

For the time being though, Colonel Holland was able to compile a camp roll. He included in it 22 men who had escaped during the march, many of whom had already arrived at Eschwege. This included the Wanfried escapees. Major Shand and others were put to work to guard the airfield before the main column arrived. Shand for one was rather irked by the limitations this put on their activities. 'Certain senior officers began flexing their muscles.' Colonel Holland's diary confirms the return of military order. On 6 April he organises the camp in its defensive positions around the airfield. The new structure includes an Officer in charge of Administration, which Shand might not have been completely at ease with. Holland counted a total of all ranks of 368 brought back from Lengenfeld unterm Stein. And that all the escapees and the others, who had to leave the column on medical grounds, were accounted for once the main body was at Eschwege.

Oflag IX A/H eventually left Eschwege on Sunday 8 April in USAAF Dakotas that had just flown in supplies of fuel and ammunition for 6th Armored. The aircraft took two days to transport the whole camp to France, some men going to Paris, others to Le Havre. The Le Havre contingent spent the night at a large American transit camp 'Camp Lucky Strike'. Ironically for men captured whilst serving with 51st Highland Division, they were 3 miles from St Valerie where they had surrendered five years before. Desmond Llewelyn also left France via Lucky Strike, which suggests that the prisoners liberated at Lengefeld had joined them at Eschwege. Whilst in Paris they were required to complete their Liberation Questionnaires, a bureaucratic task which Shand for one found less beguiling than Paris herself. The Questionnaires were in fact only two and a half pages. They had 20 questions in all, from name, rank and unit to questions on collaboration, sabotage and escape attempts. Most men would have completed them in less than 15 minutes. Some, like Frederick Corfield, added extra pages to give more details of their time as a prisoner or their escape. Others gave the minimum.

After a night at Lucky Strike the men were flown back to the UK and RAF Westcott in Oxfordshire, again in USAAF Dakotas. At Westcott they were met by the RAF. Almost every account quite understandably mentions the amazing welcome and the presence of WAAFs. Women serving in the military, especially for the men captured early in the war was a surprising innovation. If there was a phone at their family home, there was the chance to surprise families with an unexpected call. Colonel Holland closes his account with a matter-of-fact description of the reunion, presumably with his wife: 'And so to Brockenhurst and M on the platform there.' In the period they had been at Eschwege, the men had helped the Americans by providing armed guards. After the war this service was deemed sufficient for men who had spent the few days at Eschwege to be awarded the France and Germany Star, a rare distinction for prisoners of war.

Oflag IX A/H had travelled home in an organised and military fashion. Ernest Edlmann and Frederick Corfield were less fortunate. They too passed under the protection of 65th Infantry Division, but they don't make it to Eschwege, instead they are carried farther west. On the morning of Thursday 5 April they are taken past Spangenberg with its now ruined Schloß. The party is at least nine strong. Edlmann refers to Lieutenant Norman Cox, Pioneer Corps and Captain Gerry Daly, Royal Engineers, both from Rotenburg. Later still his account refers to 'about' six others in their party, but he gives no names. It is a reminder that the columns leaked more escapees than are recorded in men's diaries.

For Norman Cox the site of the ruined castle on its hill at Spangenberg is too much and he breaks down in tears. The named men had presumable escaped before the column reached Windeberg. They reach another former Luftwaffe airfield at Fritzlar, but there are no planes available to take them to France. The next day and after another airfield, Gießen, which also has no transport, Edlmann, Corfield and Daly decide to abandon the USAAF and set off on their own. They get a lift on a mail lorry going to Bonn and though they arrive safely, their independent travel gets them into trouble. Very sensibly, they report to the Military Police, but with no identification papers the police take them to a military prison holding 800 Germans. Fortunately the prison staff are inclined to believe them and they spend the night in the guard room and not the cells. Their ordeal is not over. The next day, Saturday 7 April, they are taken to a huge German POW camp near Koblenz where they are interrogated. They are finally accepted as former British prisoners and allowed to leave in the early evening. There follows a journey at breakneck speed, 250 miles in seven hours, across Germany into Belgium in a US Army lorry. Just after midnight on Sunday they arrive at Namur and are met by US and British POW liaison staff. They spend the rest of that night in a proper hotel with hot baths, whisky and sodas, and clean uniforms. After almost six days of travelling, on

Monday 9 April they are driven to Brussels and they enter the formal British system for handling returning POWs. The three men get back to the UK on Tuesday 10 April on an RAF Dakota that lands at Ford in Sussex.

Harold Ashton's experience once safely in American hands was a more speedy version of Edlmann's. Also taken by lorry to Gießen, for Ashton there is a plane. It takes him to Frankfurt and then on to Paris. Still in his old prison camp uniform he has no tie to wear. He improvises one from the tail of his shirt and then goes down to dinner and the appalled looks from other officers in rather smarter uniforms. Ashton is flown home first to Amersham and then again by air to Croydon, where he completes the appropriate paper work and he too is free to go on leave.

Now only the 400 men of Oflag IX A/Z could still call themselves kriegies.

6

NORTH THEN SOUTH

Our journey never seems to end. Our destination unknown.

Lieutenant Marcus Bruce Edwards, 2/2 Field Regiment Australian Artillery, Oflag IX A/Z, captured in Crete in 1941.

Oflag IX A/Z at Friedrichsrode were four miles beyond the Americans. Against all the odds, Brix had somehow outpaced the American tanks. Had 6th Armored continued northwards they would have overtaken the column before it had finished breakfast. They were now beyond the current American high-water mark. After eight days walking and having covered 70 miles, some of the older prisoners were finding the going tough. Thirty men had been left at Lengefeld, an unspecified number at Windeberg and another six would be left at Friedrichsrode. The prisoners are obviously fed-up, their accounts make that very clear, but that seems to be more as a result of the poor weather and the apparently aimless walking, not the near-miss of liberation.

The Rotenburg men had suffered far less than those from Oflag IX A/H. Edward Baxter, who was over 50 and Harry

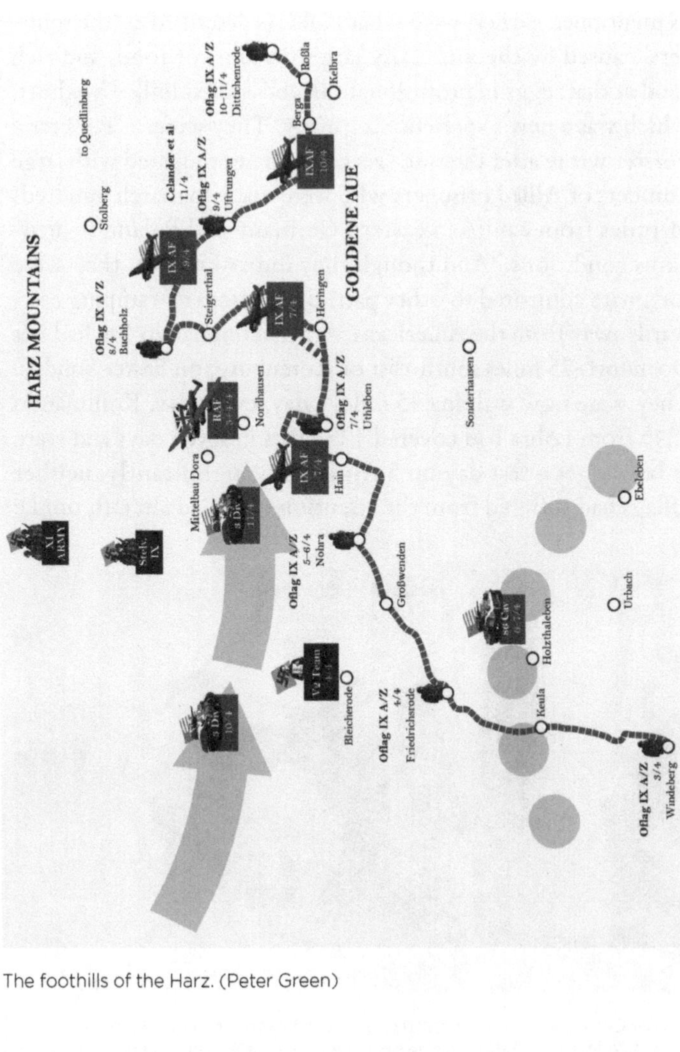

The foothills of the Harz. (Peter Green)

Roberts who was one of the youngest at 24, both refer to getting fitter through the exercise and the better food they were getting on farms The biggest medical problem most men faced, as mentioned earlier, were what Roberts described as 'the squitters' caused by the unusually large amounts of food, and rich food at that: eggs in profusion, milk and soured milk – yoghurt, which was a new experience for many. They were, as Reverend Forster wrote after the war, 'very fortunate compared with large numbers of Allied prisoners who were made to march hundreds of miles from camps in eastern Germany and Poland in atrocious conditions.' And though they didn't know it, they were fortunate compared to other parties of prisoners tramping eastwards away from the Americans. Arbeitskommando 106 had left Dorndorf, 25 miles south-east of Rotenburg, on Easter Sunday. They were now walking 15 miles a day, every day. Kommando 1249 from Lohra had covered 125 miles in seven days and were at last to get a rest day on 5 April. Most significantly, neither Oflags had suffered from the attention of Allied aircraft, unlike

Gunnar Celander (centre with briefcase) watches the trailer being hitched to the YMCA lorry in Friedrichsrode on the morning of 5 April. Today, only the addition of pavements and the heavy quarry lorries heading downhill has changed this scene. (Marion Gerritsen-Teunissen Collection)

Little has changed at Friedrichsrode, apart from the addition of pavements and a less muddy road surface. (Peter Green)

other columns of prisoners strafed by mistake by the RAF and USAAF.

Gunnar Celander and his Danish colleague Niels Jörgensen continued to provide an ambulance service to the column, carrying sick and tired men and their kit, as well as helping to find the overnight billets. On at least one day there was also a tractor and trailer provided by the Germans to carry those who could not walk. In his post-war report to the Swedish YMCA, Celander wrote that they also provided spiritual help to the men: 'Our YMCA-humour in a way as never before touched the prisoners of war and helped and encouraged them.'

The uneven American advance and the gaping hole in the German defences between the encircled Ruhr and the south meant that the prisoners were now walking into a military void.

Much of the remainder of the German Army that had been defending first the Fulda and then the Werra was still to the south-west of them. Other units were retiring north-eastwards towards the Harz Mountains.

Hitler had now declared them a fortress – 'Festung Harz' – to be defended at all costs. (This designation of 'fortresses' to be defended to the last drop of blood was one of the tiresome habits of the Führer – Festung Warschau, Festung Breslau, even Festung Europa.) By the end of the war there would be around 100,000 troops, Volkssturm and Hitler Youth concentrated in the Harz. It was an impressive number, far larger then the Allies imagined. But lacking equipment and organised in ad hoc units, it was not a formidable army. Eventually the shattered remnants of two army corps plus two ad hoc groups, one built around the headquarters staff of Wehrkreis IX, the other from Wehrkreis VI's staff, would retreat to the Harz. Nearest to Oflag IX A/Z was Stellvertreter IX with what was left of two Volksgrenadier Divisions, 26 and 326, and other units from the former headquarters at Kassel.

Oflag IX A/Z was also walking into a kind of moral vacuum. The southern Harz had seen a massive SS presence overseeing the supply of slave labourers to the Mittelwerk and the many other factories around Nordhausen that made V2s, jet engines and other aircraft parts. There were around 30 labour camps in the area. Even before the RAF bombed Nordhausen, the deteriorating military situation in the spring of 1945 had led the SS to begin evacuating the area. Himmler had wanted to seal the Dora tunnels and gas the workers, but there were too many tunnel entrances and too little gas. The early evacuations had been by packed trains; now later groups were trudging northwards on foot.

The slave labourers that survived the evacuations went to Bergen-Belsen or Sachsenhausen concentration camps. The SS intended that none of their prisoners would be released. Those who were too weak to travel were shot. In the worst of many hellish incidents, on Friday 13 April after a party at Gardelegen near Berlin given by local party members for the SS escort, 1016 prisoners were burnt alive in a barn. The final evacuations on foot to the north were taking place as Oflag IX A/Z reached the area. At the same time SS General Heinz Kammler, who had been in charge of the V2 and other special projects, was given responsibility for defending Nordhausen. Something he failed to do.

The managers and engineers of the V2 project had been based at Bleicherode, three miles north of Oflag IX A/Z's current billet at Friedrichsrode. On the same day that Oflag IX A/Z arrived, Wernher von Braun and his team left for Oberammergau in Bavaria. The main body of engineers travelled by the project's train and von Braun by car. Although the SS were no longer operating factories and labour camps in the southern Harz, there were still individual SS men and small groups in the area. Apart from one uncorroborated reference to SS burning documents at Windeberg, none of the prisoners had yet met the German organisation that above all others posed the greatest danger to them.

The bombing of Nordhausen had killed many labourers, but it had also freed others. They joined the growing population of French, Belgian and Russian POWs, some of them still working on farms, others just living rough, and refugees from the bombed cities surviving as best they could in the countryside. Lee Hill would see some of these refugees later in the march living in culverts under the road. The culverts provided them both with shelter from the weather and protection from the dreaded Allied fighter-bombers. Hugh Cartwright wrote of seeing 'workers in their striped pyjamas as we passed Nordhausen but [we] had no idea then of the horrors of that place.' Cartwright is unlikely to have seen concentration camp workers in their striped clothes unless they were under guard. Two slave labourers at Dora who escaped during the Nordhausen air raid published their experiences after the war. The men changed their clothing after their escape and spent their nights with groups of foreign farm workers, including French POWs. Marcus Edwards's diary entry for 6 April includes the surprising observation, 'Slave labour working in rocket factory among the hills.' The existence of the V2 factory was not widely known amongst the Allies and certainly not by POWs, so this comment must be derived from talking to villagers or forced labourers on farms.

The strong SS presence and a civilian population that had just suffered two devastating British air raids meant that Oflag IX A/Z was walking into peril. The men make some references to these twin dangers in the coming days, but by now they were seasoned travellers, confidently believing it their eventual liberation.

Lee Hill describes helping with the cart taking rations on to their next billet at Nohra. During that morning's journey there is an explosion behind him that Lee attributes to a road block being blown. If it was, the most obvious place for it would have been Keula. The Germans would not have blown one of their own obstructions on the road through Friedrichsrode. The explosion prompts his guard to try and surrender to the New Zealander, Kenneth White, whose POW diary for this period is almost entirely a list of dates and distances. He says that at Friedrichsrode the 'Town Crier warned all at 6 am.' This was a 'Panzer Alarm' a warning to the inhabitants that the Americans were close by. The distance from Keula to Friedrichsrode is 5 miles. In the article that Lee Hill wrote for *Illustrated* magazine he refers to the day when 'artillery fire rocked the German village in which we were halted. The Burgomaster gave the "panzer alarm" and I saw the whole population evacuating to the hills … A German guard promptly surrendered to me.' This could only be the Friedrichsrode incidents plus a large helping of dramatic licence. Harry Roberts made no comment on liberation. He was just pleased to leave Friedrichsrode, calling it 'this unreceptive dump'.

The column left at 1000hrs the next morning. Once on the road Roberts felt better. The scenery was becoming more pleasant, a mixture of woods and fields. The road north passed through beech woods for much of the early stage, it would have been ideal escape country, but none are recorded. 'Feeling very fit again today,' wrote Roberts. The weather was better and the column was able to stop for lunch and sit by the road close to the village of Großwenden and eat whatever they had bartered for or was left over from their own stocks. They had walked 4 miles. John McIndoe drew another Kiwi, Captain Bruce Mackenzie, NZEF and Lieutenant Peter Methuen, Queen's Royal Regiment, eating their lunch whilst a guard looks on.

The men's destination that night was Nohra. It was a state farm. These were farms, often very large, that had once belonged to the royal or noble families that had ruled Germany before its unification at the end of the 19th century. Oflag IX A/H's Lower Camp at Elbersdorf had originally been a state farm. Lee Hill with his sense for the dramatic identified their billet as stables belonging to 'the famous Baron Munchhausen'. It had certainly belonged to a Baron Munchausen, but whether Karl

Captain Bruce Mackenzie, New Zealand Expeditionary Force and Lieutenant Peter Methuen, Queen's Royal Regiment drawn at the lunch stop on 5 April near Großwenden between Friedrichsrode and Nohra. (Otago Settlers' Museum, New Zealand)

The landscape suggests that Lee took this picture on 5 April as the column walked to Nohra. Prams and other carts were a frequent feature of the evacuation of Oflag IX A/Z. This pram belonged to Lieutenant Sidney Turnbull, Duke of Wellington's Regiment. John McIndoe's drawing of the same pram has the caption 'Sid Turnbull's go-kart'. He pushed it 130km. Lee Hill's diary has 'One Duke of Well. Lt., who picked up pram about 10 days ago from the side of the road, today got a good, solid 2-wheeler & solid body made by a villager for 20 cigs, 2 tobacco, & 1 cake of soap.' So this pram was to be replaced in the next few days. (Green Collection)

Friedrich Hieronymus von Munchausen, a very real person from Thuringia, and known in Germany as the 'Lying Baron', was the creator of the extravagant fictional Baron Munchausen stories or its role model is uncertain. It fits Hill's character that he alone of all the diarists mentions Nohra's Munchhausen connection. Edward Baxter remarked that the Nohra barn was larger than many English parish churches.

It was also was a better billet than Friedrichsrode, although Marcus described it as wet. Roberts thought that Nohra a good place to trade. He managed to get five eggs, some flour and the ubiquitous potatoes. His first night's menu was: 'Sweetened porridge for supper followed by Section meal of spuds + meat paste.' In his billet there was an impromptu concert, given by a young Polish girl, of traditional nursery rhymes. There were other foreign workers on the farm. Lee Hill mentions French and Polish

The farm yard at Nohra where Oflag IX A/Z had a rest day on 6 April. McIndoe has had a problem with the perspective, but Gunnar Celander's car can be clearly seen parked alongside the barn. (Otago Settlers' Museum, New Zealand)

This steam-powered machine looks similar to one in a McIndoe drawing, however the barn itself is different. The sunshine suggests the picture was taken a midday and therefore the rest day at Nohra is the most likely candidate. (Green Collection)

forced labourers all ready to get their own back on their German masters. He wrote, 'Polish women showed me weals where she had been beaten. Some kids taken from home, when five – now ten years old…'

South of Oflag IX A/Z Mühlhausen had fallen to the Americans. And 40 miles further south, on 4 April, 4th Armored Division had solved the mystery of Ohrdruf. It was an empty communications centre. There was no sign of Hitler or any other Nazi leaders. The complex had been built in 1938 in preparation for war against Czechoslovakia but never used. Goebbels had planned to renovate it and present it to Hitler as a 55th birthday present on 20 April 1945, but the work had hardly started when the Americans arrived.

Close to it, the Americans did made a dramatic discovery. The remains of an SS-run labour camp that housed the slave labour for the renovation. The SS had marched as many inmates east as were able to walk, shot most of those that couldn't walk and then tried to burn their bodies. The horrors of Ohrdruf were only a prelude to the discovery of camps at Nordhausen a week later. But they were dramatic enough to bring the Supreme Allied Commander, General Eisenhower, and his army commanders, to view the horrors.

Oflag IX A/Z had been on the road for a week when they reached Nohra. The general opinion amongst the prisoners was that the Germans didn't know where to take them, but that they were being held hostage. If they were not hostages why hadn't they been left for the Americans? Edward Baxter laconically includes in his account for 4 April, 'We were seeing a lot of the country.' Marcus Edwards wrote rather more succinctly, 'Our journey never seems to end.' Oberstleutnant Brix still had his own troops under control. There are none of the comments about the guards' poor morale as there had been by prisoners from Oflag IX A/H. Unlike Colonel Holland, there is no evidence of Clay or Kennedy refusing to move. The interests of captors and captives coincided over the shorter distances the men were now walking. A mutiny at Windeberg might have brought them freedom, but at what cost? With no justification to disobey German orders and with Brix having full control of the guard, it would have been a risky move. Heinrich Sultan in his post-war memoir makes it clear that not all the guards were well disposed to their prisoners. Nohra is the most likely location for at least one guard to suggest shooting them.

For now by moving regular short distances, the column was avoiding a direct confrontation with German commanders and was continuing to be protected from rogue German elements. The column was also slowly being overtaken by the Americans. The Germans and the senior British officers felt that the best option was to keep together and for both parties to cooperate. They had escaped attack by Allied aircraft and apart from the beatings by the Volkssturm at Rockensuß, Brix had kept the prisoners safe from German elements that might have taken out their anger at defeat on the men. On the other hand, 10 miles a day may not sound a long distance, but to do it every day for a week, especially for those who had been prisoners for several years, was not easy. Many of the men captured in France in 1940 were Territorials. Five years on they would not have the same fitness levels of men captured at Arnhem, Italy or North Africa. Marcus Edwards noted, 'Many of us with tummy trouble & feet.' One of Lee Hill's photographs is of the New Zealand medical orderlies attending to a prisoner's feet.

If the Germans had cause to be satisfied that they had kept the Rotenburg men in their hands, they would have been less pleased about the fate of Oflag IX A/H and Oberst Schrader's overall command. Together with the leakages from Oflag IX A/Z and the liberation of the Spangenberg column, the Germans had lost control of more than half of the men who had left the camps nine days earlier on 29 March.

Oflag IX A/Z would spend two days at Nohra. The OKW orders to commandants stipulated a rest day every three walking days. Oberstleutnant Brix had failed to order a rest day at

Some prisoners from Oflag IX A/Z had already come across the German policy of conscripting labourers to work on their farms during parole walks. During the evacuation all the men saw at first hand Polish woman and children conscripted to work on farms. These women appear to be carrying hay to feed animals, whilst in the barn behind, prisoners wash and shave. (Green Collection)

Diedorf. The changes of plan that day presumably made a rest day impractical. Brix could have argued that the short amble to Diedorf was as good as a rest. But why now have a rest day whilst so close to the Americans? There are no explanations in the prisoners' accounts. The evidence points to Oberstleutnant Brix being conscientious in carrying out his military duties: he interrogates deserters; he has the guard under his control; and he would keep Oflag IX A/Z in German hands for some time to come. If he had decided the game was up, he could have waited for the Americans at Friedrichsrode or Windeberg. The prisoners now mention German troops only rarely, but there were some German troops near them. The 86th Cavalry screening the north flank of 6th Armored, were shelled on 6 April whilst just east of Keula. Presumably there were enough troops near them to give Brix the confidence that he was secure against the arrival of casual American intruders.

The following day Oberst Schrader arrived for a conference with Brix. Schrader must have left Ebeleben by Thursday 5 April at the latest, when the 86th Cavalry reached the town. That he meets the column on 6 April rather than summoning Brix to him, suggests Schrader is now nomadic. On 6 April Harry Roberts' diary contains, 'Meeting of Brix, Schrader, etc, to receive and issue rockets.' Roberts expresses no surprise at Schrader's appearance. The meeting was evidently very visible, and vocal. There would be a further meeting the next day before the column left, which involved Lieutenant-Colonels Kennedy and Clay. Harry Roberts' account suggests a disagreement between Schrader and Brix. There was certainly scope for disagreement. Why had Brix allowed his column to travel so slowly? What was their destination now? How long could they stay on the road? And from Brix, resentment born out of the fact that he had at least kept his column out of American hands, unlike Fleischmann and Seybold. It would not just be the future of Oflag IX A/Z that was under review. Schrader's future and what remained of his staff was also uncertain. Whatever the agenda of the meeting, it involved some straight talking and would lead to another route change. When they left Nohra on 7 April Oflag IX A/Z were no longer heading directly towards Nordhausen. That night the German war bulletin would report fighting east of Mühlhausen for the first time.

Heinrich Sultan's memoir describes a meeting of officers and NCOs of the guard in the later stages of the march, at which an unnamed officer suggests that whatever else happens, the Americans are not going to release the prisoners because they should shoot them first. Sultan wrote that 'the Oberst' makes it clear that the war is over and that no one is going to shoot anybody. Sultan does not give the Oberst a name, so it could have been either Schrader or Brix. Was this at the meeting at Nohra? If so, the shooting prisoners remark was sotto voce: it never makes it into any of the prisoners' accounts. Sultan's part in the discussion was the comment that 'he wasn't going to shoot the prisoners – he had a better use for his rifle.' Sultan had lived alongside many of the prisoners for three years. It would have taken a particularly ruthless man to consider mass murder. Was the massacre advocate a relative newcomer to the guard? Perhaps earlier in the march and with some regular German troops nearby Brix might have felt equally firmly that his orders would require him to open fire to maintain control. It is a reminder that the prisoners' fears of a massacre at the war's end were not completely unfounded. The Guard had its own 'hard nuts', who would follow Party orders through the ruins of the Third Reich.

The overriding practical concern for Schrader and Brix would have been the need to find a more long-term home for the column. Even with the reduction in numbers through sickness and escapes, the camp could not stay in barns for more than a couple of days at a time, no matter how large they were. The need for sanitation, water and food would all create serious problems. The air raids on Nordhausen had devastated the city and eliminated any chance that the camp could have been housed there in a factory or school. If Brix still had the objective of a train to remove the camp from close proximity to the front line, either to Bavaria or the north, where was the railhead? The local alternatives were Sangerhausen, a little further east or Sondershausen, a little to the south. Since the Germans' military focus was turning northwards towards the Harz 'fortress', railheads closer and east of the Harz would be attractive options, but so too would be a march over the Harz with an ultimate destination in the North. Brix's family came from Nordhausen and he would have had some knowledge of the surrounding country to help him plan his route and find billets.

The Germans' primary concern should have been whether rail travel was still possible at all. With Allied fighter-bombers rampant everywhere, German railways were having difficulties in just storing the wagons and coaches that had become marooned in sidings and yards, with so few trains running. The V2 team in their special train had just got away to Bavaria, but a wandering

Oflag with no train of its own was a different proposition. This would have been no concern of Oberstleutnant Brix. He would have wanted to know what were his orders. He still had rail transport as one possible solution to his problems, but for the time being he was under orders to head north. Sultan's memoirs refer to walking north for one day, but then receiving orders that because the Americans had advanced farther in the north, to keep to the south. This and the column's route for the next few days suggests that after the Nohra conference the Germans had decided to cross the Harz and take Oflag IX A/Z into northern Germany, towards Fallingbostel.

The rest day at Nohra was welcome. The farm was large, which was good, but as well as being wet, it stank. There was a midden in the centre of the yard, which ensured that the whole of the yard got an equal share of the stench. Of more concern to Harry Roberts was that he had lost his spare pair of underpants. Losing kit was not unusual. Harry Roberts lost his overcoat on the first night at Nohra and spent a cold night as a result. He found it the next morning elsewhere in the barn. 'Someone, who was an officer, but no gentleman, never got another chance to improve his body warmth at the expense of mine,' he wrote in his diary.

Whilst at Nohra, Harry Roberts and three other prisoners formed a partnership to coordinate their escape plans. They agreed that as long as they were simply being marched they would stay with the column, since they must eventually be overtaken by the Americans. However transport by train or lorry, if for longer than an hour, was another matter. Either of these eventualities would trigger their escape bid. How they would judge the length of a lorry journey in advance is not clear. Both were dangerous forms of transport beneath the Allied aircraft and would take the men too far from the advancing Americans. The little consortium agreed that it would be undesirable to kill anyone in their escape, but only because the resulting man-hunt would be that much more vigorous.

With the free time at Nohra, Lee Hill was able to photograph individual prisoners. His diary refers to photographing the SBO and cookhouse staff at Nohra. No prints of Robert Lush, who led the cooking team or his staff have come to light. Lee Hill was certainly concerned about his photography whilst at Nohra, noting that he needed more negative. The German Army took a different view of photography to the British. German soldiers were encouraged to carry cameras and take pictures for intelligence purposes; something that was often remarked upon by British POWs in 1940. Apart from questions about how he got the camera, photography would have been less of an issue for the Germans. In his diary Hill would return to the topic of photography and schemes to get more negative as the days wore on, sometimes referring to offers of help from German officers to make detours to get film.

John McIndoe only produced one drawing at Nohra. Perhaps he also used the rest day to wash and dry clothes. Reverend Forster spent some of his time with a Lutheran Pastor and his family, who entertained him with a musical evening. But another chaplain who used the parole period to milk a cow in a field was not welcomed by its owner.

There was a little more food at Nohra. They were issued with a tin of pork each on both days and some bread, sugar and potatoes. But there were other treats in store for the men: they were able to bathe and wash their clothes. Harry Roberts met some Italian farm workers from whom he traded 20 cigarettes for peas and beans. Green vegetables would be a balm to the men's digestive system after the eggs, milk and cream. Nevertheless his digestive system continue to play up and he would have yet another disturbed night.

The morning of 7 April dawned dry and later there was bright sunshine. Lee Hill's pictures begin to show sunnier days. A sunny shot of happy prisoners sitting in straw outside a barn was probably taken at Nohra. The morning also brought a potentially depressing turn of events for Oflag IX A/Z. Lee

Hill heard gunfire from 0500hrs and 0700hrs. It was the start of a German counter-attack around Struth, between Lengenfeld unterm Stein and Lengefeld. An ad hoc unit, Panzer Brigade 688 with six tanks and five assault guns launched an attack south-eastwards with the aim of cutting the American lines of communication to Mühlhausen and hopefully of reaching Eisenanch 20 miles to the south. Eleven armoured vehicles against the American armoured might and several infantry divisions was a fantasy. After initial success in the first hours after dawn against the surprised men of 260th Infantry Battalion of the 65th Division, the Americans, supported by aircraft, stopped the attack in its tracks. Two days later, the 65th Infantry, with the 69th Infantry Division coming from the west, had surrounded and eliminated the German attackers. Colonel Holland had been proved right in his concern for his men at Eschwege because of rumours of a German offensive. He and the rest of Oflag IX A/H would not leave the battle zone for France by air until the following day.

Whether Patton's halt after the capture of Mühlhausen and Ohrdruf and the counter-attack at Struth would have encouraged Schrader and Brix, if they knew of them, appears unlikely. Neither Schrader or Brix could have had any misconceptions about the progress of the war. Their actions should be seen as fulfilling their immediate obligations, not following any wider strategic background. Patton's pause and the delay whilst Hodges's 1st Army fought their way eastwards from Paderborn and the Ruhr encirclement would certainly give some breathing space to the Germans. But it would not last.

On the morning of Saturday 7 April, as they left Nohra, Lee Hill thought that they were headed for Harz Mountains. Edward Baxter agreed. He thought that the column's objective had been Nordhausen until the RAF attacks forced the Germans to change their plans. It certainly appears that the column is improvising billets from day to day. Hill gives as their destination that day the village of Windehausen. The route should have taken the men in an arc around the south-east of Nordhausen. But Harry Roberts' diary, which gives an unusually detailed itinerary for this day, shows that the column made a detour after lunch and doubled back on itself to stay at Uthleben, a couple miles to the south. Edward Baxter wrote that they were marching around the smoking ruins of Nordhausen. Marcus Edward confirms that their journey had been unexpectedly cut short. The Germans, he wrote in his normal terse note, 'tried to march us 19km, but reduced to 15'.

Before the column left, Clay and Kennedy protested to Schrader and Brix about the way the camp had been treated and the pointless walking. They accused the Germans of using them as hostages. They were no doubt given the same reply that Holland had received at Ebeleben. Why should he give up his captives whilst the war continued? Voices were raised and Marcus Edward thought it a 'fierce interview between Col. Clay & German officers'. It is the first time that there is any hint that Clay had objected to German orders.

Getting to the Harz and then crossing the mountains would not be easy. Travelling directly through the burning ruins of Nordhausen was not an option. To go west round Nordhausen would take Oflag IX A/Z across the route of the transports of slave labourers around the western edge of the mountains, and closer to the Americans. The column took the easterly route. During that day they walked close to the main Halle-Kassel railway line. The weather was fine, with bright sunshine from at least midday. During their lunch stop at Hain there was an air raid nearby. Lee Hill captured his clearest shot of the march of the men holding their 'PW' sheets on the edge of an orchard. He would also photograph an air attack on a train. Bombing and strafing in the Goldene Aue had recently become heavier. During March, overflying Allied planes had triggered alarms several times a day across the valley, but there were few air raids in the region. In April that changed. There were air raids on targets around Nordhausen and Sangerhausen every day as

US aircraft disrupted German communications and supplies in front of the advancing 1st Army. It was prudent to keep clear of the railways and main roads. The men saw bomb craters alongside the roads that they were using. During these weeks farming activities ceased in the Goldene Aue. The fields were too dangerous.

Oflag IX A/Z's destination on Saturday night was Uthleben. They arrived in the late afternoon to find the village full of refugees. According to Lee Hill they had come from as far away as Kassel and Fulda, as well as most recently from Nordhausen. Whilst they were in the village the Burgomaster – Hill describes him as the 'Fat Deputy Burgomaster' – gave a speech about ultimate German victory and new German miracle weapons. There was less than a month before the end of the war in Germany.

Part of the column, including Lee Hill's group, was billeted in the local pub, the 'Gasthaus zur goldenen Aue', others were in the village hall and yet more at the other end of what is still a long, thin village. The landlord of the gasthaus was coincidentally named Carl Spangenberg. Harry Roberts thought it a good

Several men are using their smokeless camp cookers made from 'Klim' tins to heat food or drink, 7 April. The weather has improved since the rain and hail three days previously. (Green Collection)

billet. The presence of tables and chairs was significant enough to be remarked upon. He sat down that night to eat macaroni cheese, followed by a stew of beans, potatoes, carrot and meat, washed down with Ovaltine. Food was again beginning to be a concern. They were eating well, but were becoming dependent on what they could barter with civilians. It was a fragile existence. A poor market for barter and the men went hungry. If they ran out of their 'ready cash' – cigarettes, chocolate or soap – they might starve.

At Uthleben Roberts got lucky. He swapped tobacco for a Frenchman's potatoes and onions. The Frenchman would have been a POW employed as a farm worker. The food shortages were made worse by the number of refugees, who had already depleted local food stocks. Hill thought that 20,000 refugees had passed though the village and there was little left to be traded with the prisoners. Food apart, their billet was a good one and Hill in particular was in high spirits, 'All I want is a Fraulein and I will fulfil my bet with George Goff – smacking the bottom of a fat

The *gasthaus* at Uthleben had a hall attached to it which was the billet for Lee Hill's company. Hill noted in his diary that he was close to winning a bet that he had made with another prisoner of 'smacking the bottom of a fat frau in a beer garden in Germany'. Presumably having found the beer hall he failed to find the frau. (Green Collection)

The bombing of Nordhausen by the RAF had filled the surrounding villages with survivors from the town. They joined an ever growing population of refugees from the east and escaped forced labourers from almost all the European countries, living rough in the countryside. (Otago Settlers' Museum, New Zealand)

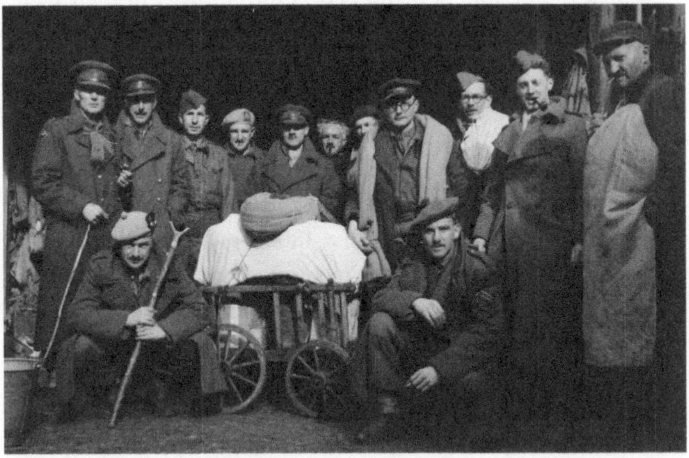

Cart being repaired at Uthleben, 7 April. Harry Roberts writes in his diary for 8 April, 'Cart was repaired last night. I now have a part share, my baccy being used to pay carpenter.' Prams and carts played an important part in Oflag IX A/Z's march, used to carry clothes and food. The prisoners appear to be mainly older men including Scots, presumably captured in northern France in 1940. The man in the centre wearing what could be an airborne beret is possibly Harry Roberts. (Green Collection)

frau in a beer-garden in Germany.' That night Lee ate a similar meal to Harry Roberts, which suggests that despite the men's anxieties there was some centrally provided food. Lee sums up the food problem: 'So far we are feeding better than ever before Kreigydom but fear it will be grim soon as cigs run out.'

Harry Roberts now had shares in a cart to help carry his kit. During the stay at Uthleben the cart was repaired by a German carpenter. Harry's share of the cost was paid in tobacco. Lee Hill took a group picture of prisoners and a German carpenter around a wooden cart. If this is the repair Harry refers to, then he must be the man in the only airborne beret barely visible over the shoulder of the older men, some Scots, who dominate the photograph. Another cart, that belonging to Lieutenant Sidney Turnbull, Duke of Wellington's Regiment, was photographed by Lee Hill and drawn by John McIndoe on 5 April. He noted on his drawing that Turnbull had pushed it 130km (80 miles). Lee Hill believed that Turnbull had 'found' the pram.

Whilst the prisoners could take some comfort in their position even if food was a growing concern, the German refugees around them were living on their nerves. The air attacks continued to terrify them. Lee Hill: 'In village just a few kilos ahead we saw an ammo train attacked by Mustangs – and it was hit. Great explosions. Refugees terrified. About 6 o'clock.' This was on the main line between Nordhausen and Sangerhausen. German records match Hill's time exactly, 1800hrs, 7 April. Explosions on the train continued over the next few days.

The destruction of their homes and the continual aircraft overhead naturally meant that some of the refugees were not friendly. Surprisingly, the civilians were not uniformly hostile. Ernest Edlmann and Frederick Corfield had spent the night in Dachrieden with refugees from the bombing of the Ruhr, who were not at all antagonistic. Beyond their immediate anxieties, the civilians feared the Americans. Nazi propaganda had built them up as monsters, especially Black Americans. The British, despite their role in the recent bombing, were a different matter.

Lee Hill described their walk as being, at times, a 'propaganda tour'. Unlike the Americans who were feared as potential rapists and looters, the 'Englische has a high reputation wherever I go here – prima, prima'. And in 1945 English could encompass any members of British Empire.

The following day, the column left Uthleben in warm sunshine. This time the men had to walk a little farther than expected. Their original destination had been Steigerthal 10 miles from Uthleben, but they had to walk another 2.5 miles to Buchholz, a village almost directly behind Nordhausen, where the ground starts to rise towards the mountains. From the village, roads led to Nordhausen or into and across the Harz near its highest point, the Brocken.

The prisoners' accounts for the day are full of descriptions of air activity and the impact it is having on the civilian population. On 8 April alone there were six raids on Sangerhausen

McIndoe's caption shows that he had his dates a little confused; this was drawn on 8 April on the route between Uthleben and Buchholz. The main railway line from Kassel to Leipzig ran just to the north and the men's diaries have several references to air raids during the day. The vehicle across the road is a Steyr-Daimler-Puch AG full-track prime mover known as a *Raupenschlepper Ost* 'Tracked vehicle East'. (Otago Settlers' Museum, New Zealand)

and Kelbra, both a few miles east of the column. Lee Hill saw USAAF Mustangs and Lightnings. As they walk north, the men see Nordhausen airfield being shot up by Mustangs. For most of the day there is the sound of bombing in the distance and all the time more evidence of the suffering of refugees. Hill was moved by the people he saw 'crouching in culverts & under fences in great fear. Pathetic really. To see old ladies & kiddies. But still, it will make them remember 1940!' During their last rest before arriving at their billet they see heavy bombers flying over. They were part of a raid by US Eighth Air Force – Flying Fortresses and Liberators – on ordnance and oil storage depots, marshalling yards and railway facilities around Leipzig.

Harry Roberts thought that they did not stop as planned at Steigerthal because it was too full of refugees. Butch Laing and Lee Hill have a different explanation – a stray bomb had hit their billet. Oflag IX A/Z walked through the centre of the village and were watched by disgruntled evacuees, but there were few insults. Lee Hill reckoned there were 1400 refugees in a village with a normal population of 200. The road had been climbing slowly as they went north, but they were still only on the edge of the Harz. It was rolling country after the flat valley of the Goldene Aue, but not yet mountainous or even as hilly as the British Pennines. From Buchholz a road led to one of the main routes across the Harz; from Nordhausen via Hasselfelde, to Blankenburg on the north German plain.

There were no central cooking facilities at Buchholz so the men were issued with oatmeal to boil as porridge. Hill found some refugees, at Buchholz who, given their situation, were amazingly friendly. Even so one old lady does shake her fist as Hill passes and shouts 'Luft Gangsters!' It was a far milder reaction than one might have expected.

Edward Baxter saw some signs that they were not welcome, but as with the other prisoners makes it clear that these were extremely unusual. 'At one village where we slept a most peculiar situation arose. We arrived at the usual large farm in the form of a square. The barns on one side were occupied by civilians, mostly women and children, who had survived the attentions of the R.A.F. at Nordhausen … At the farm pump German civilians, guards and British POWs were all queuing for water. One old woman in tears shook her fist at us. This was the only sign of animosity that I can remember seeing personally during the whole of our conducted walking tour, and I believe, also, the whole time I was in Germany, from a civilian.'

There was a potentially more serious confrontation on the way to Buchholz. Harry Roberts in his post-war account (but not his diary) recorded them meeting an SS officer. The man stepped out in front of part of the column. Most of the column stepped around him, but then a large Canadian officer just marched up to him and stopped. The rest of the column behind him came to a halt. The SS man gave an order to the Canadian, which he ignored. Others joined in the discussion, including Hauptmann Heyl. The SS men by now had his revolver in his hand and disaster threatened until at the last moment Brix returned and ordered the SS man away. Thankfully, the SS man complied and the column continued on its way. The man might have come from any of the factories and camps, some of which were still being evacuated, on the eastern side of Nordhausen. Close by at Rottleberode there were factories with slave labour at Thyraweke, which built aircraft landing gear (in what is now a cave that can be visited, the 'Heimkehle') and there were other factories at Stempeda and Buchholz at Osterode. To the east at Roßla and Kelbra there were other camps. It is significant that it was only around Nordhausen that the marchers met SS men; although Reid and Bowlby had nearly fallen into the hands of the SS at Bebra over a week earlier. Fortunately, the column met only solitary individuals: an SS officer with troops might not have been so easily intimidated by a Wehrmacht Reserve Lieutenant-Colonel and 80 Landes Shützen.

Today, Buchholz is a small dormitory village for Nordhausen. On the outskirts is a large memorial to the slave labourers who worked and died in the area. In April 1945, swollen with refugees, it is not surprising that the prisoners found bartering difficult. That they found somewhere to spend the night was close to miraculous, a barn. Harry Roberts' evening meal was porridge and then stew both cooked over his open fire.

Men were still make escape attempts. But only one is recorded in accounts for the period from 5–11 April. It had happened as they had circled Nordhausen. Lieutenant N. Gershony, Auxiliary Military Pioneer Corps, escaped from the column some time around 7 April. Gershony had been serving with a Pioneer unit raised in Palestine, when he was captured in Greece. He was Jewish. Nordhausen, after the devastating air raids and with its strong SS presence, was a bad place for Gershony to be. Lee Hill:

> Lt Geishoni [sic] was delivered back after an interesting experience of escape. He was taken into Nordhausen & saw the flattened city – thousands of corpses still lying around – mostly foreign workers, as the Germans have been shifted. They handed him back to the army [Wehrmacht] quickly, & a Lieut looked after him very well before delivering him.

This was a remarkable piece of good fortune for a Jewish escapee hard on the heels of the devastating British air raid. The descriptions of the corpses of foreign workers left unburied match those given by shocked Americans several days later, when 3rd Armored reached the ruined city. One wonders which organisation 'they' were, who had captured Gershony before handing him over to the army. Was it the police or the Volkssturm? The SS would surely not have been so magnanimous.

If there had been concerns amongst the men that their walk was aimless, then the next few days would confirm them. At Buchholz, although they were only a few miles away from one of the main roads across the Harz Mountains, Oflag IX A/Z would now about face and return down the valley. As at

Mühlhausen over a week before, the cause was the speed of the American's advance eastwards. Now it was 2nd Armored Division, part of US 9th Army, who were causing problems for the Germans north of the Harz. US 9th Army was beginning to overtake the American armies south of the mountains. On 8 April, 2nd Armored, having established a bridgehead across the Weser, had paused to resupply. They were 60 miles north of Brix and had cut the route to the north. The OKW War Diary had reported the crossing of the Weser on 7 April, presumably it had taken time for the news to reach Brix. The news that was available to everyone in Germany from the daily war bulletins simply reported pressure on the Weser, but then the same bulletins also noted that 'fierce fighting' was in progress at Mühlhausen. Mühlhausen had fallen to US 6th Armored several days earlier.

Since Oflag IX A/Z would not have been welcomed by the German troops preparing to defend the Harz Fortress, Brix's only option was to return south. Plan C had lasted no longer than Plan B. Unlike the changes of the earlier plans, this time the decision must have been made overnight: the men record no conferences amongst the guard and their departure time is not delayed whilst Oberstleutnant Brix formulates a plan.

Brix's supplies were running low. Had he been able to continue northwards he would have been travelling towards the main Red Cross depot in northern Germany at Lübeck, now he was traveling in the opposite direction. Oflag IX A/Z had set out with enough supplies to reach Mühlhausen in three days. That was almost a week before. The Spangenberg column had almost run out of food by 2 April at Lengenfeld unterm Stein. It was only Gunnar Celander with his car and lorry that had allowed Oflag IX A/Z to remain on the road for so long. Basil Clay's report to the war Office described Celander as

> ... using his own initiative, on several occasions left the column with his lorry in order to collect food from centres

> near the line of march, and was extremely successful in doing this. But for the food he collected, we would have been in a very bad way indeed. In making these journeys, Mr Celander ran considerable risks, as there was much air activity and all movement on roads was extremely dangerous.

Brix and the SBOs now agreed a desperate solution to the column's problems. Celander in his car and with the Red Cross lorry would leave the column and drive independently to Lübeck. There he hoped to have access to medical stores and Red Cross food parcels. He also planned to replenish his petrol stocks. Lübeck was almost 250 miles to the north. It was a journey that Celander had done regularly from Kassel. Assuming no major difficulties, it would still take Celander over a day to get to Lübeck. With a day to load, the total journey time would be three to four days. This ignored the fact that Allied armies were close to cutting Germany in half. Whether they would be willing to let Celander travel across their front lines was debatable. And even if Celander was able to reach Lübeck and return, how would he find the camp on his return if it continued walking across Germany? Part of the plan must therefore have been for Oflag IX A/Z to find somewhere to lay up for several days and wait for Celander to return with supplies.

The overnight billet at Uftrungen on 9 April was presumably intended as that extended stop. The village is on the edge of the foothills of the Harz. It was a mere seven miles from Buchholz. It had a good water supply from the small brook that runs through the middle of the village and several farms with large barns that could easily hold the camp. Lee Hill's description of Uftrungen could have come from a holiday postcard: 'The farm people at our barracks have been wonderful, giving us the run of the kitchen and altogether it has been a pleasant stay.'

To reach Uftrungen the column returned down the valley from Buchholz. The route was farther east than the previous day so the men might have realised initially they were returning south. The road took them through Rottleberode with its railway yard, gypsum mine and factories and onto the flat land of the tip of Goldene Aue. There were factories in the valley associated with Mittlebau-Dora and the other SS factories. Lee Hill described the column passing the gypsum factory that still dominates the southern end of the village. 'Lots of Eyetai workers around here. We passed a gypsum factory yesterday and a crowd of Soviet & Polish girls happy & well fed, were out in the yards. It must have been their lunch hour, & they gave us a very smiling "hip hip hooray".' Lunch hours are not concepts that fit easily with SS forced labour.

By now the men were reasonably confident that they could avoid becoming victims of American air attack. They describe bomb damage but no air activity that day. The USAAF diary shows that 9th Air Force was supporting 3rd Armored between the Weser and Nordhausen, which was the other side of the town to the marchers. However German records show that

This is possibly Rottelberode on 9 April; Lee Hill describes bomb-damaged trees that appear to have been lopped. This picture fits that description and could have been taken on the journey from Buchholz to Uftrungen. The contented man with his pipe leaning against the tree is Lieutenant Gerald Frost, Royal Army Ordnance Corps. (Green Collection)

On the way to Uftrungen, 9 April. The landscape suggests that this is the road from Buchholz down the valley with the branch railway line to Stolberg just a field away to the right of the road. At the right of the centre party Lieutenant Alan Green, Border Regiment, in his airborne beret, and an unknown colleague pull a heavily laden cart. (Green Collection)

This is probably the road to Uftrungen on 9 April, with the village of Rottleberode in the distance. Lieutenant Kenneth White, Royal Artillery is standing in the centre reaching for the coat held by another prisoner. (Green Collection)

The railway along the valley past Uftrungen was a clear target for Allied fighter-bombers. (Peter Green)

air activity was affecting everyone. Mrs Christa Kneißel, then Christa Walter and a 15-year-old school girl, was living on the family farm in Uftrungen. At the beginning of April she stopped going to school in Stolberg by train '[because there] were fighter-bombers that attacked everything and shot at people.' There was no bombing of Uftrungen itself, but Christa remembers the bombing of Nordhausen, when ashes and fragments of paper drifted in the air to Uftrungen.

Harry Roberts described a domestic start to their second Monday on the road, but soon there was evidence of bombing.

> Got up at 6-10 to prepare porridge. Made a couple of slices of toast + shared an egg with Reggie ... 'Found' some potatoes = small wheat. Started at 9-45 + did 4 kilos to Stempeda + then a further 2 to Rottleberode where we had 1 hrs halt for lunch (no tea) ate hardboiled egg. Bomb damage all around.

For once Lee Hill did not know their destination that day, '1 hour stop at a small village of Rottelberode on a main road. Bomb damage heavy on road & many houses damaged. Trees in Avenue lopped off as bomb hit just off road. Only 1km to go to tonight's billet, they say … Heard today that the Spangenberg crowd are still on the road. Too bad.' Where Hill got his information about Oflag IX A/H is not explained, but of course he was wrong. On 9 April the former prisoners of Spangenberg were in France. John Sewell had spent the night at the Hotel Bedford, Paris. As the Rotenburg men breakfasted over open fires and prepared for another day's walking, Sewell had eaten a leisurely breakfast – porridge, bacon and eggs – followed by a stroll by the Seine.

Christa Kneißel lived with her mother and grandfather on their farm alongside the stream in the middle of the village.

> On April 9th, 1945, without any warning a group of British prisoners of war came to Uftrungen during the morning. The guards were armed, were uniformed and were not SS-men. The POWs moved around relatively freely and appeared happy.

Fifty men were billeted on Christa's farm. Christa spoke English and she remembers that there was no hatred whatsoever on either side. The British mostly wanted to have eggs. She also remembers that the prisoners were tidy and well groomed. Harry Roberts had a good opinion of Uftrungen.

> 4 kilo more to a State Farm at Uftrungen which was the best billet of any. B.M. very good. Good start 2 bottles milk, 12 eggs, + German sausage, Beer + lemonade + sausage sandwiches. Sat in the sun. beautiful.

Each man was issued with a small amount of milk and a centrally provided supper of pea soup. Harry even tries to get his haircut in

McIndoe is surrounded by village children as he draws in Uftrungen on 9 April. Children were often more willing to make initial contact with the prisoners and handled much of the trading, but they were also the recipients of the prisoners' gifts of chocolate. (Marion Gerritsen-Teunissen Collection)

This is the picture that McIndoe was drawing in Uftrungen. Oflag IX A/Z were billeted in several barns in the village. This is one with a group of prisoners and guards standing outside. (Otago Settlers' Museum, New Zealand)

the village, but the shop is shut. That night the atmosphere eases even more and Harry has what he describes as an interesting discussion with 2 'Goones', three Dutchmen and two other prisoners. Lieutenant Baxter's description of Uftrungen includes a wonderfully condescending remark about German sausage 'It is quite wrong to regard all German sausage as bad, or poor in quality. This was quite palatable. The better kinds are supposed to be excellent.'

As in the earlier villages, it was the children who organised many of the exchanges. As soon as they had discovered what a prisoner wanted they would run home and return with one or two eggs or a piece of meat or sausage in a bit of paper. Then the bartering would start. The guard must have found this strange and difficult. Their prisoners and their chocolate, soap or cigarettes, were more attractive to German civilians than their Reichsmarks. Edward Baxter,

> All this business was a very bitter pill for our guards, who suffered considerably by our competition. Normally they would have had the first choice and the best of everything. But who wanted German marks which in a few days time might be only waste paper for the Americans and when opulent British officers were offering delicious cocoa, rare and luxurious English soap and good English cigarettes, all scarce and precious things in Germany.

Later an improvised altar was set up in front of a barn with two candles and a service was held in English. The congregation included Polish farm workers, some from Christa's family farm, and villagers. For Christa it signified that the war could not last much longer. In the late afternoon Lee Hill went to collect Celander's typewriter and some negative from his billet at a local vicarage, before Celander drove north. The parson already has other guests, a Lutheran pastor and his family, refugees from Eastern Prussia. They sit down with a table cloth and china for a civilised tea. But the idyll was not to last.

At 1900hrs Celander and Niels Jörgensen driving the YMCA lorry set off to Lübeck. To help share the driving two prisoners went with them, Lieutenant Lestock Baigent, New Zealand Expeditionary Force and Lance-Corporal W.A. Brown, RASC. Just after they left the village on their way north back to Buchholz, their little convoy of car, trailer, and lorry was strafed. Basil Clay wrote later, 'Shortly after they had departed the lorry returned to camp asking for a doctor and stating that Mr Celander's car had been shot up by American planes and Mr Celander and Lt. Baigent wounded.' One of the camp doctors went to bring the injured men back to Uftrungen. Gunner Celander had been hit in his right arm. No bones were broken, but he was in pain and suffering from shock. Lestock Baigent had a flesh wound to his groin, but seemed otherwise to be in good condition. They were given first aid and put to bed in the minister's house. Edward Baxter gives the most detailed account of what had happened: 'Not long after they left us a fighter came down to have a look at them. Both Celander and his driver got out of the car and waved to the plane. The car had the Swedish Flag painted on the top and side; Celander was wearing civilian clothes and the New Zealander was in khaki. After circling round a bit the fighter gave them a burst of machine-gun fire.' No doubt the car did have the Swedish flag painted on its sides and tops, unfortunately none of Lee Hill's pictures show them. There is, though, a picture of the YMCA lorry. It shows Swedish flags stencilled on its wheel arches. The flags are not large. On dirty vehicles the blue and yellow markings would not have been obvious.

Celander's post-war report refers to three Thunderbolts attacking them. In the article that Lee Hill wrote for *Illustrated* magazine of 12 May 1945, the attack is attributed to the Germans. 'Swedish Red Cross officials, Rev. Celander, Capt. Baigent, went with the column; provided use of car and truck; were shot up by Germans as they went to contact representatives of Protecting Power to try and get food and help for prisoners.'

FORCED MARCH TO—FREEDOM—continued

ILLUSTRATED—May 12, 1945

German Doctor (with two nurses) now friendly, was typical Nazi brute while liberating Allied armies were far away

Swedish Red Cross officials, Rev. Celander, Capt. Baigent, went with column; provided use of car and truck; were shot up by Germans as they went to contact representatives of Protecting Power to try to get food and help for prisoners

snatched a few sentences from their radio. Our guards grew nervous. We saw Allied planes circling overhead. The Nazi Kommandant was more irate than ever. We heard artillery fire in the distance.

Lt.-Col. Clay, our own senior officer, issued instructions. Our haversacks were quickly filled with all the necessities of life on which we could lay our hands, with all the available Red Cross supplies, bandages, medicines. For three days we waited. Then the Germans gave the order which we had anticipated. They told us that we would be marched away.

We set out on a march which lasted fifteen days and took us on a zig-zag route across 230 kilometres. It was a march none of us will ever forget. We could not have survived it but for the help of the Rev. Celander, a Swedish Y.M.C.A. official, who put his car and tender and a three-ton truck at our disposal.

If our men wearied and faltered under the strain, if they could no longer carry their haversacks, if they fell by the wayside, exhausted, unable to continue the march, the Rev. Celander and his Danish driver performed miracles. They drove backwards and forwards, moved the provisions, gave lifts to the weak, cared for the wounded. They saved many lives.

We slept in barns; we fed in fields; all the time we marched and marched and marched, knowing that only a few miles separated us from the liberating forces in our—and the Wehrmacht's—rear. Keula, Sontre, Nordhausen (site of the terror camp), Friedrichsrode—they were small villages which we passed. There were many more, and there were drama and excitement on every stage of our march.

Once four fellow-prisoners hid under the straw in a barn where we had spent the night, trying to "jump the column." They were ferreted out by Volkssturm and S.S. Black Guards, beaten with rifle butts, hit with whips, threatened with death. What saved them and many others was the Kommandant's determination to keep us alive—as hostages.

Then there was the day when artillery fire rocked the German village in which we halted. The burgomaster gave the "panzer alarm" and I saw the whole population evacuating to the hills within ten minutes. I found myself alone with our supplies—and a German guard who promptly surrendered to me. Alas, it was a false alarm and I was a prisoner once again.

There were the days when Thunderbolts and Mustangs, flying at zero feet, darted at us and we could see the gunners with their eyes on the gun-sights. Would they "get us"? Anxious moments passed until they wagged their tails as a sign of recognition and we watched them flying off in pursuit of truly German targets. We saw the havoc of destruction which they left behind wherever they went—burning railway engines, shot-up lorries, villages wiped out. Grand fellows, these!

Once a shout went up: "Our airborne boys are here!" But it was only an observation plane which we had mistaken for a glider. Then we knew that critical hours were ahead. We "Kriegies" sensed that the Germans were afraid. From now on we moved only by night. The Kommandant, impatient with our slow progress—so happily delayed by R.A.F. activities—made arrangements for us to be moved south by rail. This would have been the end of us.

But when he told Lt.-Col. Clay that we were to make another forced march our leader was firm. He realized that the Americans could not be far off. Men were too weak to march on, he said; he pointed to our blistered feet, to the sick and wounded. No, he could no longer order us to obey the Germans. Not a step farther!

The result was surprising. The Nazi Kommandant knew that the game was up. He announced that he would leave us and withdraw his guards. We were on our own. It was Friday, the 13th. It was Lt.-Col. Clay's birthday. What a birthday present for him—for all of us! We were virtually free.

We organized ourselves into an active, combatant unit. We sent out patrols. Soon we knew that the American spearheads were near. Some of our comrades who had managed to escape turned up again with the first American tanks. Some of us went frantic with joy, others wept, others were just silent. I think they prayed.

The rest was a "joy-ride" home. We had won the race for freedom. Weary, exhausted, sick, we were too slow for the Germans. Our fighting American Allies were too quick for them. Our forced march of fifteen days ended in glorious liberation.

Eastwards Into Germany march these British prisoners, some with their scanty belongings on strange "transport vehicles," and carrying odds and ends picked up at short stops. Allied forces were hard on the heels of this party

The article in the *Illustrated*, 12 May 1945. In the caption to the picture of Gunnar Celander (top right) the Germans are blamed for his being shot. Hill's diary and those of other prisoners are clear that Celander's car was attacked by a USAAF fighter. (Green Collection)

To suggest that the Allies had attacked Red Cross vehicles must have been too much for the editor of *Illustrated*. Lee Hill went along with the lie, probably it was a case of accept the editor's changes or the story will not be published. The Swedish paper, *Dagens Nyheter*, carried the story almost immediately and although closer to the truth, it still had errors. The article blamed British planes and located the attack close to Rotenburg.

Later that night a German Casualty Clearing Station arrived in Uftrungen and announced that the prisoners would have to move as the hospital needed all the space it could find in the village. Celander and Baigent were in no condition to travel with the column so they were handed over to the care of the German doctors, whilst remaining lodged at the Pastor's house. Lance Corporal Brown stayed to act as batman. A supply of food was also left for the invalids. In the early hours of the next morning Niels Jörgensen set off in the Red Cross lorry for Lübeck. Lee Hill has him travelling to Lübeck via Berlin and leaving at 3 am. He was driving on his own and ahead of him had a 350-mile trip north across war-torn Germany. His route would, for the time being, take him clear of the advancing British and Americans. Jörgensen's fate is not recorded in Celander's report – both driver and lorry disappear from the story. When the column left Uftrungen the next morning Celander and Baignent had both improved. They were being well looked after and had a radio to entertain them and keep them in touch with the outside world.

Oberstleutnant Brix now had a serious problem. His plan to lie up and wait for more supplies was unravelling. Even if Jörgensen avoided Allied aircraft, the attempt to get food and medical supplies might not succeed. And if it did, would he return before the Americans arrived? With US 1st Army now released from fighting at Paderborn, US 12th Army Group could once again resume its push eastwards. North of the Harz, 9th Army was pressing on towards the Elbe. In the south, Patton's 3rd Army would reach the river Saale and Weimar within 24 hours. West of Uftrungen, Hodges's 1st Army, led by 3rd Armored Division, were a day's travel west of Nordhausen. Nevertheless, it appears that that night's billet had been chosen as a replacement for Uftrungen. The village of Dittichenrode was also in the foothills of the Harz. Today it is the starting point for hiking trails into the mountains. Lying about a mile north of the main from road from Nordhausen to Halle, it was a logical place to wait for the arrival of supplies.

The column, when it left Uftrungen, includes a tractor pulling three trailers of baggage with the sick sitting on top. Celander's car also comes with them, with a German driver. Once down the valley and into the Goldene Aue the prisoners were sharing the road with streams of refugees and their assorted transport. They were also walking alongside one of the main east-west railways. Again, there was considerable American air activity. Hill sees Mustangs shoot up a column of German troops. Hill claims that the guards are pleased to be with the column of prisoners with their PW signs as protection. At the same stop Hill's lunch included 'the greatest hors d'oeuvres I've ever had. About 8 Thunderbolts came down on railway with several engines and wagons less than 400 yards away. They circled, strafed and bombed for 25 minutes attacking several times trains & other targets in the vicinity.' The shellfire and explosions disturbs five hares that Hill sees running in a nearby field. It is an incongruous battlefield image. The following day he would not that despite the aircraft noise and explosions, one of Dörrs' stallions that had come from Rotenburg with the carts had covered a mare at the farm.

Harry Roberts records a second incident on the eight-mile walk with the SS near Roßla, though this time Hauptamn Heyl got the situation under control more quickly. Butch Laing also remembered there being SS troops in the area. Roberts commented that by this stage they seem to face three ways of dying: at the hands of the SS, by Allied strafing or by shot-down German aircraft crashing on to them. This was the day that the men saw the Luftwaffe overhead for the first time in their journey. Near Roßla an Me 109 and a Mustang crashed near the column and both were still burning as the men passed. Lee Hill's optimism was now growing by the day, 'I am eating well & feel fit as a fiddle, although must admit I was glad to drop my 60lb pack tonight. The typewriter made the damn thing heavier than ever.'

On arriving at Dittincherode the men are told that the next day will be another rest day. As with the previous rest day at

Nohra, this is odd given that the Americans are closer than they have been for several days. The men were billeted in a large farm and with families elsewhere in the village. Today Dittincherode has, like Buchholz, become a dormitory village for the surrounding towns. In 1945 it was more remote. John McIndoe found time from his drawing to produce a vegetable stew for his section. The vegetables were augmented with Bovril and pork fat. Hill's verdict was that it was 'excellent'. It was cooked as other meals were that evening over an open fire and eaten by the farm pond full of croaking frogs. Hill would later describe the view as including camp fires and 'bare bottoms, as the squitters still attack some'. The latrine pits dug by the men in the meadow behind the farm are still remembered today by the older villagers.

Lee Hill used the rest day to add to his diary some reflections on their experiences so far. The comments, some of which describe events far earlier in the march, include statements more suited to describing a holiday ramble, 'Don & Jack Frazer of Nelson are doing grand job as R.A.P. on the trip.' 'R.A.P' – Regimental Aid Post – was the first aid post. 'They get time to have a lot of fun cooking great meals on the camp fire. Maj. Ted Young, London Stock Exchange, is also enjoying it. Lt. Shama of Palestine, Lt Geo Cameron of Scotland, Art Godfrey of Canada, Capt. Bruce McKenzie, Capt Cyril Butterfield both from Dunedin, are also in my platoon, & all getting fitter & browner.' Major Young was serving with the Royal West Kent Regiment – not the Stock Exchange – and whether he would have felt that enjoying the journey was an appropriate comment is moot. In a caricature drawn by Frank Slater George Cameron is holding several bottles of beer and it is captioned 'The Fechtin Provost O'Tain' – a reference to Burns and to Cameron's scavenging abilities. Art Godfrey was a CANLOAN officer who had been captured at Arnhem whilst serving with the South Staffordshire Regiment.

Hill was still trying to get more film. Whilst the column was at Dittichenrode, he persuaded Hauptmann Herman

The prisoners appear to be waiting for something to happen, which would fit early evening 11 April at Dittichenrode. Surprisingly there are no obvious guards in the picture. Nor are there horses for Dörr's carts. They must still be in the field where the men record them grazing. (Green Collection)

The church of St Anne and St Mary at Dittichenrode. On 11 April when McIndoe drew the picture the men were settling down to enjoy a rest day. The men sunbathed, with their 'PW' signs as protection against air attack laid out on the ground. (Otago Settlers' Museum, New Zealand)

McIndoe's friend Lieutenant Eric 'Podge' Webster on the hill above Dittichenrode looking at the Goldenen Aue and Roßla. (Otago Settlers' Museum, New Zealand)

Prisoners and German civilians chat and exchange food for the POWs' luxury goods – soap and cigarettes. John McIndoe is third from the left against the wall. (Green Collection)

Schwekowsky to walk back to Roßla with him to get his film processed, but Schwekowsky changed his mind after the air attacks on trains and roads. Apparently Hauptmann Hoffmann offered to try and get to Stolberg, a village 16 miles away north of Uftrungen, and buy Lee a ciné camera with sterling provided

The German decision to move the men from Dittichenrode by lorry came in the late afternoon of 11 April. The men's diaries refer to them spending considerable time with the villagers and how unhappy they were that the prisoners were to be moved. The man second from left with his wings is from the Glider Pilot Regiment. (Green Collection)

A photograph of men from Oflag IX A/Z that was left by Major J.A.S. Mackenzie, a dentist with the medical corps of the New Zealand Expeditionary Force and Captain E.E. Vaughan, a member of the medical service of the Indian Army, to provide the German family that had looked after them in Dittichenrode with names to contact for help after the war. It is addressed to 'The kind Frau who looked after us'. (Margaret Knott Collection)

Villagers leaving Dittichenrode on 11 April, A common response by German civilians to the imminent arrival of the Americans was to abandon their villages and move into nearby woods so as to be safe from any shelling or bombing. (Marion Gerritsen-Teunissen Collection)

by Hill. It all seems wishful thinking on Hill's part, unless Hoffmann had been ordered to do this by Stolberg as part of his duties. Both Hill and Colonel Holland describe Hoffmann as Welfare Officer, duties that would have brought him into contact with Hill and his film shows whilst at Rotenburg.

Harry Roberts was finding it hard to get food in the village. Although he conceded that his billets were good, the village was a poor one when it came to trading. But he had no complaint about the weather. Wednesday 11 April dawns as an apparent rest day. Roberts and others strip off and sunbathe. The men lay their PW signs out on the ground and lay in the sun to the sound of aircraft and gunfire. As with other relaxed moments during the march, it was too good to last.

7

UNEXPECTED FINALE

> Received order to move this evening by truck. Things definitely not looking so good. Had a good supper anyway, meat + onion + spud pie.
>
> Lieutenant Harry Roberts, REME, Oflag IX A/Z, captured at Arnhem, September 1944.

In the late afternoon of Wednesday 11 April the sunbathing prisoners were given most unwelcome news. Oflag IX A/Z would be moved by lorry that night. Only Lee Hill's diary records their destination, Wimmelburg, 20 miles to the east, but for everyone it was an alarming surprise, with the added worry that there was no time limit to their journey.

The leading task force from US 3rd Armored Division was six miles west of them. The Division had arrived at the outskirts of Nordhausen early that day. By late afternoon they were at Hain where Oflag IX A/Z had stopped for lunch 4 days before and by nightfall they were at Heringen, which the men had passed through three days earlier as they headed north to Buchholz. At the rate the Americans were travelling they would pass the end of the road to Dittichenrode the next morning. Once again, the prisoners were less than a day from freedom.

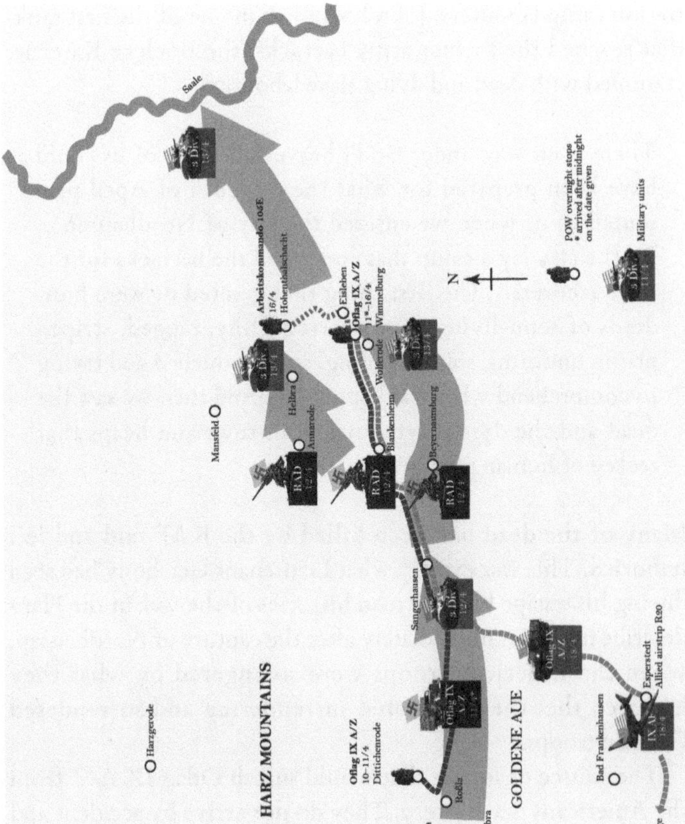

Oflag IX A/Z's final days in Germany. (Peter Green)

One task force from 3rd Armored had gone into Nordhausen. They had been appalled by the horrors it contained and the news spread quickly through the rest of the Division and 1st Army. Liberation had come too late for many of the concentration camp labourers. John Irwin was in one of the first tanks that reached the former army barracks, the Boelcke Kaserne, crammed with dead and dying slave labourers.

> There is no way under God's heaven that any of us could have been prepared for what the eleventh of April presented to us when we entered the city of Nordhausen... By the city lay a camp that contained the barracks for the slave laborers...The first thing that greeted us were hundreds of semi-living men wearing filthy, ragged, striped prison uniforms, some standing, some crouched and trying to comprehend what was happening. And then we saw the dead and the dying, lying naked in rows and heaps that reeked of human putrification.

Many of the dead had been killed by the RAF raid and left unburied. This was exactly what Lieutenant Gershony had seen during his escape bid. German histories of the war in the Harz describe incidents immediately after the capture of Nordhausen, when the American troops were so angered by what they had seen that they murdered surrendering and surrendered German troops.

The source of lorries that would snatch Oflag IX A/Z from the Americans is a mystery. They do not arrive by accident and unannounced in the village. Brix knew that they were coming early enough to give the prisoners several hours warning. Somehow he had made arrangements for the vehicles to come to Dittichenrode and transport the camp eastwards. They were not flagged down by chance by the guard as they passed the end of the road. Had they been taking supplies to the defenders of Nordhausen? Were they part of a retreating German unit, but if so why were they not carrying German troops? Hitler had agreed that POWs could be moved by lorry or train if they might otherwise return empty having taken supplies to the front. In either case it would have been impractical to arrange for vehicles from the west: by the afternoon the Americans had occupied Nordhausen. Unlike the lorries that should have taken Oflag IX A/H to Ebeleben or those expected at Lengefeld by the mixed group, Brix's lorries did arrive.

The vehicles must have come originally from the east, most probably from Eisleben. Eisleben was a hospital centre and presumably had vehicles to move wounded men, although these do not apparently have hospital markings, Butch Laing describing them as 'unmarked lorries.' If the source of the vehicles was Eisleben, Brix had established communications with the town and was not operating in isolation. The men were issued with bread, but Harry Roberts at least was unsure if this was for the journey or represented a final issue of food. Wherever they came from, the vehicles would be travelling to Dittichenrode at dusk; a dangerous time with the skies full of US fighter-bombers.

The announcement about the lorries was not welcomed by either the prisoners or the villagers. Now it was clear that the Americans would soon arrive, the villagers had hoped that the Allied prisoners would provide them with protection from what the Party described as gangsters and black men. At least two of the POWs, both with medical connections, Captain E.E. Vaughan, Indian Army Medical Service, and Major J.A.S. Mackenzie, New Zealand Dental Corps, left a safe conduct note for Frau Ida Becker. It was a photograph of themselves, taken in Rotenburg, with a note addressed to 'To the Kind Frau who looked after us', and their home addresses in the UK and New Zealand. As the afternoon wore on many villagers decided to leave for the 'safety' of the woods behind the village. Lee Hill photographed elderly villagers carrying bags walking uphill from the village towards the surrounding woods.

Harry Roberts and his escape group learned of the lorry transfer late in the afternoon, by which time the guard had been organised to prevent men slipping away. The prisoners had been under parole in the village not to escape, now with the threatened arrival of transport, Harry Roberts and his group attempted to withdraw their parole, but Lieutenant-Colonel Clay refused to allow it. His argument was that the parole was in fact his own, on behalf of the men, and he had already agreed there would be no escapes from the lorries. Clay, like Colonel Holland a week earlier, felt that they had no choice but go along with the German orders even though the Americans were so close.

Whilst Harry Roberts abided by the terms of the parole, others did not and the arrival of the vehicles triggered a series of escapes. Hamish Forbes's memoirs contain a firsthand description. In the gloom of the evening as the men were being organised to board the lorries, Forbes, Lieutenant James Russo, 3 Hussars, and Major Frederick Gray, RAMC, just faded into the background and lay low in the dark. For Forbes, this was his tenth escape attempt. 'Bullshit' Smith and Alan Smith who had failed to escape at Rockensuß made it this time. As the convoy drove off they were already in a cellar eating roast chicken with a Ukrainian girl. Others jumped over the tailgates of the lorries whilst the guards' attention was distracted. In all, nine escapees are named, no doubt there were more. Unlike earlier escapes, where the men made the way back to Britain relatively quickly, escapes at this stage of the march led to at least four men remaining and fighting with the Americans. Forbes's party served with 36th Armored Infantry. Lieutenant Terry Fairbairn, 2/1 Infantry Australian Imperial Force, who had escaped by hiding in a culvert like Edlmann and Corfield, spent several days as an interpreter with 3rd Armored, since he had a little more German than his American liberators. Fairbairn modestly described his German as 'Soldaten Deutsche'.

The lorries arrived at around 2030 hours. Thirty prisoners and two guards were put into each truck. The men had to sit on full cans of petrol for an hour in the dark before they left, which did not help their feeling of unease. Some men fainted: others were sick from the petrol fumes. 'Butch' Laing would later attribute an unpleasant ulcer to sitting for several hours on the uncomfortable lid of a can. They eventually left Dittincherode around 2200hrs. The lorries trundled down the lane to the main road and turned eastwards. After an hour they passed through Sangerhausen, still burning from air raids earlier that day. An hour later and 20 miles farther on, they arrived at Wimmelburg. It was gone midnight. Not everyone had travelled in the lorries. Lieutenant-Colonel Kennedy was in Celander's Opel along with three German officers, whilst Robert Lush went in the German ration truck. It was completely black, the night of a new moon. Heinrich Sultan and his usual advance party led the way, occasionally using a single flashlight. Ten miles an hour was perhaps an acceptable speed in the dark.

What did Brix think he had achieved? Given the speed of the Americans, the distance they had come would only postpone liberation by 24 hours, unless they moved again quickly. Lee Hill for one thought that the lorry move was only a preliminary to a train. From Wimmelburg to the railway station in Eisleben would take under an hour on foot, just a few minutes by lorry, but from the station where would they go? The railway lines south ran via Leipzig and were either already cut or were about to be cut by Patton's 3rd Army. The ones north were similarly threatened by the Americans and Russians. The other possibility was that Brix was aware that Eisleben was a hospital town and thought it would provide a safe haven. Eisleben was a town where the end of the war was likely to arrive quietly. However, the following day rumours of further travel to a railhead northeast of Eisleben spread amongst the prisoners. It is just as likely that Brix had no plan. The lorries had fortuitously given him a chance to move eastward quickly and he had taken it. Now he had to work out what to do next.

After the past fortnight it is nor surprising that the prisoners saw it as just another detour, a new way for Brix to prevent

Oflag IX A/Z's liberation. The prisoners' billet was another state farm and another smelly barn. The farm and much of the village lay in the shadow of slag heaps from a smelter that extracted copper and other minerals from rock mined a little farther north. The column had now left the Harz and was on the edge of the Mansfeld mining district. The area has some of the look of the slate mining districts of North Wales and Harry Roberts describes their being in a slate quarrying area. In fact, the heaps were of shale.

The men were led to the barn by the light of two torches. There were shouts of abuse and cat calls aimed at the guards. Tempers were frayed and the dark and confusion allowed the men to vent their anger on the Germans. Lee Hill records having a good sleep until 7 in the morning. Others were less lucky. 'Butch' Laing spent an hour deciding were to sleep and finished up with hardly any space where he could stretch out. Harry Roberts describes sharing his billet with rats, one of which ran over his face. Wimmelburg was on the western edge of Eisleben, the town where Luther had been born and where he had returned to die. The farm had been an estate and monastery in the Middle Ages. There was in 1945, and still is today, a small chapel dedicated to St. Cyriacus that had been built in the seventeenth century from the rubble of the monastery.

The farm was almost surrounded by the slag heaps from the Krughütte smelter. Today may of the heaps have gone from Wimmelburg and only some of the farm buildings remain, but they are still overlooked by a rather depressing heap of shale. In 1945 there was a muddle of buildings around several yards.

Brix had his own connections with Wimmelburg. Unknown to the prisoners, the family of one of his closest friends lived in the village. Horst Ehricht (senior) had served with Brix in 1914–18. He was now dead; his family believed killed whilst in hospital for his political views. The Brix-Ehrict connection was so strong that after 1945 Brix offered to marry Elizabeth and move her and the family from the Russian Zone. So in the early hours of 12 April, whilst the men were billeted in a barn at the farm, Brix was able to stay with the Ehricht family, at 30 Maschinenstraße.

Daylight on Thursday 12 April brought conflicting rumours about German plans for the day. Marcus Edwards thought that they were to travel onwards by train that night. Lee Hill also has them going by train, but he has more information, their destination is Hof in northern Bavaria, Later he writes that they are to travel by road north-east to Schwittersdorf, close to the Saale river. 'Butch' Laing also had the information about Schwittersdorf. He thought they would be travelling there the next day. There are no references to briefings from the SBOs or orders from the Germans. The destinations appear to have been based on rumour and supposition. Eventually breakfast comes and goes and the men are paroled to explore the farm. Any immediate move is off.

The atmosphere around Wimmelburg now relaxes. Apart from rather gleeful comments about the Germans not having any trains, there are no further references to being moved. Lee Hill learns that trains along the nearby line from Nordhausen to Halle via Eisleben stopped running four days before. The American fighters have been shooting up stationary wagons and locos in sidings along the line. As the day wears on, the men's diaries return to their favourite topic – food. Harry Roberts managed to concoct macaroni and cheese, with potatoes for lunch. From somewhere, he acquired baked scones for tea. Edward Baxter saw little fires springing up in the yards where men undertook, '…some interesting experiments in cooking. Oatmeal cakes appeared to be the favourite.'

Edward Baxter had noticed a conference between Colonels Clay and Kennedy, and the Germans, but neither he nor any of the other diarists record its outcome. He does comment though that despite the overall calm there was a 'general feeling that something was in the air'. Later in the morning the SBOs walk a few hundred yards to the post office in Wimmelburg and send telegrams to the Red Cross in Berlin and to the Swiss

A Wimmelburg farm yard, Friday 13 April. McIndoe's caption makes it clear that this was drawn on the day that they were liberated. The absence of Americans suggest that it was drawn before midday. The figure at the centre looks like a German officer, which would make him one of the guards that stayed with the prisoners, either Hauptmann Hoffmann or the Doctor, Stabsarzt Hehenkampf. (Otago Settlers' Museum, New Zealand)

George Forster: 'In the evening, about 5.30pm, I was trying to make some porridge in an old tin, on a small fire in the farmyard which I had started with a little brushwood. I was sharing rations with one of my flock, Captain Kennedy, an eye specialist. He had produced a small tin of oatmeal saved from Red Cross parcel days. He was standing over me, and had just said to me, "Do you call that stuff porridge?" – when shells screamed overhead from two directions.' The shelling, though close by, was to the west of the men. (Otago Settlers' Museum, New Zealand)

Government as the protecting power, reporting their position and objecting to the continued travelling. This is the first time that there is any hint of the SBOs communicating with the Red Cross or others beyond the column. The conference and the telegrams may in fact have been linked to a new influence on Brix. Eisleben would soon declare itself an Open Town.

The military and civilian leaders in Eisleben had decided that the town should be surrendered to the Americans. Eisleben was crammed with sick and wounded in improvised hospitals in restaurants and schools. It had always had extensive medical facilities that had been established in the first instance to support the mining industry, but these had been overwhelmed by the flood of more recent German casualties. Any fighting in the town would have been disastrous. A few days earlier Field-Marshal Kesselring had agreed that Göttingen could declare itself an Open City and surrender to the Americans without a fight. Now, despite being close to Festung Harz, Eisleben also wanted to avoid unnecessary bloodshed. On 12 April Oberst Seeger, the town commander, Herr Heinrich, the burgomaster, and Dr Hartung the senior medical officer agreed to surrender the town.

When Edward Baxter wrote his post-war account he included a 'rumour that Eisleben would be declared an open town.' This is the only reference. But if Baxter knew, then most certainly Oberstleutnant Brix knew too. Perhaps he had told Colonels Kennedy and Clay at their conference, hence their telegrams alerting the Red Cross to their location. For Brix, leaving Oflag IX A/Z to be liberated by the Americans, having been marooned in a town that has decided to surrender, gave him a satisfactory ending to the evacuation. His responsibilities both to his senior officers and to the prisoners would have been properly discharged.

West of the men the Americans had brushed aside attempts to defend Berga and Kelbra near Roßla. At Kelbra the local Party Leader barricaded himself into the Town Hall before being killed. After the shocking sights of Nordhausen the

Americans were in no mood to take prisoners. By midday on Thursday, 12 April the Americans had reached Sangerhausen 10 miles from Wimmelburg. The history of 3rd Armored published immediately after the end of the war suggests that they too had heard rumours that Eisleben would surrender without a fight. First the Americans and the civic leaders had to meet. Between the two sides were aircraft batteries either side of the main Sangerhausen–Eisleben road. The crews of these guns were either not aware of the surrender plan or had rejected the idea. In the late afternoon Combat Command B that was leading 3rd Armored along the road from Sangerhausen were surprised to come under fire. They called for artillery support.

Lee Hill and John McIndoe had made up their beds in the barn whilst there was still light and had then gone outside for a smoke and to discuss their project to publish a book that combined McIndoe's drawings and Hills photographs. Sadly, their project never came to fruition. Suddenly in the early evening there was the sight of a light aircraft to the south-west followed almost immediately by the noise of heavy shellfire. Some prisoners thought that the spotter plane was a glider and that Allied airborne troops were landing, but eventually it was recognised as a spotter aircraft for US artillery. The Reverend Forster and John Kennedy were preparing porridge for their evening meal when the shelling started. Forster thought that the shells were passing overhead in both directions. Their porridge was abandoned. The shells' target remained unclear to the prisoners. Hill thought that the Americans are shelling Eisleben. Others thought that the next village west, Wolferode, was the target.

In fact the Americans were responding to fire from the anti-aircraft batteries at Beyernaumburg and Blankenheim, five miles west of Wimmelburg along the road to Sangerhausen. The guns had originally been part of the outer anti-aircraft defences for Leipzig and Halle. They were the last defensive positions before the River Saale, Halle and the northern approaches to Leipzig. They had been camouflaged with straw bales and should have been supported by the Volksturm. But the Volksturm had melted away leaving the guns with no infantry support. The batteries themselves were manned by teenagers from the *Reicharbeitsdienst* (RAD) – German Labour Service. They were not regular troops. Nevertheless their opening shots took 3rd Armored by surprise. The American response was devastating. The Division's artillery was brought up and under the direction of spotter aircraft they fired airbursts that slaughtered the exposed gun crews. The Reicharbeitsdienst's resistance had delayed the Americans by a day at the cost of the lives of most of the young gun crews.

It is this shelling that Oflag IX A/Z could now hear. The prisoners were ordered to take shelter on the ground floor of their barn. But this meant sharing their quarters with a Friesian bull, who was neither happy with the shelling or with his new companions. At least one group of prisoners decided the bull was more dangerous than the shelling and moved into the farm house itself, which eventually became very crowded. The shelling must have also surprised Brix. Either the Americans had broken the agreement to allow access to Eisleben without a fight or the town's leaders had changed their mind. Brix decided that Oflag IX A/Z was no longer safe and that the column had to leave. He gave Clay 30 minutes to get the men together and be prepared to march.

But now, Lieutenant-Colonel Clay refuses to move. He has a very good argument against leaving. It is getting dark and there are retreating German troops on the main road outside the farm heading into Eisleben. Mixing the prisoners with these men might be an explosive combination. All Brix could do to persuade them was to argue that the countryside was filled with dangerous groups of stray SS, the Volkssturm, the Hitler Youth and other fanatics, which was exactly what the SBOs were also saying. The chopicess came down to staying and trying to lie low or leaving with the dubious protection of the guard. As a counter argument the SBOs offer the guard the protection of the prisoners and a good word when the Allies arrive.

Eventually Brix agrees to let the prisoners take their destiny into their own hands and withdraws the guards that wish to stay under his command. At 2000hrs the guards parade, Brix salutes the prisoners and then he and most of his men march eastwards. Heinrich Sultan, who opted to stay with the prisoners, remembered that they left to try to reach a fighting unit at Torgau on the Elbe. Torgau was 70 miles away. Today it is famous as the place where the Russian and American armies formally met. In April 1945 its significance was that it was the base camp for Stalag IV D. Brix was therefore taking the guard to a prisoner of war centre. As well as Sultan, around half a dozen others opted to stay with the prisoners. Lieutenant Gerald Frost, Royal Army Ordnance Corps and captured in Crete in 1941, listed the guard that stayed as 'the Doctor, his orderly, his sister, Frau Weygand, Hauptmann Hoffmannn, the Feldwebel Ruppert, Feldwebel Sultan, Censor Rauch.' Possibly Frau Weygand was the wife of the officer that Forster names as the Lageroffizier Weigand. The morale of the guard and Brix's control had by now eroded, the men were in effect deserting; although Stabsarzt Hehenkampf could argue his place as a medical officer was with the prisoners.

Edward Baxter was told that a guard had been seen trying to sell his rifle for 50 cigarettes to a New Zealander, but that the New Zealander was only prepared to offer 20. About an hour after the guard had left, one man returned on a bike. He asked for the prisoners' Adjutant, Major Burston, 2/3 Field Regiment Royal Australian Artillery. He handed over five Reichsmarks in fulfilment of a bet that Hauptmann Heyl, the Camp Security Officer, had made with him in 1944, about the eventual winners of the war. Heyl had lost his bet. Hauptmann Heyl was disliked by many of the prisoners and would eventually be transferred to the London Cage to face interrogation about alleged war crimes against the prisoners whilst they were at Rotenburg. But for Edward Baxter, Heyl had 'fulfilled a debt of honour'.

Not all the men were aware of the departure of the guard, presumably they had turned in earlier. The warren of yards and sleeping places at Wimmelburg gave some a rare chance of privacy. But for the rest the tempo of the evening picked up. Guard duties had to be arranged and procedures agreed that might offer some security against an incursion by German troops, especially any determined to carry out what Edward Baxter described as 'a jolly little holocaust of British POWs as a finale to their megalomaniac Führer'. The reality was that with no weapons there was nothing they could have done to prevent a massacre. Their best option was to lie low and not advertise their presence. But their presence was well known. The arrival of 400 Allied officers in a small village like Wimmelburg could not have failed to be noticed. Harold Schlanstedt, a 16-year-old living in Wimmelburg, remembered the arrival of the mysterious lorries and their load of prisoners on 12 April. For him it was a sign that the war was coming to an end. The village was home not only to inquisitive young people who had always provided Oflag IX A/Z with the best traders for the prisoners' luxury goods, there were also around 1000 foreign labourers at the copper smelter and the nearby mines. The prisoners might try to avoid being noticed by retreating German military units but there was nothing that they could do to stop the news spreading about their arrival and then the later news that the guard had abandoned them.

The first sign that their presence and status, free of German control, was more widely known was later that evening. Harry Roberts wrote in his wartime diary 'Commando came in'. In his post-war account he puzzles over this apparent reference to a British Army unit and presumes his memory had failed him and that they were not British Commandos but American Rangers. In fact they were neither. They were men from an arbeitskommando, British and Commonwealth NCOs and other ranks who had been working at the smelter. Lee Hill reckoned that there were 68 of them and that they marched in as a unit. The number of their kommando was not recorded but Lee noted that they were administered like the other kommandos in the area from Stalag IV D at Torgau. Over the next few days more former prisoners and forced labourers would arrive and swell the numbers at Wimmelburg to over 1000.

Oflag IX A/Z had now set itself on a war footing. Observation Posts were established around the perimeter of the farm and the men not on duty dispersed into their Company and Platoon groups, which were allocated new billets around the farm. Throughout the night there was the noise of shellfire. Lee Hill for one got very little sleep, with people knocking into him as they passed to and fro from the latrines or going on watch. The men spent an hour at a time on guard duty in the various OPs. Marcus Edwards' post was by a wall near the main road. From it he watched 'broken and weary German troops tramp past. Many old men.'

The prisoners gradually learned a little about the immediate military situation. Syme's wartime diary notes that the previous afternoon American reconnaissance units had been fired on and that since then the American main force had split into a northern and southern group and that they were attempting to link up and surround Eisleben. Syme's information would have come from local people and the new arrivals in the farm, the former prisoners and forced labourers. The prisoners also had access to a radio, which is how Marcus Edward's diary entry for 12 April closes with 'Shelling continued overhead. Roosevelt dead.'

Those prisoners who had turned in early the previous night woke to the surprise news that the guard had gone. Once again they could see American spotter aircraft, so the 'PW' signs were laid out. The morning was passed either on guard duty or in helping Robert Lush prepare a celebratory meal. At around midday the noise of machine guns and shell fire from the west became louder.

Harry Roberts and his party were not impressed by orders that they should not leave the farm. In the morning they slip out of a side entrance to do some freelance exploring. There are no German troops to be seen and so they settle down in a hollow beside the road to Wolferode. Here they doze until the sound of approaching tanks disturbs them. Not sure if it is retreating

German armour or advancing American, Roberts breaks cover and stands in the middle of the road as a tank rounds the corner. Though it is masked by trees it has the unmistakable outline of a Sherman. A second tank arrives and with machine guns trained on him he is recognised as British. The rest of Roberts' group join him and sitting on the tanks they return to the farm in style. The tank commander – Donald Malone from Burgettstown Pennsylvania – becomes the first of many Americans to sign prisoners' diaries.

The official observation posts were on the upper floors of the farm buildings and also in a small hut besides the main entrance to the farm off the main road. Lieutenant Nicolle, Commandos, was on duty there at midday. He had been given a large Union Jack painted onto a bed sheet, which he was under instructions to wave at the first sign of Allied troops. Nicolle had been captured in 1940. He had not seen any of the modern Allied armour. His instructions though are straightforward: Allied tanks have white stars. Unfortunately the tanks that passed Nicolle had no stars, but then he recognised that amongst the infantry riding on them are some black faces. They must be American. The flag is waved. Nicolle, like Roberts a few moments earlier, is met by surprised Americans.

Initially there is euphoria. Lee Hill's diary entry suddenly breaks off from a record of the members of the Guard who had opted to stay with them into: 'They're here. General Boudinot. They are going past by the dozen, by the hundred. Everything. The excitement is tremendous. Col. Clay – 49th birthday – Fri 13th Stews up, but who cares!' Captain Frederick Müller MC, New Zealand Expeditionary Force, used his YMCA diary for the first time on his liberation. He concludes the short entry for Friday 13 April, 'First sight of tanks broke me up, nearly cried.' Finding words to describe their emotions, when their military training had been to write short factual reports, was understandable difficult. Lee Hill captured the incredible excitement in the blurred image of a jeep and excited prisoners pushing to shake hands with two American soldiers. John McIndoe managed a small sketch of Brigadier-General Truman Boudinot, the commander of 3rd Armored's Combat Command B. Lieutenant Gerald Frost, RAOC, wrote that 'Grown men cried like children – my first thoughts were of home.'

The joy was mutual. John Irwin described how the welcome that the Americans got from the POWs 'gave us all a much needed lift' after the experience of Nordhausen. The kriegies were not only free, their isolation from the rest of the world was over. In the camps, the arrival of new prisoners had always been a welcome relief; the Americans were not just new people, but people from the land of Hollywood and plenty. Some of the prisoners' diaries have names and addresses scattered over the final pages, towns in Virginia, New Jersey and Pennsylvania, sometimes written in different handwriting. Lee Hill added a note to one that he must write to 'Mrs Southall about her hubby'. Hubby

Wimmelburg 13 April
A Sherman tank from the US 3rd Armored stopped in front of a house displaying a white flag, Wimmelburg, 13 April. The absence of other spectators suggests that this is shortly after the Americans liberated Oflag IX A/Z, on the other hand the two former prisoners frame the shot beautifully and were perhaps positioned by Lee Hill, especially since the tank is facing west. (Green Collection)

US Army jeep at Wimmelburg, 13 April 1945. Lee Hill captures more vividly than any words the almost unbearable excitement of liberation, as the vehicle is surrounded by men all wanting to shake hands with two of their liberators, confirmation that they are free. The picture must have been taken just after the first tanks from 3rd Armored had appeared on the road outside the farm. (Marion Gerritsen-Teunissen Collection)

A Sherman tank with its attendant infantry from the US 3rd Armored Division, the liberators of Oflag IX A/Z, being thanked by a group of former prisoners. (Green Collection)

was Leslie Southall living at Swift Creek, New Jersey. Their liberators have two immediate and standard responses. How could they have been prisoners for so long? And have some cigarettes and 'K' Rations. Suddenly the men's diet was transformed. No more reliance on bartering soap for onions or potatoes, suddenly there was instant coffee, sweets and chewing gum. And the promise of more to come.

The Americans had been warned to expect a prison camp on the outskirts of Eisleben but after their experience at Nordhausen they were expecting yet more horrors. 'Unlike the prisoners at Nordhausen, these men looked human and reasonably healthy,' was how John Irwin, 6th Armored, described Oflag IX A/Z in his post-war account. 'They wandered among our tanks and shook our hands, graciously accepting our cigarettes and generally looking us over as though we were divinities from another planet.' The prisoners certainly did find the Americans' equipment and uniforms strange. Edward Baxter described the first American to arrive in the yard. 'His helmet, clothes and equipment seemed strange to us, and he was quickly surrounded by an excited crowd of kriegies.' Men like 'Butch' Laing who had been captured in Norway at the start of the war had been trained to fight First World War battles with almost identical equipment. He had been a prisoner for almost two years before America came into the war. The career soldiers were acutely aware of how out-of-date their knowledge was. They had interrogated the Arnhem captives for information about current technologies and tactics, but now they could see it for the first time. There was general amazement about the quantity of equipment that 3rd Armored had at its disposal.

Gerald Frost heard the first American officer into the yard say, 'I've just looked in to greet you boys.' Frost found this southern comment rather 'quaint'. Given the American worries that they would encounter another Nordhausen, the understated remark carries an understandable relief at what the Americans had found.

In a gesture of defiance to their former captors, some prisoners demanded that their liberation be formally recognised by the Americans writing 'Cancelled' on their German POW identify cards. They were now no longer *Kriegsgefangene*. Their guards were now Prisoners of War. Of those who had stayed with them at Wimmelburg, Heinrich Sultan was singled out for praise by the British. His American captors were less inclined to treat him differently from any other German after having seen Nordhausen. Edward Baxter learned of concentration camps from the Americans who had come for Sultan. 'So far as I know none of us had any suspicion of these places until we were freed. German military prisons were said to be very strict, as most military prisons are, but of these civilian hells we knew nothing. Personally I believe the majority of German soldiers and

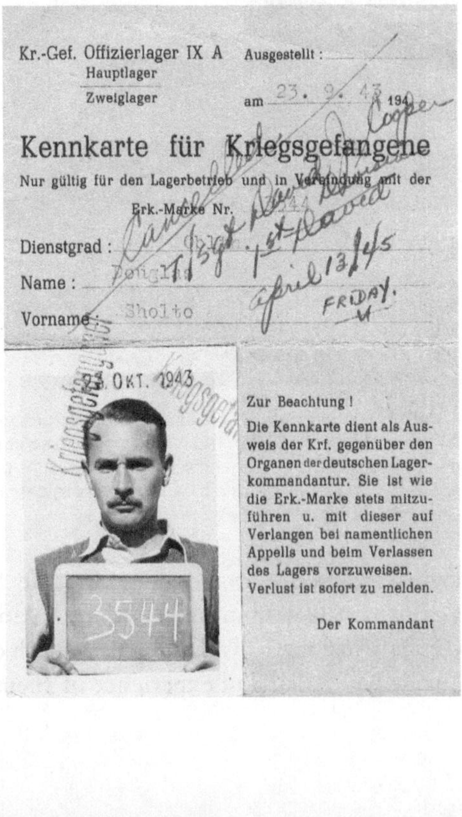
Kr.-Gef. Offizierlager IX A Ausgestellt:
Hauptlager
Zweiglager am 23. 9. 43 194

Kennkarte für Kriegsgefangene

Nur gültig für den Lagerbetrieb und in Verbindung mit der Erk.-Marke Nr. 3544

Dienstgrad:

Name: Douglas

Vorname: Sholto

Cancelled T/Sgt David Cooper

April 13/45

FRIDAY.

23. OKT. 1943

3544

Zur Beachtung!

Die Kennkarte dient als Ausweis der Krf. gegenüber den Organen der deutschen Lagerkommandantur. Sie ist wie die Erk.-Marke stets mitzuführen u. mit dieser auf Verlangen bei namentlichen Appells und beim Verlassen des Lagers vorzuweisen. Verlust ist sofort zu melden.

Der Kommandant

Lieutenant Sholto Douglas's POW card issued on 23 September 1943, the date that Sholto arrived at Rotenburg, and cancelled by Temporary Sergeant David Cooper, 3rd Armored Division, on Friday 13 April 1945. (Douglas Family)

A Sherman armed with a 105mm howitzer from US 3rd Armored. The civilian spectators suggest that this picture was taken during the afternoon and not at the time of liberation. (Marion Gerritsen-Teunissen Collection)

A mixed group of German civilians and former prisoners watch a bridging pontoon pass on its trailer. The men were amazed at the amount of equipment travelling behind the tanks of US 3rd Armored. Harry Roberts noted that the initial column took four hours to pass the farm at Wimmelburg. (Marion Gerritsen-Teunissen Collection)

civilians were equally ignorant. Certainly Sultan and the other Germans at Rotenburg had nothing to do with them.' Sultan certainly had not had anything to do with operating the camps, but he had first-hand experience of them. When the SS had taken 68 Polish priests from Rotenburg to Dachau in 1940, the SS officer in charge of the transport had made it clear that this was not a simple transfer of POWs.

The column of vehicles behind the leading tanks took four hours to pass through Wimmelburg. Eisleben only a mile or so down the road would surrender shortly afterwards. The German radio bulletin was for once accurate and up-to-date, when on 13 April it announced that the Americans had reached Eisleben and Jena. The city's representatives had met the Americans under a white flag between Eisleben and Wimmelburg. It cannot have been an easy meeting; after the horrors of Nordhausen, the Americans often shot first and asked questions later. Detailed information about the end of the war in Eisleben is scarce. From July 1945 the area became part of the Russian Zone. Under the communists, the history of the end of the war emphasised the achievements of the Red Army and is silent on the details of the American liberation.

As the news spread of the arrival of the Americans, other victims of Nazi Germany began to trickle into the camp. Marcus Edwards described them as including 'men in concentration camp pyjamas'. Two former concentration camp prisoners were photographed by Lee Hill at the rear of the chapel. It was a rather more quiet setting than the yard where someone had fixed up loudspeakers and dance music was playing. The two prisoners were originally from Buchenwald. From the numbers on their jackets it is possible to trace their camp records. Both were political prisoners who had been working in one of the SS factories on the southern edge of the Harz. Johann Groothuis, prisoner number 92625, had been a wood turner before being imprisoned on 20 December 1944. Martin Haug, prisoner number 8814, had been imprisoned on 5 February 1944. His prison records give his occupation as a 'buyer'. He was 35 when Lee took his photograph; Groothuis was 46. They and other former forced labourers joined the Polish farmworkers who had been working on the farm before Oflag IX A/Z arrived.

The new arrivals found a carnival atmosphere with music and radio broadcasts blaring over the yards. The first day was spent in joyful celebration and cheering the American vehicles passing along the road into Eisleben. Harry Roberts: 'What a day! Can't remember much of what happened except that we stood and waved.' In the evening there was a service of thanksgiving in the little chapel, with well-loved hymns. Reg Westcott remembered them singing 'The Magnificat', 'God Our Help in Ages Past' and 'Jesus shall Reign', which contains the line, 'The prisoner leaps to loose his chains.' A Polish farmworker too weak to sit was brought into the chapel on a stretcher. Men broke down in the highly charged atmosphere. Others just sat quietly as the chapel emptied and reflected on their good fortune. They had survived, and now they were free.

Wine was found in the farm and there were sore heads the next morning. After years, when the only alcohol was a rare chance to buy weak camp beer from the Germans, the wine was strong stuff. A Maori officer who had got hold of a guitar

Wimmelburg after liberation. In the foreground a group of smiling orderlies sit on the farm wall. Behind them are parked one of Dörr's carts and a large US lorry. The visible buildings have now been demolished. (Marion Gerritsen-Teunissen Collection)

Lee Hill photographed these two concentration camp prisoners in a quiet corner of the farm in the shadow of the chapel. Johann Groothuis (left) prisoner number 92625 was living in Emden and working as a wood turner before being imprisoned on 20 December 1944. He was married with two children and was 46 when the picture was taken. Johan had served in the 73 Hanover Infantry Regiment in the First World War. Martin Haug (right) prisoner number 8814 was imprisoned on 5 February 1944. His prison records give his occupation as a 'merchant' and notes that he had 'no criminal record'. He was 35 when Lee took his photograph. The grounds for their detentions are given as political on their camp records. (Green Collection)

sat with Lee and others around an American tank singing and drinking. But others had guard duty. Edward Baxter spent the early hours of the next morning in one of the American tanks. After instructions on the use of the .50 calibre machine gun, the crew adjourned to a nearby house to get some rest. Baxter describes the few hours spent in the tank as his only combat duty in North West Europe.

Lieutenant-Colonel Clay imposed a curfew and ordered the men to stay close to the farm for their own safety. The curfew also extended to the Polish farmworkers who were now under the command of Oflag IX A/Z's Polish officers. Friday had been a day of improvised celebration: Saturday brought the chance to explore beyond Wimmelburg. The Krughütte smelter had baths that the men could use as they tried to get rid of the effects of two weeks on the road. The baths were very close to Eisleben and it became impossible to prevent the men going into the town centre only a mile further on. It was only natural that after being given their freedom that they were not happy to be confined to the farm and the bath house. And so men slipped into Eisleben to enjoy their freedom and have a beer. One group somehow found a collection of Nazi ceremonial swords as souvenirs. The description of the men's trips into Eisleben, some by US jeep, have the tone of naughty children disregarding the instructions of their teacher, in this case the SBOs. Eisleben town centre was now full of American vehicles and would for a month or so be under US Military Government, before the Allies implemented the Potsdam agreement and the boundary of the American zone moved west to the Werra, leaving Thuringia and Saxony to the Russians.

The men's main concern was when they would be going home. Some worried about retrieving their belongings from the store room at Rotenburg. Both of these questions could not be answered immediately by their liberators, but from Saturday onwards plans for their future began to be decided. They would be flown home, possibly via Belgium. For that to happen the immediate area had to be secured and the infrastructure put in place to cope both with the needs of the fighting troops close to the Elbe and the repatriation of all the prisoners in the area, not simply Oflag IX A/Z. This would take two or three days.

As for their possessions at Rotenburg, Lieutenant-Colonel Kennedy believed that they would not see them again. In the meantime the men had to prepare to travel once more. This time there would be no carts. The men would be limited to 25 kilos each. But they could expect to be in the UK in 48 hours from the time they left Germany. The itinerary given to Lieutenant Frost on Sunday evening for the next day was Breakfast 0600hrs – Lorries 0800hrs to aerodrome – Planes 1000hrs – Lunch Paris – London during the evening. Parts of the plan would prove to be correct. The prisoners continued to provide sentries for its own security and by now they were armed with American rifles, however the threat from rogue German units failed to materialise.

Whilst the men of Oflag IX A/Z were enjoying their freedom, it is sobering to note that Arbeitskommando 1249, which had also left its camp on 29 March and had followed the two Oflags towards Mühlhausen, was still on the road. On 13 April they had the fourth of their rest days at Muntscha in southern Thuringia. Unlike Oflag IX A/Z, their guard continued to move them onwards, on one day travelling at the rear of a column of concentration camp prisoners, They would continue to walk south for another 10 days, before being liberated on 22 April. Kommando 1249 were very unlucky. Another party from Stalag IX C that had started out from the east of Mühlhausen on 2 April reached its parent camp at Bad Sulza and was liberated by the Americans on 11 April.

North of Wimmelburg Arbeitskommando 105 was not marched away as the Americans approached. It was working in a copper mine near Hohenthalschacht. The story of the

A group of former prisoners, some obviously New Zealanders from their hats, on the steps of the now demolished Gasthof in Wimmelburg on 14 or 15 April. The children are obviously intrigued by the situation and overall are pleased to see their visitors. (Green Collection)

This group of celebrating orderlies are probably inside the Gasthof near the post office in Wimmelburg; it was the nearest bar to the farm. The woman is more likely to be a former Polish forced labourer rather than a German. (Marion Gerritsen-Teunissen Collection)

The Union Flag had been painted before the men left Rotenburg. Initially it had been given to Lieutenant Nicolle to wave before Allied troops, but once the column had been liberated it was displayed from a linden tree outside the farm. The German children may have been prepared to be photographed under the British flag but in fact they were not pleased by it hanging from a German tree. They pulled it down overnight, then worried that they might be thought of as members of the 'Werewolves', the Nazi resistance movement. (Marion Gerritsen-Teunissen Collection)

kommando was recorded in detail by Private Frederick Daniels, Queen's Royal Regiment. The kommando mined the copper ore that was smelted at the Krughütte. Daniels had been an insurance clerk in Rochester before the war. Captured in North Africa in 1942 he had been sent to the kommando in 1943. Daniels, who was 33, seems to have coped surprisingly well with the change from clerk to miner. His unpublished manuscript 'Round Trip' describes the hard and dangerous work, the Miners' Galas, and the literary competitions that they somehow fitted into their six days of labour each week. The Americans had also reached them on Friday 13 April.

Next to the British kommando at Hohenthalschacht was a compound holding Russian prisoners who were also employed at the mines. With their guards gone the Russians set out to loot the surrounding area and take revenge on anyone who had mistreated them. In contrast to Wimmelburg the situation around Helbra was chaotic: cows are stolen and slaughtered by the Russians; the local bakery broken into and its stock liberated; tobacco and wine looted; and a German who had mistreated the Russians is murdered. The British in contrast had retained more of their discipline. The camp Medical Officer Captain Macmillan assumed command. On the Saturday the kommando also got their travel orders. They were to march to Wimmelburg to join Oflag IX A/Z. The kommando's orders included the creation of passenger lists for the American planes. Frederick Daniels has the task of typing six copies of lists of 25 men's names with their regiments and army numbers. These were to be the passenger lists both in the lorries and aircraft. Checking the lists proved difficult since despite Captain Macmillan assuming command, some men had decided not to wait for processing by the military bureaucracy and they had already set off westwards hitching lifts on US vehicles.

At Wimmelburg the number of former British and Commonwealth prisoners had grown. Oflag IX A/Z had been joined by at least two kommandos. Although Lee Hill in the

Eisleben Market Square; Lee Hill and Cyril Butterfield hitched a lift on a US jeep into the town in the hope of finding some souvenirs. The watching crowd are in the best clothes – respect for the Americans or celebration of the war's end? Martin Luther was born here and his statue still dominates the market place. (Green Collection)

The statue of Martin Luther still stands in the square at Eisleben, though now it overlooks the market. (Peter Green)

American vehicles continued to pass through Wimmelburg and Eisleben in large numbers for several day after the arrival of the 3rd Armored Division, as this photograph of Eisleben taken by Lee Hill no earlier than 14 April shows. The lorry with its 40mm Bofors anti-aircraft gun is travelling east, whilst the vehicles outside the Rathaus appear to be parked. (Marion Gerritsen-Teunissen Collection)

article in *Illustrated* magazine claimed that there were 1400, it was more likely that the group of British and Commonwealth men was smaller. Peter Brush heard Brigadier-General Truman Boudinott, Combat Command B, reporting over the radio that they had recovered '480 of them – 450 with pips and 30 without.' But this sounds like the nominal roll of the camp when it left Rotenburg. Lee Hill's diary recorded the same man as reporting '360 with pips'. Given the reduction of the column through escapees and those left behind unable to continue to walk, the strength of Oflag IX A/Z would have been around 400, which, with the two kommandos joining the camp, gives a total of around 500.

Frederick Daniel and his comrades left the mine at 0700hrs on the Monday morning to march through Eisleben to Wimmelburg. Although the kommando had compiled passenger lists for each plane, they failed to arrive. Corporal Baker,

Wimmelburg, Monday 16 April. No evidence of any guards and the yard filled with men ready to travel means that this is a picture of the prisoners waiting for the lorries to take them to Esperstedt. (Green Collection)

A GMC AFKWX tractor and trailer carrying the former prisoners from Wimmelburg to Esperstedt airfield. Not the most comfortable form of transport but given the high spirits of the men not something that bothered them, since none of their diaries refer to standing in open vehicles. (Marion Gerritsen-Teunissen Collection)

who had the lists, had become involved in a row with American Military Police over whether he was allowed to sit on the front wing of the lorry. He arrived at the airstrip after the rest had left. The lists were in any case superfluous. None of the Oflag IZ A/Z accounts refer to any kind of plane lists. For them the relative anarchy of the flight is what registered most about their departure.

Their destination was a former Luftwaffe airfield 20 miles away, near to Bad Frankenhausen. The grass airstrip was littered with the burned-out wrecks of German aircraft. Until the end of March 1945 the airfield had been the home of *Ergänzungs-Jagdgeschwader* 2, a training unit converting pilots to the Me 262 jet fighter. After a journey in open lorries back through Sangerhausen to Eichstedt, the men were surprised to find that the USAAF did not stand on ceremony getting them on board. Edward Baxter remembered 'no red tape, blue forms, green documents'. '"Cargo out – POWs in – Go", was their motto.' Peter Brush did not approve: as soon as the Dakotas had unloaded the petrol they were carrying the men were packed in. 'There seemed to be no particular orders about anything – everybody was very lighthearted, everybody smoked. The Dakotas absolutely stank of petrol, but fortunately, none caught fire.'

The Dakotas were supplying the 3rd Armored with petrol and lubricants. Flying was a new experience for most of the older men, but like Edward Baxter they knew that flying could be very cold. So they put on lots of clothes, but at the height they flew back the planes were in fact warm. The warmth and the petrol fumes made the aircraft stuffy and unpleasant. Peter Brush was one of several who was sick as the planes hedge-hopped back across Germany. The low flying was to avoid Luftwaffe aircraft that were still active. In the previous week a group of Dakotas from 98th Squadron had been attacked and one aircraft forced down on fire at Wenigenlupnitz south of Mühlhausen. A week before that, on 8 April, two planes of the 97th had been strafed whilst on the ground and both destroyed.

Douglas Dakotas from the 97th Squadron USAAF 440 Troop Carrier Group wait to take the former prisoners to Liège. The aircraft had brought in petrol and lubricating oil for the US 3rd Armored Division. (Green Collection)

The airfield at Esperstedt is now a flooded sand and gravel pit. (Peter Green)

The former prisoners queue to board a Dakota of the US 97th Squadron. The men all remarked about the lack of official procedures in getting them onto the aircraft. The planes stank of petrol, but even so many of the men smoked during the flight to Belgium. Others felt sick. (Green Collection)

From their low altitude the prisoners had wonderful views of the German countryside in spring, with swathes of white blossom. Rotenburg was on their route to Liège and some of the men spotted their previous home by the Fulda as they flew westwards. They were in the air for about an hour, before they landed at Ans on the northwest edge of Liège.

They were not expected by the ground staff. The British authorities were expecting them in Paris or Namur. Even so, the Americans at Ans gave them a tremendous reception. The formal RAF evacuation of former POWs, Operation *Exodus,* did not get underway for another week. The Wimmelburg men were guinea pigs. They were fortunate that the RAF only mislaid them for one day. Many Australians and New Zealanders had bad memories of the RAF from the Mediterranean. Lee Hill recorded one as saying, 'We waited for the RAF in Greece and Crete and we're waiting for the bastards now.' For the time being they enjoyed American coffee and doughnuts. Eventually at 0100 hours it was decided that they would stay at Ans overnight. The American ground staff gave up their tents to the former prisoners. The next day, 17 April, they were moved by lorry and train to Brussels and joined the formal repatriation programme of recovered Allied military prisoners.

For Lee Hill his brief time in Brussels went 'like a blur'. Most crammed sightseeing and shopping into their 24-hour leave, but only after they had been deloused. George Forster thought it was 'Keatings Powder', a well-known insecticide before he was captured, but it was the new discovery, DDT, that the men were dusted with to kill lice. For Harry Roberts the chance to eat white bread was worth noting. His entry for 17 April has, 'Ice cream etc. Delousing + intelligence'. Presumably the 'intelligence' referred to a debriefing. All the men were given a Brussels leave leaflet that had their hostel and bed details as well as the location of bars, restaurants, theatres and cinemas. It included the information that all brothels were strictly out of bounds to service personnel, as was smoking in the cinema or buying food from civilian shops.

It was in Brussels that most men completed the 'General Questionnaire for British/American Ex-Prisoners of war'. Although most are dated 17 April, when they were in Brussels, others have later dates. Form filling was evidently not completely regimented and some men managed to avoid military matters for a few hours in the relatively undamaged surroundings of a major European city. 'Butch' Laing describes having a short walk in the city, before being taken by British Army lorry the next morning to Melsbroek airfield outside Brussels. They were flown home by aircraft from RAF 38 and 46 Groups. Lee Hill photographed the converted Stirling bombers of 570 Squadron. Like the American 97th Squadron that had flown them from Germany, 570 Squadron, along with others from 38 and 46 Group, had taken part in Operation *Market Garden* just over six months before.

Whilst the flights home were uneventful for most, Lieutenant Symes's recorded in his diary that he was in a Handley Page Hampden that crashed from 30 feet. It is an odd reference:

All returning former prisoners were required to complete a three-page questionnaire describing their experience of capture and captivity. Lieutenant 'Butch' Laing is fourth from the left in the queue at the rear, but it is a mystery why his epaulets have the two pips of a Captain. (Green Collection)

Hampdens had gone out of service in 1943. There were Handley Page Halifax's employed on bringing former POWs home, but given that Symes wrote of the undercarriage coming through the floor of the aircraft it seems that he was a passenger in one of the last of the pre-war Handley Page Harrows, which were still in use by 271 Squadron to evacuate stretcher cases. 'Butch' Laing also had a crash to contend with. The aircraft he was in – he calls it a converted bomber – hit something on take off. They were hurriedly evacuated, given a tot of whiskey and bundled onto another plane. On top of this scare, the ulcer that he had developed from sitting on the petrol cans in the German lorries that had moved them to Wimmelburg was again causing him pain.

Peter Brush: 'We came within sight of the Cliffs of Dover, an unforgettable sight after five years, to have seen them so near and yet so far in 1940, and never imagined that you would see them again, they suddenly hoved in sight, and the whole cabin broke into a cheer.' Laing's aircraft took them back over London. They were low enough to see St Pauls surrounded by bomb damage.

Page 5.

☐ *Map Key*—in red on map *Map Ref.*

CLUBS and CANTEENS

Officers' Clubs.

1. Allied Officers' Club (E.F.I.), 82-84, Rue d'Arlon ... E.3
2. British Officers' Club (E.F.I.), Boul. Ad. Max ... D.6
3. Atlanta Hotel, Palm Room (Cdn. Army), Boul. Ad. Max ... E.6
4. English Tea Room (C.W.L.), « St. George's », Boul. Ad. Max ... D.6
5. R.A.F. Officers' Club, Hotel Gallia (R.A.F. *only*), Avenue des Arts ... E.3
6. The Rendez-vous (Cdn Army), Rue de la Science ... E.3

All Ranks.

7. The Marlborough (E.F.I.), Boul. Ad. Max ... D.6

W. Os. and Sergeant's Club.

8. The Vauxhall (E.F.I.), Behind Theatre Royal du Parc ... E.4

Other Ranks.

9. Montgomery Club (E.F.I.), Palais d'Egmont, Rue aux Laines ... G.4
10. Café Blighty (E.F.I.), Boul. du Jardin Botanique ... D.5
11. Club for Allied Soldiers (Belg. Red Cross), Rue des Princes ... E.5
12. Red Shield Club (S.A.), 28, Quai aux Pierres-de-Taillel (15 tram) ... D.6
13. Toc H, 28-30, Boul. de Waterloo ... G.4
14. Methodist Club, Rue du Champ de Mars, Porte de Namur ... G.3
15. Café Ancien Scheers (Church Army), Place Ch. Rogier ... D.5
16. Canada Club (Cdn. Army), 32-33, Boul. du Régent ... E.4
17. Station Canteen, Gare du Nord (Belg. Red Cross) ... C.5
18. Station Canteen, Gare du Midi (Belg. Red Cross) ... H.6
19. Malcolm Club (R.A.F. *only*)), Rue Leopald ... E.5
20. Services Club (J.H.C.), 33, Rue de la Caserne ... G.6
21. Albert Canteen (Y.M.C.A.), Place Ch. Rogier ... D.5
22. Canteen Club for H.M. Forces, 11, Rue Brialmont (C.W.L.) ... C.4
23. The Corner House (S.A.), Boul. Ad. Max ... D.6
24. Grand Scheers (C.A.), Boul. Ad. Max ... D.6

A.E.F. Club.

25. Hotel Metropole, Boul. Ad. Max ... E.6

Womens' Services (Officers and O.R.s).

26. Y.W.C.A., 20, Avenue des Arts ... E.3
27. Y.W.C.A., 6, Rue du Buisson (off Rue de la Vallee) ... H.3
28. Belg. Y.W.C.A. and Girl Guides Club, 126, Avenue Louise... H.4

SHOPS

Welfare Gift Shop, 45, Boul. Bischoffsheim ... D.4
Officers' Shop (Ordnance), Rue Neuve ... D.3

STUDY CENTRES

1. Army Study Centre, 103, Rue de la Loi ... E.3
2. Y.M.C.A. Study Centre, Rue Neuve (Nr. Pl. Rogier) ... D.5

CHURCHES

1. Church of England, Rue Capitaine Crespel ... G.4
2. Methodist, Rue du Champ de Mars ... G.3
3. Church of Scotland, Rue Buckholtz (off Avenue Louise) ... H.3
4. Roman Catholic (At. C.W.L. Canteen), 11, Rue Brialmont ... H.4
5. Salvation Army, Rue Duquesnoy ... A.5
6. Christian Science, Place du Chatelain ... F.5
7. Hebrew, Rue de la Regence ... G.5

BATHS—

1. St Sauveur, Rue Montagne-aux-Herbes Potagères ... E.5
2. Bain Royal, Rue de l'Enseignement ... D.4
3. Bain du Centre, Boul. Anspach ... E.6
4. Blue Pool (Cdn. Army), 27, Rue St François (Valet Service) ... C.5
5. Military Bath House, 32, Boul. d'Anvers ... D.6

SSAFA (Soldiers' Sailors' and Airmen's Families Association). Office : 22 Boulevard Maurice Lemonnier. Men and women of the British Forces may consult SSAFA on family problems G.6

MONTGOMERY CLUB.

Palais d'Egmont, rue aux Laines. — Map Ref. G.4.

350 Rooms, Facilities include Restaurant, Tea Lounges, Cafeteria, Beer and Wine Tavern, Games, Music, Shop, Valet Services, Ladies' and Gents' Hairdressing and Baths, Photographic Studio, Library, Writing and News Rooms.
Trams: From Gare du Nord 1, 3, 7, 10, 11, 14, 15
From Jardin Botanique 8.

One page of the leaflet issued to returning prisoners. On the front cover it had the name of hostel to which the man had been allocated. The rest of the leaflet included a map of Brussels, places of interest and a list of dos and don'ts that included the instruction that brothels were out of bounds. (Green Collection)

Stirlings at Melsbroek airfield. Although their squadron codes are not visible these aircraft would have been from the RAF's 38 Group. The Group had delivered British airborne troops from 1943. At the end of the war they took part in Operation *Exodus* carrying returning prisoners to the UK. However at this date *Exodus* had not formally started. (Green Collection)

The planes took them to a hero's welcome at RAF Westcott. Edward Baxter described a vast hangar where 'a beauty chorus of pretty W.A.A.F. girls fed us sumptuously on tea, sandwiches, buns, cakes, biscuits, etc.' And for those whose families had telephones there was the sudden realisation that they could talk to their wives and families for the first time in many years. Peter Brush was perhaps the most fortunate. His wife had a car and enough petrol to drive from Gloucestershire to collect him and drive him home in the moonlight. Laing's bad luck pursued him to the end. He was able to ring his parents from Westcott, but then had to meet them in hospital. His ulcer that he had first noticed at Dittichenrode would finally receive attention.

8

AFTERWARDS

I was met by my sister at Newcastle Central Station and taken by car to my mother's home in Byker. After greeting me my sister exclaimed, 'Where on earth have you picked up that accent?

Reverend George Forster, Royal Army Chaplains' Department, captured Tobruk, 1942.

Information about the former prisoners, their guards and their liberators after April 1945 is sparse. Of the 1000 prisoners and guards who walked eastwards in March 1945, less than 50 left any kind of record of their experiences. The situation becomes even worse once the camps were liberated. Men who played a major role in the camps' stories, for example Colonel Holland, SBO Oflag IX A/H, are today remembered for earlier military activities – in his case the defence of Calais. Even so, enough men have left accounts of this period to sketch a little of the impact of captivity on the former 'kriegies'.

Many of the longer-term prisoners, George Forster included, were concerned that their time in camps had changed them. The men's existence had been so closely regulated and the opportunities for new relationships limited for so long that they worried that they would not be able to fit back into civilian life. Many of the cartoons in Ted Beckwith's *Quill* are on this theme: post-war British homes with prison camp bunks in bedrooms; children not recognising their fathers; and men continuing to scavenge for food or tools whilst surrounded with relative plenty. For some men, the change created far more serious problems.

Captain John Le Mesurier was 35 when he was liberated. He had worked at a racing stables before the war in the Channel Islands, but now he found it impossible to settle at his home on Guernsey. His first post-war job was with the Transjordan Frontier Force, where his love of horses was fulfilled in a mounted cavalry unit. When it was disbanded in 1948 he returned to Guernsey and tried his hand at growing tomatoes, before returning again to the Middle East as a Locust Control Officer in Yemen. There followed a period when he became embroiled with drug smugglers in the Arabian Gulf. He followed this with a time teaching at a Preparatory School in Surrey before leaving again for the Middle East and a post with the Sultan of Muscat and Oman's army. Finally, in 1957 he took a job teaching Latin and Mathematics at a school in Guernsey and against all local expectations stayed for 28 years. His pupils thought him a kindly eccentric. Perhaps his love of riding and of animals, the environment and above all wide open spaces, had been inhibited to such an extent by captivity that he had to cram a normal life time's experience into 12 years.

Captain Corrie Halliday, also Tank Corps but at heart another cavalryman, had been liberated at Wimmelburg. In an interview for the Imperial War Museum he described his mental state at the end of the war as 'dreadful'. He rejoined his old regiment, the 11th Hussars in Berlin, after trying to return to the war in the Far East with the SAS. He found policing drunken Russian soldiers and the other activities of the regiment's peacetime routine pointless. He was then posted to an almost non-existent unit in the countryside outside Lanark, where he went for long walks trying to work why he, and so few of his friends, had survived the war. He contemplated suicide. Eventually after further army postings he emigrated to New Zealand. He tried sheep farming and then dairy farming before joining the New Zealand Army. He married in New Zealand, but returned to the UK, where he sold insurance and had other brief jobs. He believed that he never fully overcame the effect of the war.

Captivity does not seem to have affected the post-war lives of the career soldiers so much. Major Peter Brush, the prisoners' security officer at Rotenburg, was another horse lover. Whilst at Rotenburg he had written the text of a book about breeding and training horses, but as he got into the Dakota at Esperstedt he realized that he had left the text at Wimmelburg. Thanks to an American transport officer the manuscript was found and returned to him three weeks late in the UK. 'The Hunter-Chaser: An Authoritative Guide to Breeding, Making and Training' was published by Hutchinson in 1947. It was his love of horses that led to a reunion with a man who had escaped from one of the lorries at Dittincherode. Captain Carol Ramsden had waved as he jumped off the tail board of a lorry. Ten years later they bumped in to each other at the Balmoral Show.

Brush retired as Lieutenant-Colonel having commanded 8 Rifle Brigade. The regular soldiers had their own concerns about blighted careers. As prisoners they were concerned that their knowledge and skills were becoming out-dated whilst in the camps. They went into captivity from a world of officers in puttees and Boys anti-tank rifles and emerged to airborne troops and blanket bombing. Ernest Edlmann's career recovered and he went on to become Colonel of his regiment. He served in Aden in the late 1950s. He followed this with stints in army administration. He was still very much the Colonel when, over 90 years old, he was interviewed for this book. The two senior British Officers at Rotenburg also continued to serve. Lieutenant-Colonel Kennedy commanded a training centre at Kingston before retiring in 1948. On completing his military service, Lieutenant-Colonel Clay emigrated to the USA.

The men most affected by their imprisonment were those captured early in the war. They had to face the twin pressures of an indefinite spell in captivity as Britain lurched from one disaster to another and then three or four years of actual captivity. The Arnhem captives arrived in the camps knowing that the war could not last much longer. They were incarcerated for only six months and appeared unaffected by their experiences. Although there were exceptions, for example 'Butch' Laing and the SBOs in 1945, the men captured in France, Greece and North Africa fared far worst.

The immediate post-war period saw several books published by returning prisoners from the two camps. Ted Beckwith's omnibus edition of the *Quill* combined creative writing and artwork produced in the camps. Beckwith continued to combine writing poetry with senior management at Wills Tobacco in Nottingham, retiring as a director of the company. *Backwater*, by Guy Adams, Lieutenant-Colonel East Surrey Regiment, was a slimmer volume that contained only work by men from the Lower Camp at Spangenberg, including Ted Beckwith. It was printed in the UK by Frederick Muller in 1944 from material posted home from Germany.

One of the post-war POW best sellers, *Escape to Freedom*, was co-written by Terence Prittie and Bill Edwards. The book culminated with their escapes from Wanfried and Lengenfeld unterm Stein. Terence Prittie went on to become the cricket correspondent of the Guardian and to develop an interest in the new Germany of the 1950s and 1960s. He wrote a biography of the then German Chancellor, Konrad Adenhauer. The author of another best seller, Ian Reid, faced some of the same problems as Le Mesurier and Halliday. He overcame his demons by writing an account of his life on the run in Italy and Germany. *Prisoner At Large* was published in 1947 and republished in 1976. He joined the BBC Monitoring Service where he was Senior

Editor on the Russian and East European desk until he retired in 1976. In 1970 he fulfilled a lifetime ambition by being appointed Point-to-Point correspondent to *The Times;* yet another prisoner with a love of horses.

For some former prisoners the war provided a chance to take stock of the lives and start new careers. As mentioned earlier, Peter Conder, who had escaped from Oflag IX A/Z on the first day of the march, simply carried on recording and studying birds. He would not return to advertising and eventually became the Director of the Royal Society for the Protection of Birds. Michael Langham also did not return to his pre-war job. Instead of following a legal career, he went on to become a leading theatre director; working in several British theatres including the Royal Shakespeare at Stratford. He then went to direct at Stratford Ontario and on Broadway.

Captain John Logan, Argyll and Sutherland Highlanders, published his POW diary covering the period from June 1940 until his last full day in Rotenburg on Wednesday 28 March 1945. One book that was planned during the evacuation took 70 years to be published. Lee Hill and John McIndoe intended to publish their photographs and drawings of the march. They were discussing it at Wimmelburg when the surprise artillery bombardment had triggered the withdrawal of the German guard. Now with this book McIndoe's and Hill's objective has finally been achieved. There was a market for POW picture books. *As You Were: a Book of Caricatures* by Frank Slater, Queen's Own Cameron Highlanders and latterly at Rotenburg, was published by Hutchinson in 1946.

John McIndoe had contributed to an exhibition of POW art posted back from Germany in May 1944, organised by the *Daily Telegraph*. A year later he had a one-man show at Simpsons on Piccadilly. McIndoe came from an artistic family. The family owned one of New Zealand's pre-eminent printers. It was a family that also included the pioneering plastic surgeon Archibald McIndoe. Outwardly John McIndoe's creative work was a blessing during his imprisonment, but in fact his time as a prisoner had cultivated demons. Back in New Zealand he hated being indoors, spending longer and longer on a smallholding, living in a tent. He found sleeping difficult. His son believed that his wartime experience had destroyed his confidence. He retained the POW's habit of not wasting anything and of mending rather than buying new. McIndoe and the other New Zealand POWs spent time recuperating at Puttick Wing at Broadstairs, part of the New Zealand Reception Centre, before returning home. He painted one of his last wartime pictures whilst at Broadstairs: a view of the harbour with its sandy beach and a sunny sky.

Relaxation was not Lee Hill's style. His records show him allocated to Puddick Wing initially, but by 28 April his army records have 'Appointed War Correspondent (Photographic duties) with pay & allowances of a 2nd Lieut'. Hill's must have led a whirlwind existence. Not just his official duties – there are eight changes to his army record on 28 April alone and that was a Saturday – before his return to New Zealand in 1946, he met and married his second wife. He was 39 and on the wedding certificate is described as a Lieutenant with the New Zealand Army – Cinema Photographer, Eva his wife was 20 and from Chingford. He also fitted in a brief trip to Rotenburg, photographed returning POWs in Brussels and toured the UK as official photographer with the New Zealand Army rugby team. A news reel of the period includes footage of returning POWs in Brussels that is unattributed. It is highly likely that it was Lee's. There is a photograph of Lee in Brussels with a 16mm ciné camera. Back in New Zealand and out of the army, he formed a company called Television Films Ltd, long before New Zealand had television and bought the 'Vogue Theatre', Brooklyn, Wellington. He died in 1952 of a heart attack outside the theatre as he was putting up film posters. His widow, Eva, returned to the UK with her children in the early 1950s and has contributed her memories of a man for whom the phrase 'larger than life' is inadequate.

The post-war experiences of one of the diarists is known in considerable detail. Harry Roberts stayed with REME until 1947, serving in Palestine. He then left the army and returned to work in the railway workshop at York. After the railways were nationalised he worked at other railway workshops in ever more senior positions, before becoming the last Works Manager at the former Great Western Railway works in Swindon. He had the difficult task of managing the final years of the workshop before it closed. In his retirement he wrote his account of his experiences at Arnhem and in Rotenburg. He died immediately after a trip to London, where he had been arranging a journey to Germany to revisit Rotenburg and the route of the evacuation.

Edward Baxter went back to his native East Riding and once more took up his writing, although there is no evidence any of his work was published. However because of the demands of his writing, he persuaded the Post Office to install a post box next to his house in Hessle outside Hull to handle his correspondence. He is still remembered locally as having been slightly eccentric.

Rotenburg had a more or less peaceful transition from war to American occupation. Spangenberg was less fortunate. The town had been briefly a battleground until the USAAF bombed and destroyed the castle. The Schloß remained a burnt-out shell until the late 1950s when it was rebuilt and converted into a hotel. The old farm, the site of Lower Camp, was demolished in 1966 and is now home to a pharmaceutical factory. Eisleben remains very much as it was in 1945, although with the addition of a Red Army cemetery as a reminder of Eisleben's military hospitals and its time spent in the Russian Zone and the German Democratic Republic. The farm at Wimmelburg is still overshadowed by spoil tips, but some of the buildings have been demolished and now a group of small starter unit factories make up one end of the site. The farm's owner left for the west when the Russians arrived. The chapel to Saint Cyriacus remains unchanged. The biggest change is at Esperstedt, where the airstrip that Oflag IX A/Z flew from back to Belgium has been replaced by a water-filled quarry.

At Rotenburg the US 65th Infantry Division had arrived largely unopposed on 2 April. The threat by the SS to defend the town evaporating as they found themselves nearly surrounded by US armored divisions at Spangenberg and Bad Hersfeld. The inhabitants of the school house, Major Bormann included, had by then moved to a wooded valley nearby so as to be clear of any obvious targets for shelling or air attack. From 29 June the building became an American hospital, first the 44th Evacuation Hospital and then in late August the 24th Evacuation Hospital.

Despite there being no fighting in Rotenburg between the departure of the German troops and the arrival of the hospital, the school buildings were looted. Almost all of the prisoners' possessions were destroyed or stolen. Inevitably, this was the start of a dark period for Germany. Food and clothing were scarce and the many former forced labourers were in no mood to respect German property. The prison camp barbed wire had been removed very early on by the Americans and when Björn Ulf-Noll investigated the buildings he found a black US soldier on sentry duty at the door of the original gymnasium. 'The sentry's left arm was covered with about five or six on-sleeve wristwatches and strangely enough he had an old alarm-clock with a bell on top which was dangling on the right side of his chest instead of a military decoration.' A former classmate of Björn remembered going through the old Red Cross parcel hut in the school grounds just after the 'Amis had occupied Rotenburg … when my sister and I took our handcart to go down to the camp and there to the Red-Cross-wooden hut and picked up what other looters had left. … The boxes were filled with toilet paper sent by the Red Cross to the officers in the camp.' Even Gunnar Celander explored the school to see whether anything had been left in the food supply room. He found three tins that had not been opened, but sadly they only contained delousing powder.

The buildings were thoroughly cleaned by the Americans when it became a hospital and items dating back to the days of the school and the original teacher training college were thrown away, including stuffed birds and science equipment that belonged to the school. The Americans bulldozed the rubbish into a hole nearby.

There were some successful attempts to recover the former prisoners' possessions from the store room. Lee Hill returned to Rotenburg in May and retrieved some items from Celander. Celander had managed to sort through a damp pile of books and papers to retrieve some items. These were passed on to a former prisoner, Captain, now Major Shackleton, Royal Corps of Signals, who visited the school on 22 June, including some of Lieutenant Feilding's paintings. But most of the men's possessions were burnt during the efforts to make the buildings usable as a hospital. At Spangenberg at least one former prisoner managed to retrieve the last issues of Ted Beckwith's *Quill* from the debris of Lower Camp.

In his report to Stockholm, Celander estimates the cost of the lost and damaged property at around 75,000 marks. In 2012 values close to £120,000. It included musical instruments and gramophones. 'I heard the discouraging reports on the subject day after day and could trace some material, but was not given official permission to recover it. I heard of twelve-year-old boys who had YMCA-marked gramophones and accordions which they hired to American soldiers against two cigarettes for an evening.' Celander complained that he was treated with suspicion by the Americans. He was a foreigner and one that was liked by the Germans: two reasons for concern to the new Allied Military Government.

The Schwedenheim had been looted by civilians and, it seemed to Celander, by the American soldiers sent to guard it, whilst he was still in hospital in Saxony. Gradually as life returned closer to normality and with the help of German friends Celander reassembled his life. In mid-May he got news of his car. One of the interpreters for the Military Government had formerly been an interpreter on the camp staff and taken part in the walk to Wimmelburg. Eventually with a civilian car and driver he returned to Wimmelburg and retrieved his own car. It was a close call. The Polish workers who had been using it were planning to drive it away to Poland and Wimmelburg was due to fall into the Russian zone from July.

Before his return to Rotenburg, Celander along with Lieutenant Baigent and Corporal Brown had been caught up in German attempts to defend Festung Harz. When the German field hospital left Uftrungen they took their guest patients with them to the Gebrüder Dippe Stiftung hospital at Quedlinburg on the northern edge of the Harz Mountains. On the same night that George Forster reached Newcastle – 19 April – Quedlinburg and the hospital were shelled by the Americans, believing it to be a barracks. At dawn, Celander, as an English speaker and a neutral, was sent out under a white flag to negotiate the hospital's surrender, which he eventually did. His ordeal was not yet over, for shortly afterwards he caught pneumonia and was confined to bed for three weeks. He did not return to Rotenburg until 20 May, two weeks after VE-Day. During this period Baigent and Brown were employed by the American military government in the Harz.

All the original occupiers of the school house were allowed to stay during the time the buildings housed US hospitals. However, they had to make room for US Army nurses, which made the cramped quarters even worse. In the summer of 1945 former Oberfeldwebel Heinrich Sultan was released from POW camp to resume his duties as caretaker for the US 24th Evacuation hospital. Björn recalled that this was 'because running the 24th US Evacuation Hospital, Rotenburg, was easier to do with Herr Sultan than without him.'

The Jakob-Grimm-Schule returned to its former home after the war: lessons recommenced in January 1946. Today there are additional buildings, but the original main building and the school house are still externally as they were in 1945. Though the Red Cross parcels hut has gone. Spangenberg Schloß took longer to return to normality. It was 1958 before the building was restored and habitable. It is now a hotel.

Of the guards that had either marched away on the evening of 12 April or been arrested by American Military Police, little is known of their post-war life. Oberst Schrader was recorded by the British as being in Spangenberg at the time of the Rockensuß War Crime trial. It is very likely that Brix and the rest of the guard did not reach Torgau in April 1945, but instead they were swept up in the surrender of Eisleben to the Americans.

By June 1945 Brix was being held with other more senior army officers at Allendorf Prison near Geißen pending investigations into their involvement in war crimes. Allendorf had been a labour camp but after the war it was run as an American prison camp. He was cleared of involvement in war crimes. Unmarried, Brix had lived in Potsdam before the war. Now, with Potsdam in the Russian Zone, he made his home in Rotenburg. Here he lived, like many in Germany at the time, in straitened circumstances in an attic flat; sometimes he had to beg for food. In the confusion of post-war Germany it is perhaps not surprising that British records of this period place Brix in Berlin or Potsdam. Some time in the 1950s Brix wrote to the then Lieutenant-Colonel Edlmann asking for a reference to support an application to emigrate to New Zealand. Edlmann refused. By the 1970s he had was able to indulge in his love of riding and was teaching at a local stables.

The Abwehr Offizier Hauptmann Prosper Heyl faced two war crimes trials after the war. One related to his handling of the last escape from the camp in September 1944, when Forbes and others ended up in police hands. The German police were convinced that a guard must have helped the escapees. It was alleged that Heyl had threatened to hand all of them over to the Gestapo. Heyl's evidence is a little confusing, but he blames the civilian police chief at Bad Hersfeld for sending Captain David Maude,

The Russian Military Cemetery at Eisleben, a reminder of Thuringia's time in the Russian Zone. (Peter Green)

Somerset Light Infantry, and Lieutenant Oldman, Kings Own Yorkshire Light Infantry, to the Gestapo and threatening to hand over the other four escapees. Heyl's statement stresses that he did not believe a guard had been involved – which was true – but that he knew that had there been, the British officers would never betray him. The most Heyl could expect from them was their word as British officers that no German had been involved and that he could use this to convince the Gestapo to release them. All the men were returned unharmed to Rotenburg.

Despite spending time at the London POW Cage and being found guilty, his conviction was quashed. The second trial followed from the incident that also led to his bet with Major Burston over who would win the war. A low flying Allied aircraft had shot up a train on the railway line on the east bank of the

Fulda a few fields away from the camp, to the cheers of prisoners, many of whom were leaning from the upper windows. The camp standing orders were for men to move away from the windows during air raids. Heyl had ordered them to move away, but he had been ignored. He then took a guard's rifle and put a shot through what he claimed was an empty upper window of the art room. Once the aircraft had gone and the camp had returned to normal, Burston and Heyl had the conversation that led to the bet. Other prisoners remembered the shooting incident.

The trial of Volkssturm members Adam Diegel and Rudolf Funk for the attacks on the Rockensuß escapees took place in August 1946. The files from the trial are extremely rich in preliminary information and detail the British dealings with the Americans, within whose zone Rockensüß then lay, but sadly they are sketchy on the trial proceedings and its aftermath. The trial took place in Hannover with two defendants. Herr Diegel and Herr Funk were charged with committing a war crime against three men: Maud – Somerset, Light Infantry; Quass-Cohen – the Commandos, and Smith – South Lancashire Regiment. Adam Diegal was found guilty and sentenced to five years imprisonment. Funk was acquitted. In July 1947 Diegal appealed against his sentence, but then the paper trail goes cold. There are no official records of whether Diegal served all or any part of his sentence. In Rockensüß, though, he was remembered as only serving a short sentence.

Oberfeldwebel Heinrich Sultan remained at the school as caretaker in 1946 on the departure of the American military hospital. He retired a well liked and respected member of the Rotenburg community. On the remainder of the 80 guards there is nothing, but since Brix, Heyl and Sultan made it back from captivity, it is unlikely that they did become involved in the final battles of Hitler's Reich. Presumably they were still in Eisleben when the town surrendered.

Germany was split into four after the war. The evacuation routes of the camps had taken the men from Hesse, which became part of the US zone, to Thuringia and then to Saxony, which become part of the Russian Zone and in time part of the German Democratic Republic. The Potsdam agreement settled the part of the western border of the Russian zone broadly along the railway line south from Göttingen to Bebra. In places though the railway crossed the border briefly and this caused problems for long distance trains. So in the autumn of 1945 representatives of the four powers met at the Kalkhof, where Oflag IX A/Z had spent much of Easter Day, and agreed an additional treaty that swapped Russian and American areas to the north of Eschwege so that the railway line no longer crossed over into the Russian zone, with the consequent disruptions to travel. Exchanges of land like this occurred at several places in Germany during this period, but the Kalkhof agreement was uniquely a treaty. Known as the Wanfried Treaty, it has equal legal status to the Potsdam Treaty.

Until spring of 1945 Spangenberg and Rotenburg had been in the centre of Germany. They would spend the next 40 years on the eastern edge of the Federal Republic. For Eisleben and the other towns their few weeks of occupation by the Americans would be airbrushed from their history, replaced by a liberating Red Army.

APPENDIX

PEOPLE

The personal histories of the Oflags are in the writings, diaries and papers of over 40 men. In some cases their accounts provided only background to life in the camps and do not describe the marches.

Ashton, Lieutenant Harold W., Royal Engineers

Harold Ashton was a surveyor with Derbyshire County Council and a member of the Territorial Army. He was posted to 242 Field Unit part of 52 Lowland Division in October 1939. Ashton was captured during a confused night-time retreat towards the Channel coast at Arras on 29 May. He published an account of his service and captivity in the Royal Engineers Journal in 1991. **Source:** Library, the Royal School of Military Engineering, Chatham

Baigent, Lieutenant Lestock 'Stocky' Ryvers, New Zealand Expeditionary Force

Lestock Baigent was 38 in 1945. He was a farmer when he joined the New Zealand Army in 1939, but he stayed in the army after

the war, eventually achieving the rank of Captain. He was captured in Crete in 1941. In 1946 he was awarded the MBE for his service with Oflag IX A/Z. The wounds he received from the attack by the USAAF were still causing him difficulties after the war.
Source: New Zealand Military Records and National Record Office, Kew

Baxter, Lieutenant Edward H., Royal Army Ordnance Corps

Edward Baxter had fought in the First World War as a private in the King's Own Yorkshire Light Infantry. Baxter was captured in Greece in 1941, whilst serving in the Royal Army Ordnance Corps. He spent time in Oflag VB at Biberach and Oflag VIB in Warburg before finally reaching Oflag IX A/Z. His unpublished account of service in the Second World War and captivity was presented to the Imperial War Museum.
Source: Imperial War Museum

Beckwith, Captain Edward 'Ted', Sherwood Foresters

Ted Beckwith was captured with others from 8 Sherwood Foresters in Norway in May 1940. Like the other early prisoners he spent time in several camps, but started and finished his captivity at Spangenberg. After the war he returned to his pre-war employment with Imperial Tobacco and retired as a Director of the Company.
Source: unpublished diary made available by Mrs Jean Beckwith

Borrett, Major A.R., Royal Engineers

Borrett was an architect from Windsor before the war. He had the most unusual and perhaps unlucky route to Spangenberg.

Whilst on leave in the Caribbean, the ship that he was on was torpedoed 150 miles from Trinidad. He was picked up by the U-boat and then taken to Germany.
Source: Green Collection

Brush, Major Edward James Augustus Howard 'Peter', Rifle Brigade

'Peter' Brush was a Company Commander in 1 Rifles and was captured along with others from the brigade at Calais in 1940. He was the Security Officer at Oflag IX A/Z. Brush returned to the army after the war and retired in 1947 having commanded his old battalion. He served as High Sheriff of County Down and as Vice-Lieutenant of the County.
Source: Imperial War Museum

Brix, Oberstleutenat Rudolf Carl Otto Franz, Kriegsgefangenenwesen Wehrkreis IX

Rudolf Brix arrived at Rotenburg in May 1944 after service in France and the Eastern Front. He was deputy to Oberst Schrader at Spangenberg as well as commandant of Rotenburg. He was not liked by the prisoners, but this seems not to have been for any specific action, more that he was a professional soldier who was a stickler for doing things correctly. Brix was a keen horseman. He returned to Rotenburg in 1945 rather than remain in Potsdam, which was now in the Russian Zone.
Source: Bundesarchiv and conversation with Horst Ehrich

Cartwright, Lieutenant Hugh Harry Langan, South Staffordshire Regiment

Cartwright was Signals Officer of the 2 South Staffs, one of the battalions in the 1st Airborne Division's Airlanding Brigade, and was captured during Operation *Market Garden*. His account of

the camp and march were taken from a mini-story published by the Hartenstein Museum.
Source: Friends of the Hartenstein Museum, Oosterbeck

Celander, Reverend Gunnar, YMCA

Gunnar Celander graduated from Lund University with a degree in theology and was ordained at Växsjö in June 1920. From 1941 until 1947 he worked on behalf of prisoners of war in Germany, as one of six YMCA district secretaries. He was responsible for Hesse and Thurngia with an office first in Kassel and then when the Allied bombing made Kassel too dangerous he moved to Rotenburg. Prisoners from Oflag IX A/Z built his home and office, which was known as the *Schwedenheim*. As well as helping the Allied prisoners, Gunnar provided support to German civilians. He received several awards for his work in Germany, including the British King's Medal for Service in the Cause of Freedom.
Source: Swedish National Archives, Stockholm

Clay, Lieutenant-Colonel Basil, Royal West Kent Regiment

Basil Clay was born in 1896. He joined the British Army in 1914 and became a career soldier. His appointments included Secretary to the Governor of Burma, as well as commanding the 7th battalion Royal West Kents in France in 1940 where he was captured in May. Clay was the Senior British Officer (SBO) at Oflag IX A/Z. After leaving the army he emigrated to the US.
Source: National Record Office, Kew

Conder, Lieutenant Peter, Royal Signals

Peter Conder left the leading British advertising business S.H. Benson to join the Royal Signals. He was captured with

other members of the 51st Highland Division at St Valéry-le-Caux in 1940. He escaped on the first afternoon of the evacuation march and was liberated by the Americans five days later on 2 April. After the war he devoted himself to ornithology
Source: family papers

Daniels, Private Frederick W., Queen's Royal Regiment

Private Daniels was a signaller with the Queen's Royal Regiment. He came from Rochester, Kent, where his peacetime employment was as an insurance clerk. He was captured in North Africa in September 1942, aged 30. After spells in Italian camps he was moved to an Arbeitskommando in a copper mine north of Eisleben. Daniels and his fellow POWs joined Oflag IX A/Z at Wimmelburg for transport home. He wrote an account of his time in captivity, which has not been published.
Source: Imperial War Museum

Douglas, Lieutenant Sholto, Cameronians (Scottish Rifles)

Sholto Douglas was born in 1916 in Kuala Selangor, Malaya. Sholto was commissioned into the 1st Battalion the Cameronians (Scottish Rifles) and volunteered for the Special Services Battalion, later No 3 Commando. He arrived in Egypt in 1941 as a member of Force Z and took part in the Layforce raid at Bardia before being captured in Crete on 1 June 1941.
Source: family papers

Edlmann, Captain Ernest L.C., Royal East Kent Regiment (The Buffs)

Ernest Edlmann was a career soldier. After Sandhurst he joined Royal East Kent Regiment (The Buffs) in 1934. The battalion

went to France in 1939. He was captured in May 1940 at Cassel as the battalion defended the Dunkirk perimeter. Following his release from prison camp, he rejoined his regiment. Colonel Edlmann was interviewed for this book and kindly provided access to his diary covering the march and his escape. The drawing of Ernest Edlmann was made by Aubrey Davidson-Houston in 1943, whilst Edlmann was at OflagVIIB.
Source: interview, Imperial War Museum and personal papers

Edwards, Lieutenant Marcus, 2/2 Field Regiment, Australian Artillery

Marcus Bruce Edwards was captured in Crete in 1941. Marcus was one of those that the Reverend Forster described as a 'hard-nut', with very strong anti-German feelings. His diary entries are short, written in staccato sentences, often with anti-German comments. Marcus was a keen violinist, who also made violins.
Source: Australian War Memorial Archive

Edwards, Captain William 'Bill', Queen's Own Royal West Kent Regiment

Bill Edwards was captured near Amiens in 1940. After time in several camps he was sent to Spangenberg in 1942. During a stay at Obermaßfeld hospital he escaped and nearly reached Switzerland. Edwards collaborated with Terence Prittie on a post-war best seller *Escape to Freedom*.
Source: *Escape to Freedom* by Edwards and Prittie

Ehricht, Horst, Schoolboy, Wimmelburg 1940s

Horst's family were close friends with Rudolf Brix and Horst has provided most of the background to Brix's life. The families were so close that to Horst, Brix was always 'Uncle Rudolf'.

Horst's father died in hospital during the war. The family suspected that he had been murdered because of lack of sympathy with the Nazi Party. After service in the German Army in the closing months of the war, he eventually left the Russian Zone and is at the time of writing living in Canada.
Source: interview and Bundesarchiv

Erhard, Obergefreiter Martin Christian, Landesschützenbataillon 631

Martin Erhard was in his mid-twenties in 1945. A farmer from Oberthalhausen, a village about 10km south west of Rotenburg, he had a deformed or possibly even missing hand that prevented him serving in a front line unit. He accompanied the marchers with his dog. At some stage either before or on the first day of the march he had given his address to Captain Quas-Cohen and Lieutenant Smith and offered to shelter them.
Source: National Archives, Kew

Fairbairn, Lieutenant Terry, 2/1 Battalion, Imperial Expeditionary Force

He was born in Ireland and 18 years old when his family arrived in Australia and settled in Sydney. He joined the Militia – NSW Scottish Regiment – and when war broke out was a sergeant. He was wounded and captured in Crete. It took him a long time to recover from his POW experience. After the war he worked for an Australian charity for the blind.
Source: Australians at War Film Archive

Forbes, Lieutenant Hamish, Welsh Guards

Hamish Forbes, a Scot, joined the Welsh Guards as a regular army soldier in 1938, although he had been on the Welsh Guards Supplementary Reserve for sometime. Forbes was captured

in May outside Dunkirk, when the battalion headquarters was overrun. He was the regimental intelligence officer. He was also an inveterate escapee involved in 11 escapes from camps across Germany. His eleventh and successful attempt was from the march on the 11 April 1945.
Source: Forbes family papers

Forster, Reverend George W., Royal Army Chaplains' Department

Father Forster was a Roman Catholic padre. He was born around 1910 in Sunderland. He trained for the priesthood at Ushaw College in the early 1920s. From 1940 until the end of the war he was a Chaplain to the forces. He was captured at Tobruk in North Africa in June. After the war he returned to the North East as a teacher and parish priest. Forster wrote several accounts of his wartime experiences as articles for the Ushaw College Magazine.
Source: *Ushaw College Magazine*

Frost, Lieutenant-Colonel John, Parachute Regiment

John Frost was a career soldier. He was commissioned into the Cameronians. In 1942 he volunteered for the Special Air Services and by 1944 was commander of 2 Para. He was captured after a fierce fight for the road bridge at Arnhem. By the spring of 1945 as his wounds were slow to heal he was at Obermaßfeld prison hospital.
Source: *A Drop Too Many* by John Frost

Fuller, Fusilier James 'Jimmy', Royal Northumberland Fusiliers

Jimmy Fuller was a miner from Bedlington, north of Newcastle. Though a coal miner and therefore in a reserved

occupation he volunteered and went to France with the 7th Battalion, which formed part of 51st Highland Division. The Division was forced to surrender at Saint Valery-en-Caux on 12 June 1940. He was eventually transferred to Oflag IX A/Z as an orderly. His notes of the march were written in a small diary that includes letters received and sent, money and family birthdays. After the war Jimmy returned to Bedlington and mining.
Source: family papers of Michael Fuller

Green, Lieutenant Alan Thomas, Border Regiment

Alan Green was born in Leicester. He joined the army in 1942 and was commissioned in the 1st Battalion Border Regiment who were part of the 1st Airborne Division's Airlanding Brigade. He was captured and spent the rest of the war in Oflag IX A/Z. He was a close friend of 'Butch' Laing whilst in the camp.
Source: *A Fragment of a Life* by Peter Green

Halliday, Captain Corrie Alexander, Royal Armoured Corps

Corrie Halliday was captured in North Africa in May 1942 whilst serving in 11 Hussars. He had been born in August 1918 at Worthing in Sussex and had served in the Inns of Court Regiment, a Territorial unit, in 1937. He was a bank clerk at the time. He arrived at Rotenburg directly from Italy in 1943 after Italy surrendered, when the Germans moved their former ally's prisoners to Germany. Halliday served with his regiment in post-war Berlin, but found settling back into military or civilian life after the war very difficult.
Source: Imperial War Museum interview

Heyl, Hauptmann Prosper, Wehrkreis IX

Prosper Heyl had served in the First World War, where he was injured in the leg. Many of the prisoners thought that he had a wooden leg, but in fact a war wound had left him lame. Although disliked by many of the prisoners, some of whom swore affidavits about his alleged behaviour that led to his facing a war crime trial, he comes over as a man trying to perform his military duties honourably for an evil regime. Following the transfer of control of the Reserve Army and POW to the SS after the bomb plot against Hitler, he tried on several occasions to be transferred from the camp to active service. George Forster in particular found him a fair man.
Source: National Archives, Kew

Holland, Colonel Rupert 'Pixie', Royal Artillery

Colonel Holland was Area Commander Calais. Defence of Calais town and harbour had been improvised at short notice following the German breakthrough in May 1940, when 30th Brigade led by Brigadier Nicholson was despatched to the town. Holland surrendered with the rest of headquarters staff including Nicholson. Holland was Senior British Officer at Spangenberg from May 1944. His diary was kindly made available by Mrs Jean Beckwith.
Source: Jean Beckwith Collection

Hill, Lieutenant Leighton McLeod 'Lee', New Zealand Expeditionary Force

Lee Hill was born in Carterton, near Wellington, on 13 March 1907. Soon after leaving school he started working in the New Zealand film industry. He was captured at Sidi Azei near Tobruk in late 1941. Following the liberation of the camp he returned to Germany as a war correspondent and took more

stills and some ciné footage of former prisoners being processed in Brussels. On his return to New Zealand he created the Television Films Ltd and bought a cinema. He died in 1952.
Source: family papers and the New Zealand Film Archive

Irwin, Gunner John, 33rd Armored Regiment US

John Irwin was born in 1926, in Norristown, a manufacturing town close to Philadelphia. He was 18 when he joined the army. He was one of the men who eventually liberated the men of Oflag IX A/Z. John left the army in July 1946. He re-started his education in 1952 and gained a doctorate in Philosophy from Syracusse University. From 1964 till 1990 he taught philosophy at Lock Haven University near Philadelphia.
Source: *Another River, Another Town: A Teenage Tank Gunner Comes of Age in Combat 1945* by John Irwin

Kennedy, Lieutenant-Colonel Geoffrey Walshman, East Surrey Regiment

Kennedy, known as 'Bart', was born in 1895. He served in the East Surrey Regiment in France, where he won the Military Cross in 1918. He served with the regiment in France again in 1939, but in March 1940 took command of 4 Ox and Bucks Light Infantry. He was captured whilst the regiment was defending Cassel in May 1940. Kennedy was deputy SBO at Rotenburg. The camp's nominal roll for January 1945 is in Kennedy's papers at the Imperial War Museum. He was awarded the OBE for his work in camp.
Source: Imperial War Museum

Laing, Lieutenant W.K. 'Butch', Sherwood Foresters

'Butch' Laing was a school teacher at a public school who joined the Territorial Army in January 1939. Called up in September,

the regiment formed part of the Allied Expeditionary Force to Norway and Laing was captured at the end of the month. Soon after his capture Laing and others were interviewed by Hitler, who told them of his unhappiness that Germany and Britain were at war.
Source: Imperial War Museum

Langham, Michael, Lieutenant Gordon Highlanders

Langham had been a solicitors' clerk before the war. He joined the Gordon Highlanders and was captured with the 51st Highland Division in France in 1940. He shared his imprisonment at Rotenburg with his brother Geoffrey. After the war Michael had a distinguished career as a theatre director in Britain, Canada and on Broadway. Michael kindly gave interviews for this book.
Source: interviews

Le Mesurier, Captain John Stuart, Royal Tank Regiment

Le Mesurier was working at a racing stables when he joined the Royal Tank Corps in 1939. After service in France he was captured in North Africa in 1941. He found settling back into a peacetime routine difficult. His daughter kindly made his unpublished autobiography available.
Source: family papers

Llewelyn, Lieutenant Desmond 'Ham', Royal Welch Fusiliers

Desmond Llewelyn was a professional actor before the war. He had joined the Royal Welch Fusiliers in January 1940 and was captured in France five months later. He acted in many prison

dramas and earned the nickname 'Ham'. At Rotenburg he played Theseus in Michel Langham's final production, 'Midsummer Night's Dream'. After the war he returned to the theatre and films. He played the role of 'Q' from the second James Bond film *From Russia with Love* onwards.
Source: *Q: The biography of Desmond Llewelyn* by Sandy Hernu

Logan, Captain John, Argyll & Sutherland Highlanders

John Logan was captured whilst serving with 51st Highland Division at 5 June Saigneville on the Somme. Collins published his POW diary as *Inside the Wire* in 1948. His account finishes on Wednesday 28 March, the day before the camps were evacuated. He had arrived at Rotenburg in June 1943.
Source: *Inside the Wire* by John Logan

Lush, Lieutenant Robert, Royal Army Service Corps EFI

Lush had been captured in France in 1940 whilst serving with the Expeditionary Force Institutes, the NAAFI service that operates in war zones. He had been manager of the Droitwich Spa Hotel. Lush provider the central catering for Oflag IX A/Z.
Source: men's diaries and *Inside the Wire*

McIndoe, Captain John Leslie, New Zealand Expeditionary Force

John McIndoe was born in Dunedin in 1898. After studying art he joined the family printing business, which he eventually ran. During the Second World War he enrolled with the 1st Echelon of the Second New Zealand Expeditionary Force, serving in Egypt, Libya and Greece. He was captured by German forces in Crete in May 1941. John McIndoe's father and mother were

both were artists. His brother, Sir Archibald McIndoe, pioneered plastic surgery on burns victims in the UK.
Source: family papers and the New Zealand War Art Collection

Martin, Private 'Bert' H.L., RAMC

Bert Martin was captured in France whilst serving with the 21st General Hospital Unit, immediately south of Boulogne. By 1944 he was working as a medical orderly at Obermaßfeld. His unpublished manuscript 'Lasting Impressions' is held by the Imperial War Museum.
Source: unpublished manuscript

Montgomery MC, Captain Robert, Royal Engineers and Commandos

Montgomery was captured after Operation *Chariot*, the raid on the dry dock at St Nazaire in 1942. The Germans thought that the raiders must be Navy personnel and so he and his fellow survivors were taken first to the Kriegsmarine prison camp at Marlag und Milag Nord. A regular soldier, Robert Montgomery returned to the Engineers after the war. Robert kindly gave an interview for this book.
Source: interview

Mountford, Lieutenant John, South Staffordshire Regiment

Mountford was a platoon commander who was captured at Arnhem in October 1944. His fractured arm was slow to heal and he was transferred from Oflag IX A/Z at Rotenburg to the Reserve-Lazarett at Obermaßfeld. He remained in the army postwar and after retiring he remained Commandant of the Army Cadet Corps in Merioneth and Montgomery.
Source: family papers

Muller MC, Captain Frederick H., New Zealand Expeditionary Force

Captain Muller was born in New Zealand in Mar 1905. He was working as an engine driver and living in Hamilton when he joined the NZEF, as part of the 4th Reserve Mechanical Transport Company. He was wounded and captured in April 1941 in North Africa. His diary's short entries cover the period of liberation and return to the UK.
Source: Peter Doyle

Nicolle, Lieutenant Hubert F., Hampshire Regiment and Commando

Hubert Nicolle was born on Guernsey. In 1940 he volunteered for the Hampshire Regiment and then for the newly created Commandos. He was captured following the second of his reconnaissance missions to Guernsey with his fellow-Guernsey man, James Symes. Nicolle left the army in 1946.
Source: *The Commando who came Home to Spy* by William Bell

Noll, Björn Ulf, Rotenburg 1945

Björn was born in 1931 in Korbach, a town to the west of Kassel. His father was German: his mother Swedish. Björn was educated at Rotenburg an der Fulda Secondary School, where his father was also a teacher. During the war he continued to live in the family home, which was in a house attached to the school building that housed Oflag IX A/Z. Postwar he worked in banking, before becoming a civil servant for the Hesse regional government.
Source: personal papers

Page, Captain Richard, Royal Artillery

Captain Page was captured in France in 1940. Originally with 6th Heavy Anti-Aircraft Battery Royal Artillery, he had been

transferred to the British Expeditionary Force's Headquarters at Arras, from where he was sent to Calais with orders for newly arrived troops. Caught up in the surrender of the garrison on 26 May, he spent time in several camps before arriving at Oflag IXA/Z. His unpublished memoir was kindly made available by Jane Torday.
Source: Jane Torday

Prittie, Lieutenant Terence Cornelius Farmer, Rifle Brigade

Lieutenant Prittie was captured at Calais in 1940. He made the first of his five escape attempts whilst still in France being marched eastwards. In January 1943 Prittie, as a repeat escapee, was to have been transferred to Oflag V C at Colditz, but at the last moment it was found that there was no space and he was sent to Spangenberg instead. After the war he was the Bonn correspondent of the *Guardian* and continued to write on cricket as he had done whilst a prisoner. With Bill Edwards he wrote the post-war best seller *Escape to Freedom* that described their time as prisoners.
Source: *Escape to Freedom*

Redway, Captain Theodore A., Durham Light Infantry

Theodore Redway was born in 1919 in Exmouth, Devon. He joined the 4th Battalion The Devonshire Regiment, part of the Territorial Army, as a private in 1938 along with the rest of his rugby club. After war broke out he was selected for officer training and eventually joined the Durham Light Infantry. Theo was captured in Sicily in 1943. During the evacuation march, Redway was paired with Captain John Le Mesurier for escapes. After the war he moved to Canada.
Source: Alan Redway

Quas-Cohen, Captain A., 9 Commando

Lieutenant Quas-Cohen was originally with the Royal Artillery. He volunteered for special operations with the Commandos. He and his partner were captured whilst reconnoitring the Normandy coast by canoe. He adopted the name 'Smith' and regimental affiliation 'Royal Artillery' as his work as a Commando or his Jewishness could have resulted in his being shot. His apparently outrageous stories led to him being given the camp nickname of 'Bullshit' Smith, Royal Artillery.
Source: Commando Veterans Association

Reid, Captain Ian D., Black Watch

Ian Reid was captured in Tunisia in April 1943 whilst serving with 7 Black Watch. After time in Italian POW camps he was transferred to Rotenburg in June 1944. It was at Rotenburg that he met his escape partner Lieutenant George Bowlby, Royal Scots Fusiliers, who had been captured in 1940. Reid's *Prisoners at Large; the Story of Five Escapes* was published by Gollanz in 1947 and reprinted in 1976. In 1948 he joined the BBC Monitoring Service where he was Senior Editor on the Russian and East European desk until he retired.
Source: *Prisoners at Large: the Story of Five Escapes*

Roberts, Lieutenant Harry, Royal Mechanical and Electrical Engineers

Harry Roberts served with the Royal Mechanical and Electrical Engineers (REME) from February 1944 as part of 1st Airborne Division. In civilian life he was an engineer at the railway works in his home town of York. He was severely wounded and paralysed soon after landing at Arnhem with 1st Airborne Division, with a bullet close to his spine. He gradually recovered the use of his legs and by the time he reached Oflag IX A/Z was fully mobile. In 1990 Harry wrote a book of his wartime experiences,

but died before he had found a publisher. Thanks to the considerable efforts of his widow, Muriel Roberts, it was eventually published as *Capture at Arnhem* in 1999. The text used here is from Harry's original diary and is reproduced with the generous permission of his widow, Muriel Roberts.
Source: Muriel Roberts

Robertson, Private Leslie, New Zealand Expeditionary Force

Les Robertson was a carpenter from Auckland. He took part in fighting in North Africa in 1941 before being sent to Greece. Evacuated from Greece he was wounded in Crete and captured on 27 May. He spent time in military hospitals at Schleitz and Haina, before being transferred to Rotenburg during 1944 as an orderly. Les wrote several poems whilst a POW. His diary and poems were kindly provided by his niece Thelma McCurchy.
Source: McCurchy family papers

Schrader, Oberst Kurt, Kriegsgefangenenwesen Wehrkreis IX

Kurt Schrader had served on staff and administrative appointments before his transfer to command of the Spangenberg and Rotenburg camps. He was separated from his wife and whilst acknowledging that no blame could be attached to him for the situation, his military records make it clear he would not be an acceptable candidate for a front line command. He returned to Spangenberg after the war.
Source: Bundesarchiv

Sewell, Captain John H., Royal Engineers

John Sewell was captured in Greece in April 1941. In civilian life he worked for the London and North Eastern Railway Company at

York. He shared a room at Spangenberg with Captain Wilbraham, who also wrote an account of his wartime experiences. Sewell retained his railway associations as a POW. His papers at the Imperial War Museum include a hand-drawn map of the railways of southern Lancashire and a photograph of fellow prisoners with their signatures and the names of their peacetime railway employers.
Source: Imperial War Museum

Shand, Major Bruce M.H., 12th Lancers

Bruce Shand was a pre-war career soldier. He was commissioned in the 12th Lancers as a second lieutenant in 1937. During the war he served in France before being evacuated to England and then in North Africa. He was captured in November 1942. After the war Shand did not return to the army, instead he pursued a business career. He is the father of Camilla, the Duchess of Cornwall. He wrote an account of his wartime career.
Source: *Previous Engagements* by Bruce Shand

Slater, Lieutenant Frank, Queen's Own Cameron Highlanders

Frank Slater was captured in 1940 whilst serving with 51st Highland Division. Originally from the Wirrel on Merseyside, he returned there after the war. In 1946 Hutchinson published a collection of his drawings, *As You Were: A Book of Caricatures*. The pictures here are taken from it and from the omnibus edition of the *Quill* published in 1947 by *Country Life*.
Source: Green Collection

Sultan, Oberfeldwebel Heinrich, Landesschützenbataillon 631

Heinrich Sultan was the Jakob-Grimm-Schule caretaker in 1939. He had been captured during the First World War and had spent

time in a British POW camp. He was released from captivity very shortly after the end of the war. The Americans used the school buildings for hospitals until 1946. He retired as school caretaker in 1951.
Source: Björn Ulf Noll

Sumners, Technician 5th Grade Charles, 166th Signal Photo Company

Charles Sumners was drafted into the US Army in January 1943. He joined 166th Signal Photo Company as a driver and photographer. Charles saw service in Normandy, Belgium, the Ardennes and Germany. The pictures that he took in March and April 1945 include several of 6th Armored and 65th Infantry Divisions. Sadly, many of his negatives that appear in unit histories produced immediately after the war have been lost, probably mislaid at the printers.
Source: Sumners' family collection

Symes, Lieutenant James M., Hampshire Regiment and Commandos

James Symes came from Guernsey in the Channel Islands. He was captured with Hubert Nicolle. His YMCA diary describing the march from Rotenburg was reprinted in William Bell's biography of Hubert Nicoll.
Source: *The Commando who came Home to Spy* by William Bell

Watson MC, Lieutenant William 'Tiger', Black Watch and 2 Commando

Bill Watson was one of the youngest officers on Operation *Chariot*, the St Nazaire Raid. He had been commissioned into the Black Watch before joining the Commandos in 1941. He spent a brief period in the Kriegsmarine's POW camp at Marlag

und Milag Nord. After the war he trained at Guy's Hospital and by the 1950s was in general practice in Shrewsbury. William kindly gave an interview for this book.
Source: interview and *We Forget so Much* by William Watson

Westcott, Captain C. Reginald, Royal Artillery

Reg Westcott came from Perranporth in Cornwall. He served in Norway and then in the Middle East. He was captured after the fall of Tobruk in 1942. He trained as a teacher in Exeter and then taught in the East End of London. After the war he returned to teaching and his last post was as headmaster of the Edinburgh School, a school for the children of British service personnel in Munster. The notes for his unwritten biography were kindly provided by his widow.
Source: Westcott family papers

Wilbraham MC, Captain Ralph V., Pioneer Corps

Ralph Wilbraham was born in 1893 in Cheshire. Educated at Wellington College, he served in the Cheshire Yeomanry in Palestine during the First World War, where he won the Military Cross. He was called up in 1939 and went to France as a Captain in the Auxiliary Military Pioneers. He was captured near Rouen in June 1940. After the war he was Director of Cheshire Red Cross. Ralph Wilbraham's unpublished manuscript was provided by his son Hugh Wilbraham.
Source: Wilbraham family papers

White, Lieutenant Ken G., Royal Artillery

Ken White was captured at Arnhem whilst serving with Light Battery, Royal Artillery. His YMCA POW diary was published by a Dutch friend, Marion Gerritsen-Teunissen. He had worked

in insurance before the war but could not settle back into his old job. He retrained as a market gardener. Ken's diary and his collection of Lee Hill photographs was kindly made available by Marion Gerritsen-Teunissen
Source: *Dagboek in krijgsgevangenschap* by Marion Gerritsen-Teunissen

SOURCES AND BIBLIOGRAPHY

Personal Contacts

Contact	Material
Gillian Barnard	papers of her late husband John Mansel
Jean Beckwith	diaries of Rupert Holland and her late husband Ted Beckwith
Bob Cardinell	information about the US 65th Infantry Division
Ingemar Björklund	translation of Swedish Red Cross papers relating to Gunnar Celander
Kathleen Biddle	papers of her late father, Ronald Cheetham
Fred Dittmann	history of Esperstedt airfield
Sholto Douglas	papers of his late father, Sholto Douglas
Ernest Edlmann	papers and conversations
Horst Ehrich	conversations regarding Rudolf Brix
Mags Fewkes	unpublished manuscripts by her late father John Le Mesurier
James Forbes	papers of his late father, Hamish Forbes
Anthony Foster	papers of his late grandfather Gerald Frost
Eduard Fritze	information regarding the Eichsfeld in the spring of 1945
Michael Fuller	papers of his late father, Jimmy Fuller
Bob Gerritsen	material relating to Lieutenant H.H.L. Cartwright
Marion Gerritsen-Teunissen	papers of Kenneth White
Eva Hill	conversations

Christa Kneiß	personal experiences of Uftrungen in 1945
Michael Langham	papers and conversations
Peter Lindner	local history of Eisleben
Thelma McCurchy	papers of her late uncle, Les Robertson
John McIndoe	information regarding his late father, John McIndoe
Sheena MacDonald	papers of Robert Jeffrey
Paul Milner	information regarding Spangenberg
Robert Montgomery	conversation
Simon Mountford	papers of his father, John Mountfort
Brenda Norris	information regarding Edward Norris
Robert Patton	information about the US 65th Infantry Division
Sally Phun	information regarding her grandfather John Kennedy
Alan, Tim and Julie Redway	information regarding Theodore Redway
Muriel Roberts	papers of Harry Roberts
Sarah Rhodes	papers of her father Peter Conder
Harald Schlanstedt	the liberation of Oflag IX A/Z at Wimmelburg
Haide Schreiber	local history of Rotenburg an der Fulda
Professor Hans-Heinz Seyfarth	The Eichsfeld in the spring of 1945
Mrs Henrietta Taylor	papers of her father, Denis Faulkner
Björn Ulf Noll	eyewitness accounts of Oflag IX A/Z and the town of Rotenburg. Also his extensive assistance with information gathering across Germany
Grace Westcott	information regarding her late husband Reg Westcott
Hugh Wilbraham	access to the personal papers of his late father Captain R.V. Wilbraham MC
Theo Ziegler	Local history of the Sangerhausen district

Archives and Museums

Americans in Wartime, Virginia, USA
Australian War Memorial, Canberra, Australia
Australian Film Archive
Bundesarchiv, Freiburg, Germany
Imperial War Museum, London
ITS Internationaler Suchdienst

Bad Arolsen, Germany, Oflags IXA/H and A/Z and concentration camp victims
Kings Own Border Regiment Museum, Carlisle
Maidstone Museum, Kent
National Archives, Kew
National Archives, Stockholm
The New Zealand Film Archive, Wellington
New Zealand Defence Force, Trentham, New Zealand
Otago Settlers Museum, Dunedin City Council, New Zealand
Royal Army Chaplains Museum, Andover
Royal Engineers Museum, Chatham
The Alexander Turnbull Library, Wellington
Additional pictures by Lee Hill,
Ushaw College Library, Durham
War Art, Archives of New Zealand, Wellington
Zoological Library, University of Oxford

Published Works

Adams, Guy, *Backwater Oflag IX A/H* (Frederick Muller, 1944)
Air Ministry, *Rise and fall of the German Air Force 1933–1945* (Air Ministry 1948, reprinted National Archives, 2008)
Altner, Helmut, *Berlin Soldier* (Tempus, 2007)
Ashton, Harold, 'Wasted Years' (*Royal Engineers Magazine*, 1991)
Barber, Noel, *Prisoner of War: The Story of British Prisoners held by the Enemy* (George Harrap, 1944)
Barnouw, Dagmar, *Germany 1945* (Indiana University Press, 1995)
Beckwith, E.G.C., Captain (ed), *The Quill* (Country Life, 1947)
Bell, William, *The Commando who Came Home to Spy* (The Guernsey Press, 1998)
Bennett, Gill (ed) *The End of the war in Europe 1945* (HMSO, 1996)
Berg, Erik, *Behind Barbed Wires* (Augustana Book Concern, 1944)
Biddiscombe, Perry, *The Last Nazis: Werewolf Guerrilla Resistance in Europe 1944–1947* (Tempus, 2006)
Bornemann, Manfred, *Schicksalstgae im Harz, Piepersache Druckerei und Verlag* (GmbH, 1997)
Bouchery, Jean, *The British Tommy in North West Europe 1944–1945* (1998)
British Red Cross, *Prisoner of War, Horace Marshall and British Red Cross* (1942)
Burleigh, Michael, *Death and Deliverance: Euthanasia in Germany 1900–1945* (CUP 1994)
Cardinell, Robert (ed), *The 261st Infantry Regiment in World War II* (65th Infantry Division Association, 2007)

Cardinell, Robert (ed), *The 65th Infantry Division Headquarters, Special Troops* (65th Infantry Division Association, 2006)
Cardinell, Robert (ed), *The 65th Infantry Division in World War II* (65th Infantry Division Association, 2004)
Cartwright, Hugh, 'Cartwright mini-story', (Airborne Museum, Hartenstein)
Controvich, James, *The United States Air Force and its Antecedents: a Selected Bibliography of Published and Printed Unit and Command Histories* (Air Force Historical Agency, 1991)
Cooper, Belton, *Death Traps: The Survival of an American Armored Division in World War II* (Presidio, 2000)
Crome, L, *Unbroken: Resistance and Survival in the Concentration Camps* (Lawrence and Wishart, London, 1988)
Dancocks, Daniel, *In Enemy Hands: Canadian Prisoners of War 1939–45* (Hurtig Press, 1983)
Davies, Norman, *Europe at War 1939–1945: No Simple Victory* (Pan Books, 2006)
Davis, Brian, *British Army Uniforms and Insignia of World War Two* (Arms and Armour Press, 1983)
Dittmann, Fred, *Bad Frankenhäuser* (Fliegerbuch, 2008)
Dover, Victor, *The Silken Canopy* (Cassell, 1979)
Doyle, Peter, *Prisoners of War in Germany* (Shire, 2008)
Dyer, George, *XII Corps: Spearhead of Patton's Third Army* (1947)
Eggers, Reinhold, *Colditz: The German Story* (Robert Hale, 1961)
Folcher, Gustave, *Marching to Captivity* (Brasseys, 1996)
Forster, George, *Priest Behind Barbed Wire* (Sunderland, 1993)
Fox, Don, *Patton's Vanguard* (McFarland and Co, 2003)
Franck, Harry, *Winter Journey through the Ninth* (1946)
Fritze, Eduard, *Die letzten Kriegstage im Eichsfeld* (Verlag Rockstuhl, 2002)
Frost, John, *A Drop too Many* (Stackpole, 2008)
Gilbert, Adrian, *POW: Allied Prisoners in Europe, 1939–45* (John Murray, 2006)
Gillies, Midge, *Barbed Wire Universities* (Aurum, 2011)
Goldhagen, Danile, *Hitler's Willing Executioners* (Abacus, 2006)
Green, Alan *A Fragment of a Life* (Green, 2008)
Hamlin, John, *Support and Strike: a Concise History of the US Ninth Air Force in Europe* (1991)
Hastings, Max, *Armageddon: the Battle for Germany 1944–45* (Pan Books, 2005)
Haworth, Jennifer, *The Art of War: New Zealand War Artists in the Field 1939–1945* (Wiley 2008)
Heiber, Helmut and Glantz, David, *Hitler and his Generals: Military Conferences 1942–1945* (Enigma Books, 2004)
Herbert, Ulrich, *Hitler's Foreign Workers* (Cambridge University Press, 1975)
Hernu, Sandy, Q: *The Biography of Desmond Llewelyn* (SPB Publications, 1999)

HMSO, *Prisoners of War: Armies and Other Land Forces of the British Empire 1939–1945* HMSO 1945, facsimile reprint (Hayward Press, 1990)
HMSO, *Prisoners of War: British Army 1939–1945* HMSO 1945, facsimile reprint (Hayward Press, 1999)
Hofmann, George, *The Super Sixth* (6th Armored Division Association, 1975)
Hogg, I.V. (ed) *German Order of Battle 1944* (Greenhill Books, 1994)
Höggemann, Josef, *Eisenbahnchronik Harz* (EK Verlag, 2007)
Holzhauer, Jürgen, et al, *75 Jahre Jakob-Grimm-Schule* (Rotenburg, 1999
Houston, Donald E, *Hell on Wheels* (Presido Press, 1977)
Hughes, Thomas, *Overlord: General Pete Quesada and the triumph of Tactical Air Power in World War II* (The Free Press, 1995)
Hunt, J. and Pringle A., *Service Slang* facsimile reprint of 1943 edition (Faber and Faber, 2008)
Hunt, Leslie, *The Prisoners' Progress* (Hutchinson, 1941)
Hutching, Megan (ed), *Inside Story: New Zealand Prisoners of War Remember*, Harper Collins, 202)
Irwin, John P, *Another River, Another Town: A Teenage Tank Gunner Comes of Age in Combat – 1945* (Random House, 2002)
Jackson, Ashley, *The British Empire and the Second World War* (Hambledon, 2006)
Joslin, Lt-Col H., *Orders of Battle of the British Army* facsimile reprint (Military Library Research Services, 2007)
Kater, Michael, *Hitler Youth* (Harvard University Press, 2004)
Kennedy, John, 'Experiences of a Medical Prisoner of War' *The Medical Press and Circular*, 2 January 1946
Klemperer, Victor *To the Bitter End: the Diaries of Victor Klemperer 1942–45* (Phoenix, 1999)
Kochavi, Arieh, *Confronting Captivity: Britain and the United States and their POWs in Nazi Germany* (University of North Carolina Press, 2005)
Koyen, Kenneth, *The Fourth Armored Division: from Beach to Bavaria* (1946)
Kurowski, Franz, *Hitler's Last Bastion* (Schiffer Military History, 1998)
Levine, Alan, *D-Day to Berlin* (Stackpole Books, 2007)
Logan, John, *Inside the Wire* (Collins, 1948)
Longden, Sean, *Dunkirk: the Men they Left Behind* (Constable, 2008)
Longden, Sean, *Hitler's British Slaves* (Constable, 2005)
Longden, Sean, *To the Victor the Spoils* (Robinson, 2004)
MacDonald, Charles, *Victory in Europe, 1945: The Last Offensive of World War II* (Dover, 2007)
MacDonogh, Giles, *After the Reich* (John Murray, 2007)
McIndoe, John, drawings and paintings (Otago Settlers Museum and New Zealand War Art Collection)

Mackenzie, S.P., *The Colditz Myth* (Oxford University Press, 2004)
Mansel, John, *The Mansel Diaries* (Wildwood, 1977)
Mason, W. Wynne, *Prisoners of War: Official History of New Zealand in the Second World War* (Oxford University Press, 1954)
Mattiello, G. and Vogt W., *Deutsche Kriegsgefangenen und Internierten enrichtungen 1939–1945* (Vogt, Koblenz)
Michel, Jean, *DORA* (Sphere, 1981)
Middlebrook, Martin and Everitt, Chris, *The Bomber Command War Diaries* (Viking, 1985)
Mierzejewski, Alfred, *The Collapse of the German War Economy, 1939–1945* (University of North Carolina Press, 1988)
MLRS, 'The Liberation of Europe 1944–1945: Map File' (Military Library Research Services, 2007)
Mondey, David, *American Aircraft of World War II* (Bounty Books, 2006)
Neillands, Robin, *The Battle for the Rhine 1944* (Cassell, 2005)
Neillands, Robin, *The Conquest of the Reich* (Weidenfeld and Nicolson, 1995)
Nichol, John and Rennel, Tony, *The Last Escape* (Penguin, 2002)
Noakes, J. and Pridham, G. (eds) *Nazism 1919–1945, a Documentary Reader* (University of Exeter Press, 1988)
Padover, Saul, *Experiment in Germany (*New York 1946)
Pfeiffer, Ludwig, *Die Geschichte des Schlosses Spangenberg* (Horst Schreckhase, 1987)
Piszkiewicz, Dennis, *The Nazi Rocketeers* (Stackpole, 2007)
Pons, Gregory, *9th Air Force 1942–1945* (Histoire and Collections, 2008)
Price, Alfred, *The Last Year of the Luftwaffe* (Greenhill Books, 2001)
Prittie, Terence and Edwards, Bill, *Escape to Freedom* (Hutchinson, 1953)
Reid, Ian, *Prisoner at Large* (Futura, 1976)
Roberts, Harry, *Capture at Arnhem* (Windwood Press, 1999)
Rolf, David, *Prisoners of the Reich: Germany's Captives 1939–1945* (Leo Cooper, 1988)
Rolf, David, 'The Education of British Prisoners of War in German Captivity, 1939–1945' in *History of Education*, 1989
Rollings, Charles, *Prisoners of War: Voices from Captivity during the Second World War* (Ebury Press, 2007)
Rollings, Charles, *Wire and Walls: RAF Prisoners of War in Itzehoe, Spangenberg and Thorn 1939–42* (Ian Allen, 2003)
Rottman, Gordon, *FUBAR: Soldier Slang of World War II* (Osprey 2007)
Rust, Kenn, *The 9th Air Force in World War II* (Aero Publishing, 1970)
Rutledge, W, *The Combat History of the Super Sixth (Ripple Publishing* (1947)
Ryan, Cornelius, The Last Battle (Simon and Schuster, 1966)
Saft, Ulrich, *Krieg in der Heimat: bis zum bitteren Ende im Harz* (Militärbuchverlag Saft, 1996)

Schilling, Willy, *Thüringen 1933–1945: Der historische Reiseführer* (Christoph Links Verlag GmbH, 2010)
Schramm. Percy (ed), *Kriegstagebuch des Oberkommandos der Werhmacht* (Bernard and Graefe Verlag, 1982)
Schroeder, William, *11th Armored Division: Thunderbolt* (Turner Publishing, 1988)
Sellier, André, *A History of the Dora Camp* (Ivan R. Dee, 2003)
Shand, Bruce, *Previous Engagements* (Michael Russell, 1990)
Shulman, Milton, *Defeat in the West* (Cassell, 2003)
Slater, Frank, *As You Were: A Book of Caricatures* (Hutchinson 1946)
Smith, Wilfred, *Code Word CANLOAN* (Dundurn Press, 1992)
Stafford, David, *Endgame 1945: Victory, Retribution, Liberation* (Little Brown, 2007)
Sultan, Heinrich, *Die Erinnerungen von Heinrich Sultan an die Jahre 1939–1945* (Rotenburg)
Summers, Julie, *Stranger in the House* (Simon and Schuster, 2008)
Sumners, Anne, *Visible Darkness: Charles Eugene Sumners Memoir of a World War II Combat Photographer* (McFarland, 2002)
Thacker, Toby, *The End of the Third Reich* (Tempus, 2008)
Trevor-Roper, Hugh, *The Last Days of Hitler* (Pan Books, 1995)
Torday, Jane, *The Coldstreamer and the Canary* (Black Cat Press, 1995)
Turner, Barry, *Countdown to Victory* (Hodder and Stoughton, 2004)
US Army, *Right to be Proud: 65th Infantry Division WWII Unit History*
US Army, *65th Infantry Division Pictorial History*
US Army, *Spearhead in the West: the Third Armored Division*
US Army, *The XX Corps: its History and Service in World War II* (reprinted WEBS Inc, 1984)
US Army Air Force, *Army Air Forces 440th Troop Carrier Group, DZ Europe: the story of 440th Troop Carrier Group, 194?*
Various authors, *The Official History of New Zealand in the Second World War 1939–1945* (Historical Publications Branch, Wellington, 1959)
von Luck, Hans, *Panzer Commander* (Cassell, 1989)
Vourkoutiotis, Vasilis, *Prisoners of War and the German High Command: The British and American Experience* (Palgrave, 2003)
Warrack, Graham, *Travel by Dark after Arnhem* (Harvill Press, 1963)
Watson, William, *We Forget So Much* (self published, 1996)
White, Kenneth (Gerritsen-Teunissen ed) *POW Diary* (Oosterbeek 2010)
XX Corps personnel, *XX Corps* (WEBS Inc, 1985)
Zaloga, Steven, *US Armored Divisions: The European Theatre of Operations 1944–45* (Osprey, 2004)
Zeigler, Thilo, *Unterm Hakenkreuz* (self published, 2004)

Zeitfuchs Robby and Schirmer Volker, *Zeitzeugen* (self published, 2004)
Ziemke, Earl, *The US Army in the occupation of Germany 1944–1946* (Center of Military History, 1975)
Zumbro, Derek, *Battle for the Ruhr: the German Army's Final Defeat in the West* (University of Kansas Press, 2006)

Unpublished MSS and Diaries

Baxter, Edward, unpublished manuscript, Imperial War Museum
Hill, Lee, diary and photographs, The New Zealand Film Archive
Brush, Peter, unpublished manuscript, Imperial War Museum
Baigent, Lestock, papers, The National Archive
Beckwith, Ted, diary, Mrs Jean Beckwith
Celander, Gunnar, papers, Swedish National Archive
Clay, Basil, papers, Maidstone Museum
Edlmann, Ernest, diary and papers, personal collection
Edwards, Marcus, diary, Australian War Memorial
Fuller, Jimmy, diary, family papers
Forbes, James, unpublished manuscript, family papers
Holland, Rupert T., diary, papers of Mrs Gilian Barnard
Laing, Butch, unpublished manuscript, Imperial War Museum
Le Mesurier, unpublished memoirs and articles, family papers
Martin, H.L. *Lasting Impression*, 1990, unpublished manuscript, Imperial War Museum
Muller, Frederick, diary, private collection
Roberts, Harry, diary, Muriel Roberts Collection
Sewell, John, diary, Imperial War Museum
Wilbraham, Ralph, unpublished manuscript, family papers

INDEX

ABOUT THE AUTHOR

Peter Green's father, Alan Green, served in the Border Regiment at Sicily and Arnhem. He was captured and imprisoned in Oflag IX A/Z at Rotenburg an der Fulda. Cuttings from *Illustrated* magazine of May 1945 describing the camp's evacuation featured in the family album kept by his mother. After the death of his father, Peter discovered his father's POW diary and an album of photographs of the march.

Peter was born in Leicestershire, although the family's roots go back to Nidderdale, Yorkshire. Following a career in government science and technical public relations, he created an internet news service for research. Now retired, he edits Cumbria's Museum of Military Life's magazine, *The Lion & the Dragon*. Peter has published a survey of prisoners of war from Operation Market Garden and now lectures on Second World War prisoners of war. He is married and lives in Swindon.